Y0-CWM-220

A Christian Pedagogy

By

EDWARD W. A. KOEHLER

Instructor in Concordia Teachers College
River Forest, Ill.

Train up a child in the way he should go;
and when he is old, he will not depart from it.
Prov. 22, 6.

St. Louis, Mo.
CONCORDIA PUBLISHING HOUSE
1930

PRINTED IN U. S. A.

LC368
.K77

Foreword.

The child is the most important problem of any generation. As we gaze upon the new-born infant, the question comes to us, "What manner of child shall this be?" And in answer to this question we read, "Train up a child in the way he should go; and when he is old, he will not depart from it." What we are to-day we owe, in a measure, to the training we received in our youth, and the future of our children will be determined largely by the type of training they are receiving at our hands. The education of our children therefore is worthy of our best thoughts and efforts.

The science and art of leading, guiding, and training children is called Pedagogy. Its chief purpose is not to impart information and knowledge, but rather by means of such knowledge so to influence and train the child that his endowments are drawn out and developed, permanent habits are formed, and a definite character is fashioned.

Nobility of character is the most valuable personal asset any man can have. It ranks higher than nobility of birth or of station; it is more to be desired than much wealth and great honors; it is more precious than profound learning and heroic achievement. It is character that makes or unmakes the man. Whoever lacks a good moral character is a miserable wretch, though he live in a royal palace, while the poorest peasant is a prince of a man if he has a noble character.

Character-worth must not be measured by a man's erudition or his social accomplishments, but rather by the manner of life he leads and especially by the motives that prompt such a life. For it is the heart that determines the ethical value of the deed. The noblest type of character is that which, void of all selfish considerations and controlled by the love of God, is actuated to do what is pleasing to God and helpful to man.

Character-building is the chief aim of education. Popular conception, however, to which many institutions of learning have yielded, limits education to the mere acquisition of knowledge and the development of skill for the purpose of attaining practical advantages in life. While this phase of education is indeed necessary for material advancement and economic progress, it is a most serious mistake to stress it to such an extent that moral and religious education is neglected or regarded as being of minor importance. Moral and religious training is of greatest consequence to the youth of our land. It must be the groundwork and the backbone of all education. It alone will insure stability and permanency to our culture and civilization. "Righteousness exalteth a nation." The breakdown of religion and morals will bring ruin and disaster to any people, as we may well learn from the pages of history.

Several of our Presidents have in recent years voiced the same opinion and have emphasized the necessity of moral and religious education.

"People educated in the intellect, but not in morals and religion will become a menace to the nation." (*Theodore Roosevelt.*)

"Our civilization cannot survive materially unless it be redeemed spiritually. It can be saved only by becoming permeated with the spirit of Christ and being made free and happy by the practise which springs out of that spirit." (*Woodrow Wilson.*)

"I believe in religious instruction for American children. The future of our nation cannot be trusted to them unless their education includes spiritual development." (*Warren G. Harding.*)

"All our learning and science, our culture and our art, will be of little value unless supported by high character. A trained intelligence can do much, but there is no substitute for morality, character, and religious conviction. Unless these abide, American citizenship will be found unequal to its task." (*Calvin Coolidge.*)

Foreword.

During the last few decades, education has received much professional and popular attention. States have passed compulsory school laws. Parents desiring to prepare their children for life want them to "get an education." Professional men have not been slow to study the various problems of education and have written scholarly and useful books on the school curriculum, on methods of teaching, on educational psychology, on intelligence and achievement tests, etc. However, we have not very many books that set forth, and stress, the principles of true Christian pedagogy.

The reason is that there is not so large a demand for books of this kind as there is for educational helps. In the first place, public schools and institutions do not teach religion and train their pupils according to Christian principles. Professionally therefore their teachers are not interested in books of this type. They are to be pitied. They are expected not only to teach their pupils useful knowledge, but also to train them morally. However, they may not teach what must always constitute the foundation of morality — religion. "Nobody knows how to teach morality effectually without religion. Exclude religion from education, and you have no foundation upon which to build moral character." (*Charles W. Eliot* of Harvard.) If the training of our youth is to be effective morally, it must be religious.

But the lack of interest in Christian training is especially due to the general indifference in matters spiritual. We are living in an age that is decidedly materialistic. Material prosperity is a gift of God, but because of the perverseness of men it is fraught with evil. "This is a fair land to live in; let us secure of its riches as much as we can and let us enjoy them. Get an education that you may be able to make money; make money that you may enjoy yourself." This seems to be the modern philosophy of life. Morality and religion are theoretically recommended, but practically ignored whenever they interfere with the pursuit of pleasure, of gain, and of glory.

And what has education done to counteract this materialistic tendency? At first it yielded to it, and finally it furthered it. "We have been excessively busy seeking for information that could be turned to practical advantages in matters of dollars and cents, rather than for that wisdom which would guide us through eternity. Our higher educational institutions have turned their thoughts especially to the sciences and our secondary schools to vocational training." (*Calvin Coolidge*.)

Alarmed because of the imminent danger of the materialistic trend of modern education, statesmen and educators have of late stressed the necessity of moral and religious training.

But at once we are confronted with the question, What constitutes the right kind of moral and religious training, and who is to give it? Without entering upon a detailed discussion of these points, we would say that the responsibility for the moral and religious education of children rests with their parents and with the Church and not with the State and the State-controlled schools. As to the type of training, there can be no doubt in the mind of any sincere Christian. Accepting the Bible as the inspired Word of his God, he knows that the educational principles laid down in this Book are not only the best, but also the only right ones to be observed in the training of children. No matter how far we may advance in knowledge and science and art, the educational principles of the Bible never become antiquated. They have permanent value and can never be surpassed. Christian educators therefore will also be interested in a Christian pedagogy.

It is the Biblical principle of education the author has endeavored to set forth in the chapters of this volume. The reader will therefore understand the frequent references to the Scriptures. Psychological problems were touched on only to the extent that it was necessary to make clear the fundamental functions of soul-life.

Foreword.

The general groundwork of the present volume and much of the subject-matter was taken from J. C. Lindemann's excellent chapters on *Schulerziehung*. Also other books were consulted and quoted liberally: *How to Teach Religion*, by G. H. Betts, *The Teaching of Religion*, by P. E. Kretzmann, *Beginning Teaching*, by J. E. Avent, and others. The author is also indebted to Prof. Alb. H. Miller and to Superintendent A. C. Stellhorn for their encouragement and valuable suggestions.

The author would gladly have left the task of writing a book on so important a matter to an abler pen. But finding no suitable text for his classes in Christian Pedagogy, he was compelled to write his own. The German text, Lindemann's *Schulpraxis*, which formerly served as a basis of instruction at our Lutheran normal schools, is out of print. Moreover, it was deemed advisable to have an English text for our students. Thus the author was requested to prepare his manuscript for print.

To some, a Christian pedagogy or, for all that, any book on pedagogy might seem quite superfluous since they know exactly how to train children. Perhaps they do and have nothing more to learn in this respect. But there are others who are not so fortunate. Though very successful in their work, they realize that there is room for improvement. And then there are many beginning teachers and students preparing for their life's work who are eager to learn more of the art of training children. To these the book may be of some service. It does not prescribe a specific recipe for every case that requires pedagogical treatment; it merely lays down the general principles that should be observed. No book on the training of children can or should be followed mechanically. The individuality of the teacher and that of the child, the peculiar circumstances of each case, are important factors. But the better one understands the child, knows the aim, and is skilled in using the means of education, the more likely will one's efforts produce positive results.

Whatever may be the shortcomings of the book, — and the critical reader will, no doubt, find some, — the principles of Christian education as set forth are correct and true because they are in agreement with the Word of God. And the author hopes that the present volume may bring home to all that are engaged in the noble work of training children the supreme significance of real Christian education and character-building, that it may inspire them with greater zeal and be of some service to them in their work.

River Forest, Ill., January 15, 1930.

E. W. A. KOEHLER.

Table of Contents.

PART I. INTRODUCTION.

I. Teaching and Training, pp. 1—9.

Instruction. Education. Phases of education: physical, social, intellectual, cultural, moral, religious. Interrelation between teaching and training.

II. Moral Education, pp. 9—21.

Education presupposes a rational being. Results of education not uniform. The education of a child cannot be forced. Life an education. The moral effect. The experiences of life must not be ignored in the training of children. Mutual influence. Childhood the most opportune period for training. Education a purposive endeavor. All training must be consistent, *zielbewuszt*. Training must be persistent. The moral type of the character depends largely on the moral type of the influences that fashion it. Individual training. Group-training.

III. Christian Education, pp. 21—40.

Education not exclusively Christian. Christian education. Agencies of Christian education: the Christian Church, the Christian home; the school; the non-religious school, religious schools: the Christian Sunday-school, the Christian parish-school. A fundamental difference between secular and Christian education. Cooperation of home and school.

PART II. THE EDUCATOR.

IV. Christian Education a Duty, pp. 41—50.

The pedagog. Christian training a duty. Children need such a training. Parents expect such a training for their children. The call of the teacher enjoins such a training. God demands such a training. The Fourth Commandment. Consecration to one's calling.

V. Natural Qualifications, pp. 51—61.

Necessity of certain qualities and abilities. Ability to teach. Liking for children. Cheerfulness. Kindliness. Sincere interest. Unselfishness. Patience and perseverance. Equanimity and self-control. Common sense. Ability to gain respect and confidence.

VI. Spiritual Qualifications, pp. 61—76.

Necessity of these qualifications. Knowledge of the Scripture doctrines necessary. Ability to "divide the Word of Truth." Personal faith. Christian experience. Love of Jesus. Christ-mindedness. Sincere love for children. Meekness and lowliness. Christian character. Christian life. — Legalism. Indifference. Worldly-mindedness.

PART III. THE CHILD.

VII. The Psychic Nature of the Child, pp. 77—97.

Knowledge of children is necessary. Children are creatures of God. Children have a body that is "wonderfully" made. Children have a soul. The rational, or cognitive, activity of the soul. The emotional, or affective, activity of the soul. The volitional activity of the soul. The psychological process. Temperaments. Natural gifts.

VIII. The Sinful Depravity of the Child, pp. 97—103.

The depravity of the human nature a fact that must be recognized in education. Bible proof. The body imperfect. The soul depraved. Temperaments vitiated; natural gifts weakened. Each child potentially capable of all sins. Education begins in the heart.

IX. The Regenerated Child, pp. 104—110.

The state of grace. This state of grace must be recognized in education. Regeneration does not make Christian training superfluous. Regeneration makes Christian training possible. Every Christian child has a twofold moral nature. Diagnosis of the child's behavior.

PART IV. THE AIM OF EDUCATION.

X. The Aim of Christian Education, pp. 111—124.

A clear understanding of the aim of education necessary. Various aims or principles: the eudemonic, the utilitarian, the rationalistic, the humanitarian, the naturalistic, the social or national. The Christian principle. The preliminary, or medial, objective is knowledge of Scripture truths. The first major objective is faith in Jesus Christ. The second major objective is godliness of life. Bible proof. The relation between first and second major objectives. The proper motive for a Christian life. Leading a Christian life must become a habit. Quotations. The reason for Christian training. The purpose of such training: the glory of God, the welfare of mankind, the temporal and eternal happiness of the child.

PART V. THE MEANS OF EDUCATION.

XI. A Criticism, pp. 125—130.

Fear of punishment. Expectation of reward. The sense of right. Love of mankind.

XII. The Word of God Is Profitable for Education, pp. 130—144.

The Word of God is efficacious. The Law and the Gospel. The Law as a curb. Insufficiency of the Law. The Law as a mirror. The content of the Gospel. Effect of the Gospel on the heart. What is faith? The functions of faith. The Gospel the only effectual means for positive Christian education. The Law as a guide and rule of conduct.

XIII. The Use of the Word of God, pp. 144—162.

Doctrine. Reproof. Correction. Instruction in righteousness. Comfort. The Word of God must be taught clearly. Selection of proper material. The Word of God must be taught in its purity. Teach Bible doctrines as divine truths. Teach the child to know the Scriptures. Teach to convince the child. Teach to impress and move the child. Teach to train the child. Quotations. Meditation. Memory work.

XIV. Secondary Means, pp. 163—168.

Praise. Exhortation and admonition. Censure and correction. Warning.

XV. Punishment, pp. 168—177.

Scriptural basis. Purpose of punishment. The right to punish children. Punishment, to be effectual, must be individual. Punishment must be corrective. The nature of punishment. The measure of punishment. Kinds of punishment. Corporal punishment. The educational value of punishment. A few general rules respecting all manner of punishment. Expulsion from school.

XVI. Other Means of Education, pp. 178—184.

Prayer. Example. School discipline. School-work. Music and singing.

PART VI. THE EDUCATIONAL METHOD.

XVII. How to Preserve the Child from Sin, pp. 185—198.

The educative pressure. Prevention. Preparation. The fear of God. Abhorrence of sin. Conscience.

XVIII. How to Preserve the Child from Sin (continued), pp. 198—211.

Self-will. Pride. Dishonesty: lying, deceiving, stealing. Other sins. Instruction is necessary. Watching. A word to the teacher.

XIX. How to Save the Child from Sin, pp. 211—222.

Teach children clearly the way of salvation. Save the child from the power of sin. The penitent child. The impenitent child. The backsliding child. Sins whose perpetrators cannot be discovered. Parents not agreeing with the educational procedure of the teacher.

XX. How to Train a Child in Christian Virtues, pp. 223—232.

The general scope. The fundamental prerequisite. How to make children willing to serve God in good works. Teach children to know the will of God. Train children to observe the will of God. Recognize every effort and improvement on the part of the child. Strengthen the child in his efforts to improve.

XXI. How to Train a Child in Christian Virtues (continued), pp. 232—246.

Respectfulness. Obedience. Truthfulness. Diligence. Charity. Mission-work. Cleanliness, neatness, orderliness. Punctuality and regularity. Manners.

XXII. Conclusion, pp. 247—251.

Two extremes. Success comes slowly. Success is sure. Education a glorious work.

Part I. INTRODUCTION.

I. Teaching and Training.

1. Education, says Webster, is the "impartation or acquisition of knowledge, skill, or the development of character, as by study or discipline." From this definition it appears that the term education, in its generally accepted and wider sense, includes both teaching and training. However, there is a vast difference between these two activities, which is not always sufficiently recognized. In actual practise, teaching and training should not, and, in fact, cannot, be separated; still, in order better to understand the purpose of each, it is advisable to distinguish clearly between instruction and education, taking the latter term in its proper sense.

2. **Instruction.** — Derived from the Latin *instruere,* which means to "build in," instruction denotes that activity by means of which we impart knowledge, teaching the pupil to know what he did not know before. It includes all those efforts and devices which cause the child to learn. The teacher imparts, the pupil acquires, knowledge. Teaching and learning are therefore correlatives. Instruction addresses itself to the intellect, which responds by learning, and its immediate purpose is accomplished as soon as the pupil has intelligently grasped and understood what he was taught.

Whoever can easily impart knowledge to others, so that they obtain clear and definite ideas and form correct concepts of the subject-matter and hence can also intelligently speak of what they were taught to know, is a good instructor. His purpose is accomplished the very moment he succeeds in conveying to the intellect of his pupil that knowledge which he wishes to impart. Many a teacher is merely an instructor, having no other purpose in mind than just to impart knowledge. Whoever wishes to educate children has a purpose beyond the mere "impartation and acquisition of knowledge."

Education. — Derived from the Latin *educare,* which means "to lead out," education signifies that activity whereby we endeavor to educe, to lead out or draw out, the latent powers of the individual. Potentially man possesses certain aptitudes and capabilities, and it is the purpose of education to quicken them, to draw them out, to develop and strengthen them, and thus to create definite attitudes and habits. Education therefore implies a great deal more than instruction. Teaching and learning, whether this be by formal instruction or by the experiences of life, is but a means by which the end and aim of education are attained.

Education is the entire physical, intellectual, and moral or spiritual development or culture of a person, in so far as this is effected by external influences upon which the person reacts favorably, *i. e.*, to his betterment, regardless of whether this takes place with or without the special effort of parents and teachers.

"Education does not mean teaching people what they do not know. It means teaching them to behave as they do not behave. It is not teaching the youth the shapes of letters and the tricks of numbers and then leaving them to turn their arithmetic to roguery and their literature to lust. It means, on the contrary, training them into the perfect exercise and kingly continence of their bodies and souls. It is a painful, continual, and difficult work, to be done by kindness, by watching, by warning, by precept, and by praise, but above all — by example." (*John Ruskin.*)

"Education is any process of changing a human being for the better." (*J. Avent.*)

"Generally speaking, every one is being educated, his powers, intellectual and moral, are being developed for good or evil, by all he sees, hears, feels, or does. In this sense education begins when one enters the world and continues all the time he is in it. In a more specific sense the term is applied to a premeditated effort on the part of parents and teachers to draw out one's intellectual and moral endowments, encouraging what is good to oneself and society and discouraging what is hurtful." (*Eclectic Dictionary.*)

To educate man, then, does not simply mean to teach him to know things, but rather to train him to do things. It means to exert a definite influence, upon which he is to react in a definite way, to quicken and stimulate dormant powers and endowments, to exercise and train them so that they function in his life and conduct. By instruction we give to man something he did not have before; by education we draw out and develop those capabilities which he, potentially at least, possesses. Instruction imparts, education draws out.

Phases of Education. — While education aims to develop the whole man, we may distinguish six general objectives: *physical, social, intellectual, cultural, moral,* and *religious.*

a) With respect to the physical development of the body by means of gymnastics, calisthenics, sports, etc., we prefer the term *physical training.* The importance of physical culture was recognized in ancient Greece and Rome. *Mens sana in corpore sano* was an axiom generally observed in the training of the young, and it is again being stressed in our day. Those to whom children are entrusted must have a due regard for their bodily well-being and therefore make provision for sufficient and proper physical exercise to keep the children also bodily fit and healthy — a sound mind in a sound body. A total lack of wholesome physical exercise will retard the bodily development of children, endanger their health, and hinder their education otherwise.

b) As a child is not to live in seclusion, like a hermit, but is to live and move among his fellows as a member of the human family and especially of his immediate community, it is necessary that he learn to know and observe whatever makes such social life possible and agreeable to all concerned. *Social education* therefore respects the child's relation to society and includes whatever would fit him into the social organism. Hence it also aims to train the child in the conventional proprieties and courtesies of life. Good breeding makes one more polished and agreeable; want of it unfits him for the society of the cultured. By nature the child knows nothing of all this, nor is he inclined to submit to those restrictions and to observe those rules which social life imposes upon him. He must therefore be taught these matters and trained in them. It is the duty of every one engaged in the training of children to pay special attention also to this phase of their education.

c) *Intellectual education* does not primarily denote impartation and acquisition of knowledge, but rather the mental and intellectual training and development resulting therefrom. If our teaching is to be effective, the various mental faculties of the pupil must respond, and as they respond, always grappling with, and mastering, the problems presented, they develop and grow. As the muscles of the body, so the mind must be exercised. We learn to use the mind by using it, to think by thinking, to remember by remembering, to reason by reasoning, etc. The mental efficiency resulting from such methodical exercise of the several functions of the mind is the objective of intellectual training.

In order to train children intellectually, the teacher will not give all information outright, but he will do it in such a way that the pupil, in trying to acquire this knowledge, must exercise his mental faculties. The teacher therefore will not solve the problem and give the correct answer, but will lead the pupil to do the thinking and to find the solution himself. Beginning with what the child knows, the teacher will lead him on to find what he is to learn. In this manner he draws out and develops the mental endowments, or educates and trains the mind. A person will forget many things he has learned at school, but the mental training received in learning them is of abiding value.

d) In this connection the *cultural phase of education* must be mentioned. While the acquisition of factual knowledge and the development of mental abilities is indeed a part thereof, cultural education has respect chiefly to the effect such knowledge may have on man. For knowledge is rarely the end of knowledge; we know not merely to know. But knowledge is to mean something to man; it is to be useful to him and to function in his life. The cultural purpose of our teaching is to widen man's vision, to improve his tastes, to develop skill and ability, and to create attitudes and habits.

Thus we do not teach language, grammar, composition, etc., in order that the child may just know these things, but that he may use them habitually. We wish to create in him a sense of, and bent for, correctness of language, a literary conscience, the ability and habit of using the language correctly. Our aim therefore is not mere knowledge of language, but correct use of the language. The same applies to many other studies. Whatever we teach should mean something to our pupils and students, should benefit them somehow, improve their tastes, and develop their skill. For this reason it is important to select such subjects and subject-matter as can readily be converted into worth-while cultural values.

A truly cultured person is he who not only knows what he has learned, but who by such knowledge has been bettered in his tastes, attitudes, and habits.

e) *Moral training,* while also cultural, does not pertain to literary tastes, scientific or mechanical skill, etc., but to the moral life of man. It does not consist in merely teaching the child to learn a set of moral rules and principles, but in training him to observe them in his life. Moral training is essentially a matter of influence, whether this be by precept or example or experience, an influence that makes an impression on the heart, creates an emotional response, and tends in a certain direction. Via the mind we seek to reach the heart, inducing the child to practise what he knows to be good and right. If such influence is sufficiently strong and continuous, a permanent moral attitude, mindedness, *Gesinnung,* is achieved, which, in turn, stimulates the will and determines the conduct of life. The moral tone of this result, whether good or evil, depends upon the moral tone of the impressions first received and upon the manner in which the individual reacts to these impressions.

Whatever these impressions may be, it is apparent that moral education is of greatest consequence to the child, inasmuch as thereby his character is fashioned and his moral life is determined. "Instruction makes one wiser, but a good moral education makes one really good. A want of instruction is of more or less inconvenience, according to circumstances; but a want of a good moral education will always be to the injury, if not to the ruin, of the sufferer."

f) *Religious education,* which, as a sequence, includes a corresponding moral training, does not consist in teaching children merely to know a number of religious truths and doctrines, but rather in this, that by means of these truths a personal relation and reverential attitude to God is effected in the individual. This personal religion, taking the word in its subjective sense, cannot be taught at all. It is an experience of the heart, and the most revolutionary experience at that, which is brought about, and wrought, in the soul of man by means of doctrines he learns concerning God and which he regards as true. Mere knowledge of religious truths therefore is by no means identical with religion itself. Such knowledge may be instrumental in bringing about religion, it is the foundation on which religion rests, but in itself it is not religion. Religious education, then, can only mean to teach religious truths with a view to producing thereby that personal religion of the heart.

While every personal relation and reverential attitude of the individual to his God is truly religious, it is by no means always the true religion. True religion is that personal attitude which the true God wants every human being to have toward Him; it is essentially faith in Jesus Christ. He who knows himself to be a lost and condemned sinner in the sight of God, but trusts in the merits of his Savior for the forgiveness of his sins and, by reason of such faith, knows himself to be a dear child of his heavenly Father, whom he loves and is willing to serve all the days of his life, — such a one has the true religion.

This true religion no man can work in himself, nor can any other man produce it in him; it is the work of the Holy Ghost, who operates by means of the Gospel. What we are to do is to teach the Gospel-truth with a view to thus making our hearers "wise unto salvation through faith which is in Christ Jesus."

As the type of religion a man has depends upon the type of religious doctrines he has been taught, it is of utmost importance that we teach the true doctrines of the Bible, by which God Himself will work true religion in the heart of man.

Interrelation Between Teaching and Training. — While it is perfectly proper that in theory we clearly distinguish between instruction and education, we cannot separate them in actual practise.

In the first place, all manner of teaching requires learning for its counterpart. Learning, however, is a mental process, involving several distinct mental activities, each of which is being developed by being exercised. Therefore all effective teaching will also train the mind.

By teaching we furthermore impart knowledge. But knowledge is power. Indeed, as long as knowledge remains merely intellectual, it is dead and does not function. But at any time it may become alive, awaken in the heart an emotional response, and begin to exert an influence which will ultimately prompt action. Thus knowledge is power, not only inasmuch as it tells us how to do things, but also inasmuch as it prompts us to do things by influencing the heart, creating attitudes, and inciting action.

Whether such influence will be in the direction of social, cultural, moral, or religious education, depends upon the content of what man learns. Instruction in manners will affect one differently from a course in appreciation of literature and art. And the study of ethics will not necessarily result in religious education. Not everything man learns and knows has the same educative value. The study of mathematics and logic may be an excellent means for the training of the mind, but it is of no value as far as moral or religious training is concerned. But from a reading-lesson, a poem, a story, or a proverb the child may learn, besides language and grammar, also a lesson that will influence his moral life. Therefore, even though it may not be the intention of the instructor to train the child, the very content of the lesson he teaches possesses potential power to influence him in some way. For as soon as the knowledge he imparts means something to the child personally, this knowledge exerts an influence and helps to train the child. Hence we cannot teach the child effectively without training him at least potentially.

As it is impossible to teach without effecting some sort of training, it is likewise impossible to train without teaching. Whether it be by formal instruction or by personal experience and observation, in some way the child must learn if he is to be educated. We may not expect any reaction on the part of the child if there is not some stimulating action which produces it. If it were possible to cut off every contact of the child with the outside world, making it impossible for him to receive any sense impressions whatever or to acquire any knowledge, then also education would be impossible. It is by means of the things we learn that we are being trained. There must be impression before there can be any expression. We teach the child lessons adapted to his mental age, in the getting of which his intellectual powers are exercised and developed. In some way the child must also learn those moral and religious truths which are to influence his heart and mold his character.

Instruction and education are so closely interwoven that they cannot be separated. The difference is in placing the emphasis. Instruction appeals to the intellect and emphasizes the mere acquisition of knowledge. Education has a higher aim; knowledge is but a means to the end. Education endeavors to train man physically, socially, intellectually, culturally, morally, and spiritually.

II. Moral Education.

Education Presupposes a Rational Being. — We can raise plants and train animals, but we can educate only man. And this is one of the things that clearly distinguish man from the irrational brute. True moral education is concerned with the deepest things in man, with his real ego. For we do not wish merely to stock his mind with intellectual knowledge of moral truths; we thereby also seek to influence his inner man, his heart, his emotional nature, so that, prompted from within, he habitually lives in accordance with the views and principles imbibed. Moral education aims to mold a moral character, which is possible only in a rational being endowed with intellect, emotion, and will.

Results of Education Not Uniform. — There is an approach to the soul life of every rational being which makes it possible to teach and to train him in some way. But we must not conceive of education as a mechanical procedure, which, if its rules be but faithfully observed by the teacher, will infallibly produce exactly the same result in all children. For children are not inanimate clay, which may be fashioned at will, but are rational beings. Mentally and emotionally each one is differently constituted, each has his own individuality, and each will react to impressions in his own way. This we must take into consideration in the teaching and training of children. A certain method of presenting and teaching a subject may be very successful with the greater number of pupils, but with others it is not. What convinces one will not always convince also the other. What impresses and moves one child will not always impress and move another in the same way.

The reason for this phenomenon of different reaction on the part of children to similar or even identical stimuli is the difference in the mental and emotional complex of individuals. For besides the truths we teach and the influences we exert, the child possesses knowledge which he previously acquired, there are inborn qualities and inclinations and former experiences and impressions, all of which may be very different and over which we have no control.

These, however, affect his reception of, and reaction to, our influences. Hence it is impossible to guarantee in advance the exact result of our efforts.

While the results of the same system of training will, in general, be similar in all children, they will never be uniformly alike, as, for instance, the imprint of the same letter type is on separate pages of a book. There will be individual differences, because each child reacts to impressions in his own way. This explains, in a measure, why children of the same school, even of the same family, who have received the same type of training, are, after all, so very different.

The Education of a Child Cannot be Forced. — "You can lead a horse to water, but you cannot make him drink." We may create conditions most favorable for training, employ means most approved, and exert the right kind of influence, still we cannot force the desired emotional response and consequent action of the will. Though we can force a man to do something against his will, though we might perhaps force also a certain knowledge on him, we cannot make that knowledge function so that it impresses and moves him in the direction we desire. We can teach him truths that possess the power to touch the heart and move the will, but we cannot make these truths do so. We may do all we can to educate man, still we cannot force his being educated. It is here that we encounter the rational "self" of man, which, though highly susceptible to impressions and influences, does not yield to force, but may even defy all our efforts.

Educators therefore are certainly responsible in this, that they are faithfully to do whatever is profitable for effectual training; but having done so, they are not responsible for the results. This responsibility rests solely with the individual that is being educated.

Life an Education. — Because man is not a senseless block or stone, but a rational being, he is continually adjusting himself to impressions received and reacting upon them in some way. "Education is a constant and continuous adjustment of the human organism to human environment, to the end that the human organism may be enriched and perfected and the human environment understood, penetrated, and advanced by persistent and lofty human effort." (*Nicholas Murray Butler.*)

Every experience in life helps to educate and train man in some way and in some direction. Whatever he observes, learns, and experiences, whatever enters his consciousness, and whichever way he reacts to impressions, whatever he feels, wishes, and does, — all this helps to develop his personality and character. The determining influence of the individual experience may not always be traceable nor perceptible, but the sum total of all his experiences no doubt makes a deep and lasting impression on him, each one doing its bit in fashioning his character. Therefore life is a school in which all men are daily being trained and educated.

This personal adjustment and reaction to the conditions and experiences of life affects all phases of man's education. Manual labor and physical exercise will help to develop his body, much study and deep thinking his mind. The social circles in which he moves will affect his manners and also his morals. For customs and habits, moral ideas and practises, obtaining in a certain community will not fail to make some impression on every one living in that community and to call forth on his part a response, so that he will either accept or reject them, though in most cases he will modify them to suit himself. Man is continually adapting himself to his environments as he personally experiences them, and there lies in them a tremendous educative power, which he cannot escape.

The home and the school, after all, touch but a small, though the most important, portion of man's life. But he continues in the great school of life as long as he remains in this world. And since the experiences of life figure so very prominently in the education of man, no one engaged in the training of children may ignore them.

The Moral Effect. — We are at present chiefly concerned about the moral effect the influences of life may have on children. It is true, by observation or personal experience the child may learn that "crime does not pay" and that "honesty is the best policy," etc. But "the hit-and-miss method, which functions in the child's contact with the unorganized influences of life, does not achieve for him any sort of dependable moral education." On the contrary, the tendency of these influences is only toward evil, toward sin-service or toward self-righteousness.

The demoralizing influence of the world is quite apparent from what the Scriptures say about the world. "All that is in the world, the lust of the flesh and the lust of the eyes and the pride of life, is not of the Father, but is of the world" (1 John 2, 16). And again we read: "Woe unto the world because of offenses! For it must needs be that offenses come; but woe to that man by whom the offense cometh!" (Matt. 18, 7.) There lies in the things of this world an alluring and seductive charm, which does not fail to make an impression on every one living in this world. And since by reason of his natural depravity man is inclined toward all that is evil (Gen. 8, 21), he will yield much more readily to these baser influences than to those that can elevate and educate him. A child therefore, untutored and untrained and depending for his education solely on the experiences of life, cannot develop a good moral character.

The Experiences of Life Must Not be Ignored in the Training of Children. — Neither the home nor the school can so thoroughly protect and shield the child that the influences of the world cannot touch him. For the child is not to live the life of a hermit, but he is to live in this world, to take his stand among men, and to assume the duties and responsibilities of his position in life. Parents and teachers may therefore not ignore the experiences and influences of life, thinking that children will of themselves learn their lesson, but they must reckon with these experiences and with the influence they may possibly have on children. No doubt each child will learn his lesson, but will he learn the right lesson? Those responsible for his education must therefore teach him to view the things of this world in the right light and to evaluate them properly. They must help him to interpret the experiences of life correctly and to react upon them in the right way.

Whatever affects the child must be a matter of concern to parents and teachers. Whenever it is possible, the life experiences of the child must be made subservient to the proposed aim of education. Impressions must be corrected, modified, or deepened, as the case may be, in order that the child may obtain a right view of life and learn to react upon his experiences properly. For this reason the child should be encouraged to speak his mind freely on what he has observed and experienced, to disclose his heart to his parents and teachers, so that they may instruct, advise, and guide him in the way he should go.

Mutual Influence. — In the great school of life man not only is influenced, receiving impressions, but he also exerts an influence on those with whom he associates. And to the extent to which, and in the manner in which, he influences others, he also helps to make them better or worse. The strength of this influence varies and, in a measure, depends on the position a person holds. The influence of parents and teachers on children is stronger than the influence of children on their superiors. But as no one is totally immune from influence, so he is also not absolutely without influence. In their daily intercourse all men by word or deed exert a moral influence on one another. Thus the detrimental effect of bad company on the moral character is generally admitted; for "evil communications corrupt good manners" (1 Cor. 15, 33). Because of the influence his conduct may have on others, it behooves every one to "walk circumspectly" (Eph. 5, 15), to be "the salt of the earth" and "the light of the world" (Matt. 5, 13. 14). Also children must learn this lesson in order that they may view their lives also from this angle and be an influence for good.

Childhood the Most Opportune Period for Training. Childhood and youth constitute the formative period of life. It is then that man is most susceptible to all manner of influences. Not yet set in his views and ways, he more readily yields to strong impressions. Children and young people, as a rule, are more impressionable and plastic, as they have not yet developed that firmness of character which resists an influence and effaces an impression. They are controlled less by sober reflection than by impulses and emotions. This, then, is the most opportune time to bring a firm and steady moral influence to bear on them, which will determine their character in the making. "Education belongs to the period of childhood and youth." (*Crabb*.)

However, many fond parents let the days of childhood, which are most favorable for effectual education, pass by without any serious attempt to train their children. "The children are so young," they say; "they do not know better. Let them have their way; when they are older, they will have more sense, and then we shall put the reins on them." This foolish fondness accounts for the failure of training in many a home. The children grow up, and because they are hardly ever curbed in their waywardness, but have their own way whenever they so desire, they never learn to obey and to submit to authority. After these children have grown up, parents often find to their sorrow that it is too late to train them. We can easily bend a twig, but not a tree. Training must begin at an early period, and by the time the child is four or five years old, the foundation for his entire future training must have been laid. The importance of early training is recognized also in the Scriptures. "Train up the *child* in the way he should go, and when he is old, he will not depart from it."

Education a Purposive Endeavor. — When we speak of child-training, we do not mean the haphazard impressions received by the promiscuous influences of life, but rather the premeditated and purposive efforts on the part of educators and parents to impress and to influence children in a certain direction. This implies that there must be, in the first place, a clearly defined aim, a definite goal toward which we would lead them. As in travel we must know our destination, so in education we must know what we are aiming to accomplish. The aim of all moral training is to mold a character which, controlled by moral principles, habitually exhibits itself in a moral life.

In the second place, the educator must wisely choose and judiciously employ such means and bring to bear upon the child such influences as, under the circumstances, promise to be most effective to accomplish the end he has in view. In every educative effort he must ask himself, How will this affect the child? What impression will it make upon him? Will it further or hinder the development of his moral character? For while, on the part of the teacher, education is an influence, on the part of the child it is a reaction to this influence. The final result depends not only on the moral tone of the influence, but also on the manner in which the child reacts to this influence.

All Training Must Be Consistent, "zielbewusst." — As the wind blows, now from the north and then from the south, so man is often influenced in opposite directions, one impression neutralizing the other. To achieve tangible results in education, the means employed must be conducive to the end we have in view, and the influence exerted must really tend in the direction of said aim. We must not rear children in a zigzag fashion, now drawing them one way and then another. Very little can be accomplished unless we are consistent, steadily tending in the same direction, not shifting, not vacillating between different objectives. For it must break the character of the child if for some time he is being led in one direction and then perhaps in an entirely different or even opposite direction; if, *e. g.*, we teach him to tell the truth always, yet occasionally encourage him to tell a little lie. To be effective, our educative influence must be steadily tending toward the end we wish to attain — it must be consistent.

Training Must Be Persistent. — Nothing can be accomplished by spasmodic attempts. No lasting impression is made if occasionally we insist on discipline and good behavior and then again allow children to do what they please; if to-day we rigorously enforce strict obedience and to-morrow let manifest disobedience go unreproved. Training is not confined to certain periods of the daily schedule, but must continue throughout the day. The educative activity need not always be in evidence, but the educative influence must be constant, the atmosphere and spirit must be ever present. The child must always feel that certain things are not proper and must be avoided, that other things are proper and should be observed. He must realize that he is under the directive guidance of his parents and teachers and that, whenever necessary, this influence will be exerted.

Lack of consistency and persistency accounts for many failures in the training of children. It is imperative that all educative influence should be steady and tend in the same direction. Home- and school-training must therefore never be an aimless and perfunctory experiment, but a conscious and persistent striving for a definite goal, giving meaning, direction, and purpose also to such other impressions as the child receives through his experiences in life. These may not be ignored, but must be drawn into the educational scheme. For parents and teachers are concerned not only with those influences which they themselves exert on children, but they must watch also those impressions which children may receive outside of the home and the school. They must correct them, modify them, deepen or neutralize them, as the case may be. Whenever possible, the life experiences of the child must be made subservient to the aim and purpose of his training.

Such education is not necessarily very spectacular, nor do the results show themselves immediately. It is rather a quiet, but firm and steady influence, tending in a definite direction and bringing forth fruit in due season.

The moral type of the character depends largely on the moral type of the influences that fashion it. It is not true that man is by nature morally neutral, neither good nor evil, and that his moral character is solely dependent on the kind of training he receives. For the Scriptures teach: "The imagination of man's heart is evil from his youth" (Gen. 8, 21). Observation and experience corroborate this truth. The moral character of man is therefore not exclusively determined by the influences to which he is exposed; it is not merely the product of his environment, as some would have us believe. His own corrupted and depraved nature is an important factor that must be taken into account.

Nevertheless it cannot be denied that to a certain degree man will be what education makes of him. The branches of a tree exposed to prevailing west winds will incline in an easterly direction. Thus the steady and directive influence of education will no doubt strongly determine the growth of the child's character. Witness the difference between children growing up in the street, exposed to all sorts of evil influences, and such as are reared in truly Christian homes, under morally wholesome conditions. The boy who is permitted and encouraged to deceive, cheat, and steal will hardly grow up to be an honest man. On the other hand, he who from his earliest youth has been taught and trained to be truthful and honest is not likely to depart from this when he is old. Since, then, the moral tone of the influence so strongly affects the moral tone of the character, it is of supreme importance for the educator to examine what kind of influence he exerts and how the child is affected thereby. The means he employs must really be conducive to the end he has in view.

Individual Training.—Education is, strictly speaking, an individual affair. It is the individual child that must be educated. There are no two children exactly alike, either physically or mentally. There is a difference in mental qualification and in temperament, a difference in the knowledge they have acquired and in the experiences they have had. Though a number of children be subjected to the same course of training, the mental reception, the emotional impression, the volitional reaction, and hence the educational result will be quite different in the individual child. Therefore every child is educationally in a class by himself, and we cannot mold two children strictly after the same pattern. Ever bearing in mind our general objective with all children, we must take into consideration the individuality of each child and do all we can to lead just this particular child to the goal we have set.

Experience teaches that an educational procedure very effective with one child completely fails with another. It is even so with grown people. In our dealings with men we take into consideration their individuality. Let us remember this also when we are training children. Education is not like the Procrustean bed, upon which we force a uniformity of training by harsh, arbitrary, and stereotype methods. The educational method must never become so rigid as to ignore the individual peculiarities of the child. Education that is worthy of this name takes the child as he is and makes of him what it can in the way of developing in him a good moral character.

Group-Training. — It would be folly so to stress the importance of individual education as to advise that each child should be trained by himself. On the contrary, experience shows that best results are not always obtained where there is but one child in a family. Children need and seek the company of other children. Pity the child which has no brothers and sisters and playmates. He is deprived not only of many of the joys of childhood, but because of too much attention he often fails to receive the proper training. One child helps to train others.

Notwithstanding individual differences, children have so much in common that group-training is not only possible, but also desirable. The individual child profits by the experiences of other children and by his contact with them. It is far easier to train a number of children, provided there be not so many as to make it impossible to give attention also to the individual child, than it is to train just one only child. And it is far better for the child to grow up together with other children than to be entirely segregated from them. Indeed, there is a possibility of evil influence, and it may be necessary to keep them from associating with those whose "evil communications corrupt good manners." However, we must bear in mind that it is not always the other child that is to blame and that sets a bad example.

Children must not be brought up in seclusion, they must mix and play with children. It is part of their training to learn to resist and overcome evil influences. It is better for them to learn this while they have some one to guide and direct them than when they must meet such influences single-handed later on in life. There are occasions when the child must yield to his playmates; at other times he must assert himself. In his small circle of friends and schoolmates he must learn both to stand on his own feet and to fit himself in with others. He must learn to show consideration, to assume responsibilities, and to cultivate the spirit of fellowship. All this is necessary later in life. And a child brought up together with other children is better prepared to take his stand in the world than one that is brought up, as it were, in seclusion. The little experiences the child may have in his association with other children are, if properly interpreted and directed, of great educative value. Best results therefore are obtained where a number of children are trained together, yet with a due regard for each individual child.

III. Christian Education.

Education Not Exclusively Christian. — Since every rational human being is susceptible to moral influences, he is also capable of some sort of moral training. It is therefore not correct to say that outside of the Christian education there is no real education. People who know nothing of the Christian religion also educate and train their children, bringing such influences to bear on them as will lead them in a certain direction and develop a definite character. The Roman citizen educated his son, the Jewish Pharisee did likewise. And also to-day there are those who, though absolutely unacquainted with the principles of

Christian education, nevertheless train their children in common human virtues and civil righteousness. In each case there is a real training, a real education, the type being determined by its objective and by the means employed. But while we grant that real education is possible apart from Christian influence, we maintain that Christian education is the only right and true education.

Christian Education. — Christian education does not mean teaching the child a number of Bible-truths so that he has a clear understanding of them, but teaching them for a definite purpose. These truths are to mean something to the child; they are to affect his attitude toward God and his life among men. While an intellectual knowledge of the Scriptures is indeed necessary, it is only a means to the end. Paul clearly indicates this 2 Tim. 3, 16. 17, saying: "And that from a child thou hast known the Holy Scriptures, which are able to make thee wise unto salvation through faith which is in Christ Jesus. . . . All Scripture is profitable for . . . instruction in righteousness." The apostle distinguishes between a knowledge of the Scriptures, which may be merely intellectual, and being made wise by them unto salvation through faith in Christ and being educated, or trained, by them in righteousness and good works. Christian education therefore means teaching children the Word of God for the purpose of leading them to Christ, their Savior, and of training them in holiness of life. Because it is God who commands that children be so brought up in the nurture and admonition of the Lord (Eph. 6, 4), Christian education is the only right and true education.

Agencies of Christian Education.

The Christian Church. — Besides the common experiences of life, which a true Christian will interpret in the light of God's Word, the Church exerts a powerful educative influence on all its members. Christ commanded His Church to make men His disciples by baptizing them in the name of the Triune God and by teaching them to observe all He has commanded (Matt. 28, 19. 20). It is the business of the Church to preach the Gospel of grace to a sin-cursed world in order that through faith in Christ men obtain forgiveness of their sins and become children of God and heirs of salvation. It is also the business of the Church to teach those who have been won for Christ "to observe what Christ has commanded." The Church must also train and educate its members to live as Christians in this world. It is interested not only in their eternal salvation in heaven, but also in the sanctification of their temporal lives among men.

The first duty of the Church is indeed to save souls, to make men "wise unto salvation" through faith in the Savior. But we are at present interested in the educational activity of the Church, in its influence on the character and the life of its members. The Gospel works and preserves faith in Christ and thus supplies that basic power which is absolutely necessary for a Christian life. Besides this, Christians are warned against sin, encouraged to resist temptation, exhorted to do good works, and to consecrate their lives to God. Thus the Church exerts a powerful influence on the lives of its members, teaching them to observe what Christ has commanded.

Like a leaven the influence of the Church extends through its members to many others. The Christians are the light of the world (Matt. 5, 14). Letting their light shine before men in good works and a holy life, they are by this very fact an educative force in this untoward generation. Never did any religion and pedagogical system or civilization and science produce such marvelous changes in the customs, habits, and morals of cannibal heathen peoples as Christianity has done and still is doing. But in the same ratio as the Church departs from the truth of God's Word, also its force and effectiveness for true Christian education diminishes.

While the educative influence of the Church is indeed powerful, inasmuch as it continues when other agencies have more or less ceased to function in the life of a Christian, it is not the influence of the Church that chiefly concerns us at present. We are interested in the training of children, and for them the Christian home and the Christian school constitute the principal educative agencies.

The Christian Home. — The home exerts the strongest and most effectual influence on the child, and it does so because this influence is continuous. The mutual relation between parents and children is also more intimate than that between teachers and pupils. Parents have greater authority over their children than any one else, and these have more confidence in their parents than in other people and will therefore more readily submit to their guidance and training than to that of a stranger. Because of this fact, parents have also a great responsibility. It is to them that Paul addresses himself when saying: "Ye fathers, provoke not your children to wrath, but bring them up in the nurture and admonition of the Lord" (Eph. 6, 4). By precept and example they should train the children in the way they should go. Like Abraham of old they should command their children and their household after them to keep the way of the Lord and to do justice and judgment (Gen. 18, 19).

Let no one underestimate the influence of the home. If this is a truly Christian influence, then the home will become the most effective agency for the Christian training of children. If, on the other hand, this influence tends toward evil, it is very difficult for all other agencies fully to counteract and set right what the home has done amiss. The child will eventually go the way of the home, especially if the home directs and trains him in the wrong way. With the breakdown of the home as a positive influence for good, every other educational agency must fail to a large extent. There is no institution that can take the place of the family, and there is no influence as effective and telling as the influence of the home. The best of schools may hope to do but little if the home does not cooperate, or if it counteracts the influence of the school. But great things may be accomplished if home and school work and train in the same direction.

Parents should always be conscious both of their opportunity and of their responsibility. Their children will in later years be what they have trained them to be in their youth. Indeed, it is not an easy task to train children properly. It is far easier to feed and clothe them and to care for their bodily wants. For this reason many parents are quite willing to do the latter, but they shirk the former, expecting the teachers at school or the pastors at church to assume the entire responsibility for the Christian training of their children. But no matter how difficult the task, the duty rests and remains in the first place with those to whom God gave the children, the parents, and it is they whom He holds responsible for the training their children receive. "These words which I command thee this day shall be in thine heart, and thou shalt teach them diligently unto thy children" (Deut. 6, 6. 7). "Ye fathers, bring up your children in the nurture and admonition of the Lord" (Eph. 6, 4).

The School. — Every school, no matter what its character, educates and trains its pupils in some way. Even though its sole purpose be to impart knowledge, to develop skill, or to train the mind, still this very knowledge, the ideas and views inculcated, the personality of the teacher, the atmosphere and the spirit of the school, all these combine to exert a powerful influence on the child and thus help to mold his character. Moral training may not be intended, but whatever it may be, it is present as a by-product, which cannot be eliminated.

In schools, however, moral education should not be merely incidental, but it should be intended. "Character-building is the most important function of the school," says Strayer. Any conception which limits the work and the purpose of schools to impartation of knowledge and cultural education, ignoring the development of the moral character of its pupils and students is woefully deficient. 'Tis true, schools must teach and impart knowledge, but beyond this they have a loftier aim. By means of teaching they must endeavor to train and educate and mold a definite moral character.

This educational aim of schools is often ignored and neglected. All teachers regard it as their duty to instruct their pupils, but some do not realize that such instruction must be educative and hence make no effort in that direction. They are more interested in seeing that the child gets the lesson than that the lesson means something to the child.

"We have been excessively busy seeking for information that could be turned to practical advantages in matter of dollars and cents rather than for that wisdom which would guide us through eternity. . . . Our higher educational institutions have turned their thoughts especially to the sciences and our secondary schools to vocational training. . . . All our learning, our culture, and our art will be of little value unless supported by high character. A trained intelligence can do much, but there is no substitute for morality, character, and religious conviction. Unless these abide, American citizenship will be found unequal to its task." (*Calvin Coolidge.*)

Having spoken of the pernicious influence of the "movies," which must be suppressed, Roger W. Babson has this to say about the schools: "We must strengthen the good influence of the schools. To supply mere information without character is like giving a pistol to a child. Yet this is what a large percentage of our so-called education consists of to-day. We are giving too much time to teaching the incidentals of life and too little to the teaching of the fundamentals of life. As young people are given more material, political, and intellectual power, they must have more spiritual power to correspond, or civilization gets top-heavy and out of balance. The ultimate result is temporary collapse. Hence the great need of the hour is not more or larger schools, colleges, and universities, but more sane religious education in those which we now have."

Because of the sad neglect of true moral education in many schools of the land a generation is growing up that is fairly well equipped with all manner of knowledge and skill, but woefully deficient in character. But as a good moral character is better than much learning, so training is more important than mere teaching. The necessity of moral training has of late been stressed very much, but many are in the dark as to what true moral education really is and how it can be achieved.

The Non-Religious School. — Any school which does not recognize the Christian principle in education nor employ the means provided therefor can certainly not train children as God would have them trained. To be sure, there is some kind of education, as pointed out in the preceding paragraphs, but whatever it may be, it is not Christian education, not the true and right kind of training.

The Word of God is barred from the public schools of our country, and rightly so. For while it is no doubt a great advantage to the state if all its citizens receive a good Christian training, rendering obedience to constituted authorities for conscience' sake, it is not the business of the state to teach any form of religion or even to insist that all the children of the land should be brought up in the nurture and admonition of the Lord. The state is concerned only with temporal and bodily things. It controls somewhat the outward relation of man to man, but it must not even try to interfere in the relation of man to his God. It is not concerned with spiritual and eternal things; it is not responsible to God for what the citizens believe or do not believe. The state demands and enforces obedience to *its* laws, but it has no authority to do so with respect to the laws of God. We must therefore resist every attempt, no matter how sincere and well-intentioned it may be, to introduce religious instruction and training into our state-controlled schools.

Because these schools do not and may not teach the Word of God, Christian training is simply impossible in them. It is for this reason that Luther writes: *"Wo aber die Heilige Schrift nicht regiert, da rate ich fuerwahr niemand, dass er sein Kind hintue. Es muss verderben alles, was nicht Gottes Wort ohne Unterlass treibt."* ("Where the Holy Scriptures do not dominate I certainly advise no one to send his child. For everything must degenerate that does not continually use the Word of God.")

We ought to be very careful in our criticism of the public schools. We must not imagine that, because they lack Christian instruction and training, they are also of no account in every other respect. Let us study their courses and their methods, their requirements and their achievements, and make use of whatever is sane, good, and profitable. However, let us not blindly copy all they have just because they have it. "Prove all things; hold fast that which is good" (1 Thess. 5, 21). Let us not be so conceited as to think that we cannot learn anything from the public-school system nor so weak as to imitate all it has.

We must not create the impression as though we expected the state schools to make suitable provision for the

Christian instruction and training of children. We oppose every attempt on the part of the state to do so. It is in the interest of the state to provide facilities for the education of its citizens. But it is no fault nor neglect of the civil authorities if they do not provide a religious education. On the contrary, they would transgress the limit of their power and trespass upon the most personal rights of individuals if they would teach and enforce upon all under their jurisdiction a certain type of religious education.

Persons that do not realize the value of a truly Christian training or are not sufficiently interested in securing it for their children may on their own responsibility send their children to the non-religious state schools. But as for us, who are in conscience bound to do all we can to bring up our children in the nurture and admonition of the Lord, both in the home and in the school, we cannot send our children there if there is a possible chance to send them to a school where they are instructed not only in the elementary common-school branches, but also in the Word of God and are trained according to Christian principles.

Religious Schools. — From the non-religious state schools we must distinguish the Christian Sunday-school and the Christian week-day, or parochial, school. We have in mind schools that are Christian not only in name, but in deed, schools in which not the theories and opinions of man, but the pure and unadulterated Word of God is taught. Because this Word of God is "profitable for . . . education in righteousness," these schools exert a positive Christian influence and assist in the Christian training of the child.

The Christian Sunday-School. — Originally the Sunday-school was never intended for the children of a Christian congregation, but only for the waifs whose secular and Christian education had been neglected. With the passing of the Christian parish-school of Colonial days and with the preponderance of the non-religious state schools, the Sunday-school has in many churches of our country become the sole church institution for the religious instruction and training of the young.

In our Lutheran Church, too, the number of Sunday-schools has steadily increased. It would be folly to deny that a properly conducted Sunday-school is of any value whatever. For the Word of God as taught in these schools is indeed a power of God unto salvation by faith in Christ and unto sanctification of life among men. And by means of the Sunday-school we can reach many children whom we could not reach otherwise. In mission-fields and in localities where it is honestly impossible, for the time being, to provide better and more effective facilities for the teaching and training of children, Sunday-schools should by all means be organized. The same holds true of congregations that have flourishing week-day schools. For it is by means of the Sunday-school that even in such localities real effective mission-work can be done among the unchurched children of the community. A Christian congregation must avail itself of every means and opportunity to win souls for Christ.

In order that the Sunday-school may be effective and its work be properly correlated with other educational activities of the congregation, the called servants of the Word should certainly take charge of it and make it as good an institution for the religious instruction of children as they can. Being commissioned to teach and train the children, our teachers should not hesitate to do so, whether this be during the week or on Sunday.

If some parents refuse to send their children to the parish-school because they are satisfied with the Sunday-school, this should nevertheless not keep us from conducting a Sunday-school. Refusing a Sunday-school to these children will not win them for the parochial school. On the other hand, many a child may be won through the Sunday-school for the week-day school.

However, it is quite generally conceded that the Sunday-school is not the most efficient institution for Christian education. If five periods a week are not held to be too much for the instruction in any secular branch of the curriculum, how, then, can a meager half hour on Sunday be sufficient properly to indoctrinate children, to inculcate upon them the principles of the Christian religion? Besides this, irregular attendance, lack of preparation and application, very much impair the effectiveness of all Sunday-school instruction.

With respect to training, the Sunday-school is even less effective. Training must be continuous. It will help the bent twig very little if it be straightened but once a week; it must be tied to a straight pole until it grows straight. The impressions made on the heart of the child in Sunday-school are not entirely lost, — they may become a power conducive to holy living, — but often they are not clear nor deep enough to last long. They are easily effaced by impressions received five days of the week in the non-religious state school. Therefore the effectiveness of the Sunday-school for teaching and training must not be overestimated.

The Christian Parish-School. — Next to the Christian home the Christian parish-school is the most effective agency for the Christian training of children. The parish-school is not in itself a divine institution. While Christ has, indeed, enjoined His Church to teach all nations — and this certainly includes also children — to observe all that He has commanded, He has not said that this must needs be done by means of such parochial schools as we have in our Lutheran Church. But the experience of the Church ever since the days of Doctor Martin Luther proves that a Christian congregation can best and most effectually perform its duty towards its children by means of a full-time parish-school. And until something still better is found, we should by all means foster these schools in our midst.

In these schools, children receive systematic instruction in the truths of God's Word. The Word of God is not profitable to any man if he does not learn it. Only those truths which we clearly understand and receive in our minds can exert an influence on our hearts and thus mold our characters. It is through the mind that we reach the heart and through the heart we control the life of a person. The parochial school offers a regular and systematic instruction, which is continued throughout school age. Thereby the child is enabled to obtain a fair and clear knowledge of the principal truths of God's Word, which in themselves possess the power to move the heart (Heb. 4, 12). Because of its thorough and effective teaching of Bible-truths the Lutheran parochial school commends itself as the ideal school for Christian children.

In these schools we have also the definite purpose and determined effort to train children in Christian living. As the case may demand, the Word of God is used for doctrine, for reproof, for correction, for training in righteousness, and for comfort. Every effort is made to have children observe in their lives what they have learned from the Bible. This is done, not only in the period set aside for religious instruction, but throughout the day whenever it is necessary. For the school must be a Christian school not only during the first period in the morning, which is given to religious instruction, but also in those periods in which secular branches are taught. The entire atmosphere of the school must be Christian, influencing the child also to practise what he has learned.

"The parish-school is a full-time educational institution, affording — what cannot be found in any other establishment of its kind — a balanced cultural program, education and training for the soul, the body, and the mind of the child.

"In working out its program, the ideal parish-school does not merely add a daily hour's work in the Catechism and Bible History to the usual curriculum of a secular education, nor does it merely append a few necessary secular branches to the daily instruction in religious knowledge. It is not a compromise, a hybrid, or a makeshift. It is a real school, with conscientious regard for the intellectual needs of the child, and a soul-winning agency, seeking to fill the pupil's heart with 'knowledge unto salvation' and the regenerating influence of the Gospel. But its purpose is single, not divided. Its one product is the character of a man of God who is 'throughly furnished unto all good works' in every walk of life.

"Upon its basic program of religious indoctrination is built up the elaborate system of training through which the consciousness of God's presence is carried into every activity of the school, all secular branches are presented in the light of Christian truth and in relation to soul life, all contacts and activities of the pupil are charged with a spiritual atmosphere, school discipline is maintained in a truly evangelical manner, and character is molded on that greatest of all patterns of spiritual excellency, the God-man Jesus Christ." (*K. Kretzschmar.*)

A school with such a program and with such an aim will certainly commend itself to all serious-minded Christian parents. Therefore it must be the constant endeavor of every one engaged in our Christian parish-schools to realize this ideal to the best of his ability. Our schools must be Christian, not merely in name, but in fact. The Christian character-building influence of the school must be felt and experienced by every one of its pupils. And it is the teacher who by his teaching and training must exert this influence.

It stands to reason that a child occupying himself so intensely with the study of God's Word and being subject to Christian influence five days a week will receive more lasting impressions and a more thorough Christian training than a child that attends Sunday-school but once a week for a brief hour. While half a loaf is better than none and a good Christian Sunday-school is better than no Christian school at all, a true evaluation of the Christian parochial school will show that both in instruction and training it is far superior to the best Sunday-school. Pastors and congregations that mean well with their children will not hesitate to organize and maintain Christian parish-schools.

"Nothing will be of greater service to us and our descendants than the maintenance of good Christian schools and the training of the young." (*Luther.*)

"The future of the Church depends largely on the kind of children that are being raised in every generation. The more thoroughly these are trained in Christian doctrine and life, the better it will be for the Church of the future. Can the Church of to-day be made safe for the generation of to-morrow without the kind of Christian education that only a parish-school can give?

"A good parish-school is worth much more than the money it costs to maintain it, not only in publicity, but even more in effective soul-winning. . . . If Christian parish-schools ever go out of existence, it will not be for the lack of merit or of possibilities; it will be because their supporters surrendered to the enemies of the kingdom of God." (*K. Kretzschmar.*)

A Fundamental Educational Difference. — It is in place here to point out the fundamental difference between secular and Christian education respecting the view of life each inculcates and therefore also respecting the attitude towards things temporal each seeks to develop.

Secular education ignores the spiritual needs and the eternal destiny of the child and aims to prepare him solely for this earthly life, training him so that he may be successful in his business or profession, be a good and honest neighbor, a loyal and law-abiding citizen, and enjoy the best this earthly life may offer. The entire educational scheme, study and play, influence and environment, is calculated to have the child look upon this earthly life as the ultimate aim of his existence. Ignoring the religious life of man, secular education is strictly mundane in its scope and purpose. *"Es ist eine diesseits orientierte Weltanschauung, die der Erziehung unsers oeffentlichen Schulwesens zugrunde liegt."*

The *Weltanschauung* of Christian education is entirely different. It is based on faith in Jesus, the Savior, by whom we have been reconciled to God, in whom we are sure of the forgiveness of our sins and of eternal life in heaven. Because we know ourselves to be God's children and heirs of eternal life, Paul writes: "Our conversation is in heaven" (Phil. 3, 20). He means to say that Christians, though *in* this world, are nevertheless not *of* this world (John 17, 16); they hold citizenship in heaven. They have here no continuing city, but seek one to come (Heb. 13, 14). Therefore they set their affections on things above and not on things on the earth; they are dead to this world, and their life is hid with Christ in God (Col. 3, 2. 3). Knowing that life is transitory, Christians live *in* this world, but they do not live *with* the world nor *for* this world, but as pilgrims *en route* they "use this world," its comforts and its inventions, its learning and its material things, and whatever may serve their purpose, as travelers use the conveniences of an inn, not setting their hearts on any of these things (1 Cor. 7, 29—31). At the same time they will do all they can to interest their fellow-travelers in things eternal and to induce them also to follow the narrow path that leads to eternal happiness, setting them an example in their own lives in faith and holiness. For true Christians this life on earth is not the chief objective, but they are looking forward to their home above.

It is evident that two educational systems based on such variant views of life are bound to conflict. Secular education is world-centered; it is confined to earthly things and evaluates them from a worldly viewpoint. Christian education is heaven-centered; heaven is the chief objective, and this earthly life is lived in the light of eternity. The one trains the child to live in this world for this world; the other trains him to live in this world as it becomes a child of God, striving to enter in at the strait gate that leadeth unto life eternal (Matt. 7, 13. 14). Each one is placing an entirely different value on the things of this life (Phil. 3, 7—11). The one teaches the child to turn his thoughts, desires, and aspirations earthward. Ignoring the beyond, he is to make his home in this world and make the best of life he can. The other teaches him to sojourn in this world as in a strange land, looking for the city whose builder and maker is God (Heb. 11, 9. 10).

The difference between these two educational systems is, aside from other things, a difference in the philosophy of life each one teaches. And this is of basic importance in the training of children. Any educational system which excludes religion from the training of the child will exclude it also from the life of the child. The secular education as it is offered in the public schools of our country is bound to produce an entirely different character in children from that which true Christian education will, which is based on the Biblical view of life and has respect to the eternal destiny of man.

We can well understand that the worldly-minded will give their children a purely secular education. But we cannot understand how it is possible for people who profess to be heavenly-minded to deny their children a true Christian education. It also must break the character of the child if during the formative period of life for five days of the week the full weight of the educational influence tends earthward and he is trained to make this world his home, while on Sunday he is told that all this is wrong, that he is but a pilgrim on earth and that heaven is his home. There is sense in training a child according to either of these philosophies, but it shows poor pedagogical judgment to subject our unconfirmed children to both educational systems, which are so divergent in their ultimate aim.

Realizing the fundamental difference between these two educational systems, Christian parents will know which to choose for their children and to which school to send them. But teachers of Christian schools must also make sure that their schools really offer children a true Christian education.

Cooperation of Home and School. — The Christian home and the Christian school are the two most effective agencies for the training of children. However, in point of importance and responsibility the home stands first. Parents may not neglect Christian training at home because their children are attending a Christian school. Theirs is the child, and theirs first is the duty to give him a Christian education. This prerogative and privilege no one may take from them, nor may they forego it voluntarily.

The Church has the same duty towards children. For if the Church is to make disciples of all nations by baptizing and by teaching them (Matt. 28, 19. 20), it certainly must not only baptize children, but also teach them to observe what Christ has commanded. However, the duty and authority of the Church does not supersede that of the parents, but is subordinate thereto, even as the authority of the mother is subordinate to that of the father in the home. As the Church may not baptize children against the will of the parents, so it cannot educate them in its schools if the parents refuse to send them. The Church must reach the children through their parents.

In order to secure for children the advantage of a Christian education, the Church should instruct the parents as to their duty in this respect and also show them wherein a true Christian education consists. The Church cannot relieve parents of their responsibility, but it must use its influence to make our homes Christian homes also with respect to the training of children. Luther prefaces each chief part of the Catechism with these words: "As the head of the family should teach it in all simplicity to his household."

To assist parents in such home-training and to perform at the same time its own duty with the children, the congregation maintains a parish-school. Pointing out the opportunities such a school offers, pastors and teachers must prevail upon parents to send their children to this school. This will require not only an initial canvass to win the children, but also a continued cooperation between home and school to keep them in school and to correlate both agencies for the effectual training of the children.

Though home and school do the same work, there are some differences. Because of the larger number of children in school there are peculiar educational problems which are not so evident in the home. On the other hand, parental authority is greater than that of the teacher; children spend more time at home than at school; parents have a more intimate knowledge of their children than the teacher. Nevertheless Christian education at home must be essentially the same as at school. Both have the same objective, employ the same means, follow the same principle. It is therefore imperative that both cooperate, one supporting the other. There must be an understanding between parent and teacher, lest each follow a different course and the child be subjected to conflicting influences. The unchristian influence of a school can easily destroy what Christian education at home has built, and the ungodly influence of the home may neutralize the good influence of a Christian school.

Lack of cooperation between home and school in the education of children is one of the chief reasons why Christian training is not always as effective as it might be. Many parents depend entirely upon the school for the training of their children; the home influence is nil, perhaps even negative. But the teacher also must watch scrupulously in order that he may not in the least undermine and counteract the Christian influence of the home.

For successful cooperation, parents and teachers must clearly understand what is the aim and objective of Christian training, which are the means to be employed, and how they are to be used. As each child presents individual problems, consultation with parents will often prove very helpful to the teacher. He can thus obtain valuable information concerning the child and learn to know home conditions and influences. The parents also may profit by the knowledge and observations of the teacher. But in giving information to parents concerning their children, the teacher should be very tactful.

Visiting the home, "you will learn many things about this child which you yourself cannot express in words. You will learn how much opportunity that child has had before for education, what his opportunities are for home study, what disciplinary control is at home, and many other things that will be of help to you. Of course, you are going to be courteous to the child at school and courteous to his home people; that is, you will try to be. You may fail, unless you really know the fundamental fact and meaning of courtesy. Remember, courtesy is a spiritual attitude, and you must be courteous to people in their way. *Your influence will be in terms of the impressions which you make rather than in the information which you give."* (*Avent.*)

The teacher should be very careful what impression he makes on the parents of his pupils, for this will affect not only their reception of what he would tell them, but also their cooperation with his work in school. A teacher may be ever so able and efficient, if the parents do not like him and the home influence is against him, then his success will, for this very reason, fall short of his best efforts, as children are very much influenced by the opinion of their parents. If, on the other hand, he enjoys the respect and confidence of the parents, this will stand him in good stead for his dealing with their children.

Beginning teachers have much to learn what cannot be gotten from books and lectures. And some experienced parents know more about actual and practical training of children than the college-bred man, his theoretical learning notwithstanding. A course in Christian pedagogy is eminently helpful to the teacher, but theoretical knowledge does by no means make him an expert educator. Hence experience is the best teacher, and we must study each case and learn at every step.

Part II. THE EDUCATOR.

IV. Christian Education a Duty.

The Pedagog. — A pedagog in ancient Greece was a slave who led his master's children to school, places of amusement, etc., until they became old enough to take care of themselves. In many cases he also acted as teacher and tutor. He was responsible chiefly for the bodily safety and well-being of his wards. The modern pedagog is principally an educator, and his is a nobler calling and a far more important work than that of his Greek predecessor. His duty is by instruction and otherwise to lead and train the child morally and spiritually and to exert such a determining influence upon his soul life that permanent habits are formed and a moral character is developed. The duty of a Christian pedagog is by teaching and training to help children to lead a Christian life in the sight of man and God.

Christian Training a Duty. — There is no doubt about it that every teacher does educate, even though he have no intention of doing so. Aside from the fact that much of the subject-matter he teaches possesses potential educative qualities, his personality, his manners, his conduct, the views he expresses, and the life he leads, all these radiate an influence for better or worse, and in the measure in which he influences his pupils he also educates and trains them. But no conscientious Christian teacher will ever rest content with such incidental training. Inasmuch as he is a real pedagog, there must be, and there will be, on his part also the intention to educate and a sincere endeavor "to bring up the children in the nurture and admonition of the Lord." He will not only teach them to know, but also train them to do and to observe, what Christ has commanded. It is not at all optional with him whether or not he should put forth any effort in this direction, but it is his plain duty, which he must not shirk.

To be sure, it is more difficult to train a child than it is to teach him. There are many disappointments, and results are not always immediately evident. The teacher may at times become discouraged. Still he must not forget that he is in duty bound to do all he possibly can to train and educate his pupils in the ways of God.

Children Need Such Training. — As children are ignorant, they must necessarily be instructed. Hence many teachers give so much attention to this phase of their work that they neglect the greater and more difficult task of training children according to the Word of God. Their pupils make excellent progress in learning, but little in holiness of life; they profit in knowledge, but not so in Christian virtues; their mind is developed, but their character neglected. Here applies: *"Qui proficit in litteris et deficit in moribus, plus deficit quam proficit"*; i. e., he who becomes proficient in learning, but deficient in morals has lost more than he has gained. Let the teacher ever bear in mind that his pupils have need not only of instruction, but especially also of education and training. By nature they are morally depraved, and unless they are properly guided and trained, they will follow the "evil imagination of the heart" in their lives. The natural moral condition of every child is to us an appeal for Christian education.

Moreover, the teacher has in his schoolroom a large number of children who live together, associate with one another, and influence one another. This makes it necessary for him not only to maintain outward discipline, but also to train them. The very fact that a number of children are gathered together may cause all manner of mischief, sins, and offenses. A spirit may develop in the school that will prove detrimental to the character of all children; and this he must thwart. There may be emulation, vainglory, envy, quarrelsomeness, etc.; and these he must curb. On the other hand, certain duties devolve upon the children. They must show consideration for others, be kind, and be ready to help and to serve one another. In these things the teacher must instruct, encourage, and train his pupils. The very fact that children are committed to his care imposes on him the duty also to give them what they sorely need, *viz.,* a Christian education. "Indeed, the child ought to be the objective of the work of the whole Church. The saving of its children from wandering outside the fold is the supreme duty and the strategic opportunity of the Church, standing out above all other claims whatever.... We do not always realize that to keep a child a Christian is much more important than to reclaim him after he has been allowed to get outside of the fold." (*Betts.*)

Parents Expect Such Training. — All parents are commanded "to bring up their children in the nurture and admonition of the Lord" (Eph. 6, 4). But during school-hours these children are under the supervision and control of the teacher, who thus shares with the parents the responsibility for the Christian training of their children. Parents therefore have a right to expect that, while their children are in the teacher's care, he exert a wholesome influence on them, that he do all he can to train them according to Christian principles, and that he mold in them a Christian character as best he can. Parents have no right to entrust their children to any one who refuses, or wilfully neglects, to do this. If incompetency to teach unfits a man for the school, manifest inability or unwillingness to train and educate still more does so.

The Call of the Teacher Enjoins Such Training. — The Church is commissioned by Christ to make disciples of all nations, which certainly includes also the children.

This is to be done by baptizing them in the name of the Triune God and by teaching them to observe all things that Christ has commanded (Matt. 28, 28). While we must concede priority of right and duty to parents in this respect, the Church also has, in its own right, the duty to teach and train its children. It may therefore devise such means as in its opinion are most adequate and effectual for accomplishing this purpose.

The best institution known for the Christian teaching and training of children, next to the home, is the parochial school. The congregation, in calling a teacher for its school, enjoins upon him that part of the work of the holy ministry which pertains to children; *i. e.*, in the name and by authority of the congregation he is to teach children the Word of God and to train them according to Christian principles. The teacher, then, as the called servant of the Church, is in duty bound, as also his call specifies, not only to instruct the children in the teachings of the Word of God, but also to educate and train them so that in their lives they observe and do what the Lord has commanded.

God Demands Such Training. — Besides what was mentioned in the preceding paragraphs, there is still a higher authority that imposes upon every teacher the duty to teach and train children in the way they should go. It is not merely the congregation that has called him, but through the congregation God Himself has put him in this office as shepherd of the lambs of Christ. His also is a divine call. Therefore, in the circumscribed sphere of his office, also to him apply the words of God: "So thou, O son of man, I have set thee a watchman unto the house of Israel; therefore thou shalt hear the word at My mouth and warn them from me. When I say unto the wicked, O wicked man, thou shalt surely die! if thou dost not speak to warn the wicked from his way, that wicked man shall die in his iniquity, but his blood will I require at thine hand. Nevertheless, if thou warn the wicked of his way to turn from it; if he do not turn from his way, he shall die in his iniquity, but thou hast delivered thy soul" (Ezek. 33, 7—9). Christ enjoins upon teachers that they teach children to observe all He has commanded and that they feed His lambs. The duty, then, to teach and train children is imposed on the teacher not merely by the congregation that has called him, but by God Himself, who has made him His servant.

"The teacher must accept responsibility for the spiritual growth as well as for the intellectual training of his pupils. . . . Indeed, the cultivation of this trend of the life toward God is the supreme aim in our religious leadership of children." (*Betts.*)

The Fourth Commandment. — It might seem strange that we should call attention to the Fourth Commandment: "Thou shalt honor thy father and thy mother," since this commandment was primarily given to children. However, it teaches an important lesson which parents and teachers also should take to heart.

When God demands of children to "honor" their parents and masters, He places these over them and clothes them with divine power and authority. Parents and teachers, both in their sphere, are God's representatives, and God would have them respected and honored as such.

But this exalted position imposes on them also responsibilities. Parents generally recognize it to be their duty to feed and clothe their children and to provide for their bodily wants. Teachers often confine themselves to the teaching of such secular matters as will prepare their pupils for their vocations in life. Both often neglect their prime duty of teaching children the Word of God and of training them to lead a godly life. Hence there is growing up in our country a generation "disobedient to parents" (Rom.

1, 30). Many do not "honor" their parents and superiors because they were never taught to do so.

On the other hand, parents may not overstep their authority. Theirs is a power under God; it is not absolute, but limited. "We ought to obey God rather than men" Acts 5, 29) applies also to the authority of parents and teachers. They have no right to demand, to expect, to encourage, to countenance, and to permit anything that is contrary to the Word of God. It is a gross misuse of parental influence and authority whenever this is done. The sons of Eli made themselves vile, but their father restrained them not (1 Sam. 3, 13). And are there not many fathers in our day who also do not frown upon the evil their children are doing? How may we expect children to honor us as God's representatives if we ourselves set aside the authority of God?

The duty of parents and of those who take their place is stated negatively and positively in Eph. 6, 4: "Ye fathers, provoke not your children to wrath, but bring them up in the nurture and admonition of the Lord"; and Col. 3, 21 we read: "Fathers, provoke not your children to anger, lest they be discouraged." This does not mean that, because correction and punishment may displease children, parents should refrain from reproving and correcting them. It is the duty of parents to correct their children when they do what is wrong, for it is written: "He that spareth the rod hateth his son; but he that loveth him chasteneth him betimes" (Prov. 13, 24).

When parents, however, use their authority arbitrarily, capriciously commanding their children to do this or that, merely to vex them; whenever they deal unjustly, unfairly, with them; whenever they use them cruelly in word or in deed, then they provoke them to wrath and discourage them. Though children will submit to such treatment for the time being, there remains a sting and a rancor in their hearts, and it is difficult for them to honor their parents and teachers as they should. Often those who complain most that children are disrespectful and disobedient have none to blame but themselves because by inconsiderate treatment they provoked their children to wrath.

"Bring them up in the nurture and admonition of the Lord." It is not at all optional with parents whether to give their children a Christian education or not to do so. God, who gave them these children (Ps. 127, 3), demands that they teach them His Word and train them in it. It is this, above all other things, He would have parents do, and He will certainly call them to account if they do not faithfully perform this duty. This applies also to teachers in our Christian schools. If we properly teach and train children according to God's Word, they will also honor and respect us.

Since God demands of children that they honor their parents and teachers, the latter must so conduct themselves as to be worthy of such honor. The sins and shortcomings of parents never justify the contempt of children (Gen. 9, 20—25). However, parents and teachers must not take advantage of this, thinking they may do as they please and still insisting on being given the honor due them. They must so live and so deport themselves that they give no occasion for contempt, but that their children and pupils will look up to them and gladly "give them honor, serve and obey them, and hold them in love and esteem."

Before impressing the Fourth Commandment upon children and pupils, parents and teacher will do well to study this commandment themselves.

Consecration. — The attitude of a Christian teacher toward his calling should be quite different from that of other men toward their profession or occupation. He should not look upon his work chiefly as a means of earning his livelihood, but rather as an opportunity to accomplish great things for the Lord. For this reason he should give himself whole-heartedly to the manifold duties of his calling, not permitting his chief interest and attention to be diverted to matters which promise larger or additional financial returns. His best energies should be devoted to the work for which he has been called. It is inconceivable how any one can do his best in so important a work if his mind is engrossed with matters that are altogether foreign to it. If any one does not care to devote his time and talents to the teaching and training of children, let him choose another profession, one which he likes better. The Lord needs and wants men who from the heart consecrate themselves to His service. This attitude of consecration must be fostered. Difficulties peculiar to this work, the small recognition it often receives, the Old Adam, and many other things combine to make the teacher lose interest in his work. To counteract such influences, it is well for him to bear in mind the superior nobility and importance of his calling. His is not a work devised by men, but one which the Lord Jesus Himself commanded and into which He calls men who truly love Him (John 21, 15), a work which He esteems very highly (Matt. 18, 5) and which He will reward munificently in the realms of glory (Dan. 12, 3). It is a work by which the teacher helps to confer spiritual and eternal blessings upon children, inasmuch as he teaches them the way to heaven and trains them to live as God's children here on earth and to "glorify the Lord in their body" (1 Cor. 6, 20). It is a work by which he does greater things for mankind in general than he would be able to do in any other profession. For if "righteousness exalteth a nation" (Prov. 14, 34), then teachers who train the coming generation to walk in the paths of righteousness surely do more for their country's welfare than any politician or captain of industry can do.

Luther's estimate of the calling of a Christian schoolteacher is well known. He says: *"Einen fleissigen, frommen Schulmeister oder Magister, oder wer es ist, der Knaben treulich ziehet und lehret, dem kann man nimmermehr genug lohnen und mit keinem Gelde bezahlen. Und ich, wenn ich vom Predigtamt und andern Sachen ablassen koennte oder muesste, so wollte ich kein Amt lieber haben, denn Schulmeister oder Knabenlehrer sein. . . . Lieber, lass es der hoechsten Tugenden eine sein auf Erden, fremden Leuten ihre Kinder treulich ziehen, welches gar wenige und schier niemand tut an seinen eigenen."* Luther means to say that a diligent and pious schoolteacher who faithfully trains and teaches children cannot be sufficiently rewarded and paid. And if Luther could have left off preaching, he would have desired no other office more than that of a teacher of children. This he regards as one of the most praiseworthy occupations on earth.

To any Christian teacher tempted to become discouraged and to lose interest in his work we would recommend a careful perusal of Luther's Sermon *That Children be Sent to School* (St. Louis Ed., Vol. X, 416—459).

Christians should appraise their calling not on the basis of what comfort and financial returns they derive for themselves, but on that of service to God and their neighbor. And one will have to look far and wide to find a calling that offers greater opportunities for real and worth-while service than does the office of a Christian schoolteacher. Next to the ministry of the Word, of which, in fact, it is a part, there is none in which a person can use his gifts to a greater advantage and can accomplish more lasting results than in this calling.

Says Betts (*How to Teach Religion*, pp. 31. 34): "The greatest business of any generation or people is therefore the education of its children. Before this all other enterprises and obligations must give way, no matter what their importance. It is at this point that civilization succeeds or fails. Suppose that for a single generation our children, through some inconceivable stroke of fate, would refuse to open their minds to instruction; suppose they would refuse to learn our science, our religion, our literature, and all the rest of the culture which the human race has bought at so high a price of sacrifice and suffering; suppose they should turn deaf ears to the appeal of art and reject the claims of morality and refuse the lessons of Christianity and the Bible, — where, then, would all our boasted progress be? Where would our religion be? Where would modern civilization be? All would revert to primitive barbarism through the failure of this one generation, and the race would be obliged to start anew the long climb toward the mountain-top of spiritual freedom.

"Each generation must therefore create anew in its own life and experience the spiritual culture of the race. Each child that comes to us for instruction, weak, ignorant, and helpless though it be, is charged with his part in the great program God has marked out for man to achieve. Each of these little ones is the bearer of an immortal soul, whose destiny it is to take its quality and form from the life it lives among its fellows. And ours is the dread and fascinating responsibility for a time to be the mentor and guide of this celestial being. Ours it is to deal with the infinite possibilities of child-life and to have a hand in forming the character that this immortal soul will take. Ours it is to have the thrilling experience of experimenting in the making of a destiny."

These considerations should move every Christian teacher to consecrate himself to his noble work. Let him be ever mindful of his duty, yea, rather of his privilege, to teach children the way of salvation and to train them to walk in the ways of God. Let him not look upon Christian training as a very desirable by-product of his work, but rather regard it as one of his chief duties.

V. Natural Qualifications.

Not every grown person is, because of his age and experience, also a competent educator. There is a great difference in men respecting their ability to educate and train children. Some parents provide lavishly for the bodily wants of their offspring, but are not very successful in training them. Some teachers are skilled instructors, but only mediocre or even poor educators. We find men who are well versed in all pedagogical lore of ancient and modern times; they know the theory of education and write scholarly books for the guidance of others, still they find it difficult to follow their own precepts, or they fail because they follow them pedantically; they lack practical pedagogical sense. Even the fact that one is personally a sincere Christian will not make him an expert educator of children and young people. Whoever, therefore, would engage in the training of the young must needs possess, at least in some measure, certain qualities and abilities.

Ability to Teach. — As children are educated by means of what they learn, it certainly is necessary that whoever would train them must also be able to teach them. It is not the knowledge the teacher has acquired and stored up in his mind, but the knowledge which he actually imparts to children that can impress and move and train them. A man of deep learning is not necessarily also a successful instructor. And a good instructor is not always an equally good educator. A good educator, however, should also be a good teacher. For it is by way of the mind that he can touch the heart, and therefore he must be able to impart to the mind that knowledge which possesses power to impress the heart, move the will, and prompt action.

The necessity of this ability is recognized also in the Bible. If children are to observe what Christ has commanded, they must first be taught. "Teach them to observe whatsoever I have commanded you," says Christ. And what Paul demands of a bishop applies also to those who are to feed the lambs of Christ — they must "be apt to teach" (1 Tim. 3, 2).

Such teaching, however, does not mean merely to present the subject-matter to the class, to teach the lesson, but it means to teach the child, to "put the lesson across," to do all we can that the child really learns what we are teaching. If no learning results on the part of the child, our teaching has not been effective.

We would here plead the cause of the weak and poorly gifted child, which is so often neglected. Every instructor prefers to teach bright pupils; it is far easier and more pleasant for him. But we often lose patience with the child of slow understanding, whose intelligent quotient is low, and we do not always give him a fair chance; we do not try to teach him as much as he is able to grasp. It is most reprehensible for a teacher to devote his attention primarily to his well-gifted pupils while just carrying along the others. These weak children need his attention more than the bright pupils; they also must be taught to observe what Christ has commanded and by no means must be neglected. It is here that the instructor may show whether he is "apt to teach."

Ability to teach certainly requires that the teacher be thoroughly conversant with his subject. It is only then that he can give his undivided attention to real teaching. As long as he is still mentally laboring with the material of his instruction, not knowing what to teach and how to teach it, he is not sufficiently at ease to watch the reaction of his pupils and to adapt his method to their needs, nor can he put that life into his teaching which carries conviction. Thorough preparation for every lesson is absolutely necessary.

Natural Qualifications.

Liking for Children.—We can readily understand that a person having an aversion to children and loathing their company is not fit to educate them. Neither is he who is so conceited in his own mind as to despise these little ones. Such an attitude will not only make his work a drudgery to him, but will also very seriously impair the effectiveness of his teaching and training. For children are quick to sense whether or not a person likes them, and they will shrink from one who does not care for them. When we were children, our hearts were closed to the influence of persons whom we believed to be proud or who, we felt, did not like us, while we were easily led by those who loved us and whom we loved in return. We should therefore bear in mind that not so many years ago we ourselves were such ignorant and untrained children and needed the loving guidance of our parents and teachers and that we certainly have no reason to despise one of these little ones (Matt. 18, 10).

Love of children will make work among children pleasant and easy. Though there will be difficulties and disappointments, if we love them, we shall not tire in our efforts to help them, but shall try and try again to do for them what we can. But it also makes work among them more effective; for they will more readily yield to the influence of one who loves them than to that of one who is cold and indifferent and shows that he does not care for them.

Such love of children will manifest itself in **cheerfulness.** Imagine a teacher who appears to be continually stern, morose, and ill-humored. A smile never beams on his face. His features are set and hard and scowling. He may not be so at heart, but the children read his face. How does it affect them? They shrink from him, their hearts are closed to him, his sullen mean frightens them. Until they have learned to know him better, it will be difficult for him to win their affection and confidence. Let every teacher cultivate cheerfulness; and if he be a Christian, he has every reason to be cheerful at all times (Phil. 4, 4). Such cheerfulness will make him feel better personally, and it will affect his pupils favorably. The cheerful countenance of the teacher spreads cheer and light in the schoolroom.

Such love of children will manifest itself also in sincere **kindliness.** The impression we make does not depend only on what we say, but also on how we say it. There is a way of speaking, curt, snappish, which arouses opposition; another, cold, mechanical, which makes no impression whatever; but there is also a way of speaking that at once wins the heart. What is it? It is the tone of truthfulness, of sympathetic love and kindliness we hear in the voice that so forcibly appeals to us. If we would win children, then let us not "be bitter against them," not crabbed and "grouchy," but sincerely kind in word and deed. Such kindliness cannot be learned from books; it proceeds from a loving heart and must be practised daily. "Out of the abundance of the heart the mouth speaketh" (Matt. 12, 34). If one is in ill humor, let him control himself and not give vent to it in the schoolroom.

Sincere Interest. — Whoever loves children will also be interested in them. He will sympathize with them in their little troubles and rejoice with them when they are happy. He will recognize and appreciate their efforts to be good and to do what is right. He will not run through the mechanics of teaching and training in a cold and matter-of-fact way, but at every step his words and actions will reveal a sincere personal interest in their progress in learning and behavior. Children have a very keen sense in this matter. And once they begin to doubt their teacher's sincerity of purpose and his interest in them, his educational influence is practically nil. If, on the other hand, they feel that he believes what he teaches, that he means what he says, that he is earnestly trying to lead them the right way and to help them as best he can, they will more readily submit to his guidance and training.

Unselfishness. — Closely allied to interest is unselfishness. The selfish man will do only what promises to be of some advantage to him; and even when serving others, he does so because of some profit or honor he expects to derive therefrom. In teaching and training, however, we are to benefit others. The entire educational procedure is calculated for the betterment of the child. There are so many little, still very important things we must do that, though they give us much trouble, bring us no profit.

Selfishness not only hampers the activity of the teacher, but will also, if suspected by the children, seriously affect his influence with them. No one, not even children, will readily follow a selfish leader. Children must be led to feel that their teacher is looking, not primarily to his own interest, but to their welfare, that he does not wish to profit himself, but to benefit them. The teacher who succeeds in convincing his pupils of his own unselfishness has done much to open the way for very effectual training.

Patience and Perseverance. — Whoever would train children will certainly need these two qualities. The results of teaching are more immediate and patent; the fruits of training develop and ripen but slowly. Evil habits are not broken in a day, and good habits and virtues are not formed in a week. Training a child is always a slow and long-drawn-out process. Let no one engaged in the training of children become discouraged when he encounters difficulties or when he does not at once accomplish the success he anticipated. Let him be patient, but let him persevere.

Patience is that calm self-possession which under adverse circumstances quietly waits for what is expected and persists in what was begun. Lack of patience is a common failing. Because children do not always react immediately or not as perfectly as they are expected to do, the teacher often loses courage and desists from further efforts, or, losing his temper, he tries to accomplish by force and scolding what he was unable to accomplish by his influence.

Patience and perseverance must be learned by practise, and, indeed, they can be learned if one honestly tries and persists in trying. The Christian teacher will remember the patience of God, who never tires in leading us in the straight path though we lapse ever so often. And since Paul admonishes us to be patient toward all men (1 Thess. 5, 14), we should certainly be patient toward our pupils.

However, patience must never become license, and love must never mean laxity. No matter how patient we may be with the child, we must also be firm in leading him to the goal we have set. No matter how much we love children, we must at times be strict with them if their welfare requires it. And though we be cheerful and kind in our dealings with them, let us not become silly and foolish and childish. As soon as patience is practised to such an extent as to defeat the purpose of education, it ceases to be a virtue.

Such love for children and its cognate qualities we find in almost all normally constituted human beings. Indeed, not all possess them in the same degree. With some they are very pronounced, as in Pestalozzi; in others they are weak. But, fortunately, there are very few who lack them entirely. The reason why they are not so manifest in some as in others may be a peculiar temperamental disposition. But whatever there may be of love in us for children, it is capable of development. Interest yourself in children, and you will become interested in them. Suppress every thought that would have you despise them and think of the great things you can do for them. Learn to love by loving them.

Equanimity and Self-Control. — Equanimity is that evenness of mind and temper which is not easily depressed, elated, or agitated by passing emotions. Self-control is the ability so to control one's feelings and passions that they do not lead to rash and inconsiderate words and actions. While emotions are indeed the chief moving power in man, they must be controlled by the will, which, in turn, is regulated by the mind.

Such equanimity or, where this is lacking, such self-control is a necessary requisite in him who would control and guide others. There are occasions where the temper of the teacher is sorely tried. But he must restrain himself and suppress violent outbursts of strong feeling. Acting in a fit of enthusiasm or of anger, he is beside himself and liable to do and say what he will be sorry for when he has regained his equilibrium. A teacher losing his temper is also at a decided disadvantage over against his class, and his influence for positive training is very much weakened.

If the teacher is unduly strict to-day and to-morrow inexcusably lenient; if one day he forbids and punishes what he tolerates and encourages the next; if he praises in the morning and rages in the afternoon, then it is evident that there cannot be that steady and consistent influence which is so necessary for effectual training. Such a teacher, moreover, will lose the respect and confidence of his pupils; for they do not know what he will do next and what they may expect. If rave he must, let him do so when he is all alone by himself, but in the presence of children he should control himself and be composed.

We influence children not only by what we teach them, but also by our manner of carrying on before them. By quiet and consistent firmness we accomplish much more than by an occasional outburst of passion. Let us therefore guard against fickleness, irritability, capriciousness, and inconsistency and cultivate that "kingly continence" of body and soul.

Equanimity and self-control are qualities which men possess in different degrees according to their temperamental disposition. But it is doubtful whether any rational being is totally devoid of them, and they certainly can be developed by self-discipline. The reason why these qualities often do not function in the lives of some as they should is that these people were not trained in this respect when they were young, nor are they making any serious effort to train themselves now that they are grown. To cultivate and to develop these qualities may be more difficult for some than it is for others, but it is possible in all sane and rational beings. And surely there is no greater victory than to conquer and control oneself.

Two things are necessary, "Watch and pray." Watch yourself and pray to God for strength. Forget yourself and think of the child. "Keep cool" and do not let any personal resentment or blinding passion obscure to your vision the noble aim of your work. Pray for divine help to control your temper and preserve that evenness of mind which is so essential to success.

Common Sense. — Under this heading, as applied to pedagogy, we would group all such qualities as prudence, tact, resourcefulness, etc. Many situations arise in the training of children for which no prescribed formulas may be found in books on pedagogy, telling exactly what to do and how to proceed. The teacher is then thrown on his own resources. His own common sense must tell him what to do and what effect his procedure is likely to have on the child. Even the advice of others, though helpful, cannot always be followed in detail. For the mode of procedure might be very successful if he who advised it were to handle the case. But as it is, the teacher must act himself, and he will act in his own way. He cannot so fully eliminate his own individuality as to follow mechanically the advice of another and the rules in the book. The fundamental line of action he may learn from others, but the detail he must supply.

It is here that he must use tact, which is that skill and adroitness in doing and saying exactly what is required under the circumstances. Improving the situation, he must be quick to turn everything to account for the benefit of the child's education. Hence he must be resourceful and clever in finding those means and ways that will best serve his purpose. Very often he must act on the spur of the moment; then he must act discreetly, never losing sight of his objective. It may be advisable in such cases to say and do no more than is absolutely necessary for the time being and to take the matter under advisement. If confronted with a complex situation, let him not act rashly, but study the case thoroughly and then act as his wisdom directs. In short, knowing his objective in education and the means he is to employ, the teacher must use ordinary common sense in applying these means; but let him be sure that it really is common sense.

Pedagogical wisdom cannot be learned from books; it is a gift of God. Any one totally deficient in this will not be successful in the training of children. However, this quality often lies dormant, not having had any opportunity to manifest itself, and it springs into action when confronted with actual educational problems. It is by practical experience in educational work that one discovers whether he possesses this precious gift, and it is by experience in the training of children that this gift is developed.

Ability to Gain Respect and Confidence. — This qualification is eminently important. Every educator should earnestly strive to win and hold the respect and the confidence of his pupils. Children will not be influenced by one whom they mistrust or despise. No matter what he may do, their hearts are closed to him.

Respect consists in this, that children look up to their teacher, that they honor him, that they "esteem him highly in love for his work's sake" (1 Thess. 5, 13). Confidence is this, that children feel sure their teacher means well with them, that they never doubt his good intentions and his ability to lead them in the right way.

A teacher enjoying the respect and confidence of his pupils holds a position of vantage. They will not ignore his words nor slight his requests, but will take them to heart and observe them willingly. Respect and confidence in their teacher opens their hearts and makes them receptive for his teaching and influence. The lack of these will very much hinder his educative effectiveness, perhaps frustrate it altogether.

Such loving respect and confidence is indeed demanded of children, but it cannot be commanded, that is to say, no one can make children respect and trust him simply by commanding them to do so. Respect and confidence must be won, and they are won by what the teacher is to the children or what they believe him to be to them. Respect and confidence are based on the opinion the children have of their teacher.

Whoever would win and hold the respect and confidence of his fellow-men must be every inch a man. By studied manners and obliging service one may deceive others for a time, but in the end only true worth will tell. Hypocrisy, duplicity, fickleness, selfishness, inability, unreliability, etc., will beget contempt and distrust. Even the appearance of these must be avoided, for the opinions men have of us are not determined by what we are at heart, but by what we appear to be. "Man looketh on the outward appearance" (1 Sam. 16, 7). But no one can for any length of time keep up appearances if there be no sterling worth behind it; some one will find him out at last.

This applies also to the teacher of children. Let him avoid whatever might destroy and do what will win and hold the respect and confidence of his pupils. He must not attempt to appear what he has neither the strength nor the purpose to be. He must not be a weakling, whom they despise, nor a tyrant, whom they fear, but a fatherly friend, whom they respect and trust. He must know what he is supposed to know and be able and willing to do what he should do. He must not only tell children what they are to do, but he must himself practise what he preaches. Because of his position the teacher should be an exemplary character.

The qualifications of which we have spoken in this chapter may be present in different persons in various degrees and proportions. Often they lie dormant, and the teacher discovers them when engaged in actual work and confronted with real educational problems. A true appreciation of their value will induce him to nurse and develop them.

While the total absence of these qualifications will indeed unfit a person for the work of training children, their presence does not yet qualify him for the work of Christian education. For this other, spiritual, gifts are necessary.

VI. Spiritual Qualifications.

"Can the blind lead the blind? Shall they not both fall into the ditch?" (Luke 6, 39.) These words of the Master apply with peculiar force to the training of children. To be sure, also he who is blind in spiritual things can and does train children in a fashion. But to give them a Christian education and to help them to become better Christians in their lives, it is absolutely necessary for the educator to possess certain spiritual qualifications.

Knowledge of the Scripture Doctrines Necessary. — As the Word of God is the chief means of Christian training, it is evident that a Christian pedagog must acquire an exact knowledge of its teachings and of their use. Whoever has but vague and indefinite notions himself concerning the teachings of the Bible certainly cannot impart clear ideas and definite knowledge to others. However, that this be done is absolutely necessary; for the heart is moved as the mind is instructed, and the child will go the way he is taught. In order, then, to teach plainly and to train effectively, the educator must himself have a thorough knowledge of the Christian doctrine.

No conscientious teacher should rest content with what he knows, thinking it is enough to carry him through the lesson. He must continue to study, ever striving for a more perfect knowledge of each individual Bible doctrine and of its relation to the other Scripture teachings. For these teachings are not a mass of loose and heterogeneous statements, but rather a compact system, in which all the doctrines are fitly framed together. The better one understands the whole, the more qualified he will be to teach the parts.

Vague and hazy knowledge is often the cause of indefinite and ineffective teaching. Let every teacher therefore "give attendance to reading" (1 Tim. 4, 13). Let him read not only books pertaining to the secular branches he is teaching, but let him read, yea, let him study his Bible. Let him read books, periodicals, and articles which clearly set forth the teachings of the Bible; let him read these attentively for his own sake and also for the sake of the children he is teaching. Even though he knew all he must know and ought to know, let him continue to meditate on what he knows that he may ever better learn to teach it to his pupils.

"Our knowledge and mastery must always be much broader than the material we actually present. It must be deeper and our grasp more complete than can be reached by our pupils. For only this will give us the mental perspective demanded of the teacher. Only this will enable our thought to move with certainty and assurance in the field of our instruction. And only this will win the confidence and respect of our pupils, who, though their minds are yet unformed, have nevertheless a quick sense for the mastery or weakness as revealed in their teacher." (*Betts.*)

Ability to "Divide the Word of Truth." — The Word of God contains two distinct principal doctrines, the Law and the Gospel. They differ as to their content and serve different purposes and therefore must be distinguished in their use. The Law tells man what he must do or not do and how he must be if he would please God. It serves as a restraining curb to the outbursts of sin or as a mirror to show man his shortcomings or as a guide to direct him in his way. The Gospel, on the other hand, reveals to man the grace of God, offers to him unconditionally the forgiveness of all his sins, and works in him the acceptance of its promise. Working and preserving faith in man, it makes him able and willing to live as the Law directs.

Because of this fundamental difference between the Law and the Gospel each has its own place and purpose in the scheme of education. The educator must therefore be able "rightly to divide the Word of Truth" and also to connect in their proper sequential order, without mixing them, Law and Gospel. The Law must not be taught as though it were possible for man to be saved thereby. And the Gospel must not be taught as though its promise of grace were contingent upon some merit or worthiness man must first achieve. Still both, Law and Gospel, must be used, each in its place and for its distinct purpose. (See chapter XII, p. 132 ff.)

While in theory it seems easy enough to differentiate between the Law and the Gospel, it is not so in actual practise. Before a physician can prescribe the proper medicine, he must diagnose the patient's disease. Before the teacher can apply either the Law or the Gospel, he also must diagnose the spiritual condition of the child. He must know whether the child understands his sins and repents of them or whether he is still impenitent. This spiritual diagnosis represents the chief difficulty. However, this diagnosis must determine whether he is to use the Law or the Gospel on the child. As it may be very harmful if a physician prescribes the wrong medicine, so it will be of serious consequence in the training of children if the teacher misapplies either the Law or the Gospel. Hence the injunction: "Study to show thyself approved unto God, a workman that needeth not to be ashamed, rightly dividing the Word of Truth" (2 Tim. 2, 15).

Personal Faith. — It is not sufficient for any one engaged in the work of Christian education and training to have acquired an intellectual knowledge of the Bible-teachings, of their use, and of the effect they are likely to have on children, but he must himself have experienced their power in his own heart, — he must be a truly believing Christian. Knowing himself to be a lost and condemned sinner, who has deserved God's wrath and punishment, he must penitently, yet trustingly, cling to the grace of God as it is revealed in Christ Jesus. This is necessary for his own sake and also for the sake of his work.

Such personal faith will enable the teacher to teach more impressively, for he knows whereof he speaks. Being himself convinced of the truth he teaches, there will be in his presentation that tone of conviction which carries conviction to those who hear him. Faith in Christ is not a matter of mere intellectual knowledge, — though such knowledge is indeed necessary, — but it is conviction, it is confidence of the heart in the forgiving grace of God. Such conviction and confidence so thoroughly affects the entire being of the believer that it cannot be hid. As little as one can hide his unbelief, so little can he hide his faith. And what a disastrous effect must it have on children if they but think their teacher does himself not believe what he teaches them! Therefore, in the interest of his educational efficiency every teacher must be a sincere Christian.

Christian Experience.—Personal religious experiences are a great help in understanding the religious experiences of others. Knowing how the Law and the Gospel have affected his own heart, the educator is able wisely to use the Word of God so as to produce similar results in the hearts of his pupils. His own Christian soul life teaches him better to understand their religious soul life. He knows how the Law worked in him a knowledge of his sins and a dread fear of the wrath of God. He also knows how the precious Gospel promises comforted him and wrought faith in him and love of God and gratitude for His mercies. And as far as Christian living is concerned, he knows from personal experience that "the spirit indeed is willing, but the flesh is weak" (Matt. 26, 41). All this is of great value to him in the training of children; for, in the main, their religious experiences will be like unto his own.

Love of Jesus. — "Jesus saith to Simon Peter, Simon, son of Jonas, lovest thou Me more than these? He saith unto him, Yea, Lord; Thou knowest that I love Thee. He saith unto him, Feed My lambs" (John 21, 15). These words of the Savior clearly indicate that love of Jesus is a necessary prerequisite for any one who would engage in Christian teaching and training. It is so important that the lack of it will unfit a man for work in our Christian schools, as he cannot be actuated by the right motive nor have the right purpose in view. Where there is faith in Christ, there will also be love for Christ and for His work.

It is well for teachers to examine themselves often on this point. They are engrossed in their work, they study to perfect their professional knowledge and skill; but have they also continued and grown in the love of Jesus? Has the work in school perhaps become a matter of routine? Do they still feel in their hearts that love of the Savior which moves and urges them to do all they can for His lambs? It is this love that keeps the teacher faithful and zealous in the work of his Master.

The world seeks honors and riches. The teacher's Old Adam also covets these things. But as there is little prospect of finding them in the profession of a Christian teacher, the temptation looms up to quit the school and to seek a more remunerative calling. Jesus asks, "Lovest thou Me?"

If a teacher is conscientious, his is not an easy task. There are difficulties with the children, at times also with the parents. There is slow progress, and, alas! there are so many disappointments. All this is likely to discourage the teacher, and he is ready to look for other employment. But Jesus asks, "Lovest thou Me?"

If the love of Jesus glows in the heart of the teacher, this will very much affect his work among children. Jesus did not ask, "Dost thou know how to use the rod?" but, "Lovest thou Me?" The love of Christ will make the teacher kindly affectioned to the children, will incite him to continue faithful under trying circumstances, and make work pleasant and easy for him. A work of love is never grievous and burdensome; and feeding the lambs of Christ is, and should be, a work of love.

Christ-Mindedness. — True faith and love of Christ will inevitably produce a Christian mind, *christliche Gesinnung,* which is that quality and state of being minded or disposed to be like Christ and to do what is acceptable to Him. The worldly-minded person is swayed in his conduct and actions by worldly considerations, and he strives for worldly aims. This will inevitably affect his educational influence in a direction away from the goal of Christian training. If, then, the personal influence of the Christian teacher is to support his pedagogical efforts, he must needs be truly Christ-minded. The ruling power of his soul must be Christ, and his thoughts, emotions, and will must be controlled by the Word of Christ. "For me to live is Christ," says Paul (Phil. 1, 21). This mind must be evident also in those who are engaged in the work of Christian education.

Such Christ-mindedness manifests itself in **sincere love for children.** As Christ loved children and said: "Suffer the little children to come unto Me and forbid them not, for of such is the kingdom of God," even so must they love children whom He has charged to feed His lambs. This love, as distinguished from that which also worldly people may have for children, seeks their spiritual and eternal welfare. Realizing their natural depravity and consequent misery, there should be in the heart of the teacher a deep compassion with his pupils and an ardent desire to help them that they may learn to know, and believe in, their Savior and to observe in their lives what He has commanded. This Christian love will urge him to do not only what he absolutely must do according to the stipulations of his call, but all he possibly can do to win children for Christ and to keep those with Christ whom he has won. He will be an active missionary for his school and a faithful shepherd of his lambs.

Christ-mindedness manifests itself in **meekness and lowliness.** Christ says: "Learn of Me, for I am meek and lowly in heart" (Matt. 11, 29). *Meekness* is that mildness of temper which is not easily provoked or irritated. Teachers who by nature, temperament, and habit are legalistic, harsh, irritable, and irascible have need of learning meekness from Jesus. For though otherwise they may be well fitted for their work, the lack of this virtue will seriously affect their influence. They know what they must do and how they must do it, but in the doing of it they do not show that meekness and kindness which wins the hearts of the children.

Yet meekness must not be confounded with weakness. Christ was meek where meekness was in place, but He was not weak to permit sin and error. These He reproved firmly and consistently. In like manner the educator must not allow wickedness to go on uncensured or connive, as did Eli, at the evil his pupils are doing. Where it is necessary, he must rebuke sharply and spare not, so that children may desist from evil.

Lowliness is the quality or state of being humble, free from pride and conceit. Whoever is proud in his heart and desirous of vainglory, coveting the recognition of men, is not qualified to be a teacher and educator of little children. The work seems so small to him, there is not much honor to be won. The results are not very spectacular and come but slowly. Cherishing very fantastic notions concerning his talents and attainments, he believes himself to be too great a man for so small a "job." In this frame of mind he is not likely to do the best he can for his pupils, and these will not be drawn to him. It is not the proud, but the humble teacher that will win the love and confidence of his pupils and be able to influence them in the right direction.

Besides, the profession of a Christian teacher is by no means such a small and insignificant "job." It is a work of supreme importance and of far-reaching consequence, which requires men of special talent and extraordinary gifts. The Christian teacher is to instruct children in the Word of God, which is able to make them wise unto salvation through faith in Christ Jesus; he is to train them that they might lead a godly life; he is to mold their character and to help fashion their course of life. He is a coworker with God; and whatever he does for the children he does to the Lord Himself (Matt. 18, 4. 5). Instead of pitying himself for having chosen the profession of a Christian teacher, he should rather humbly ask himself whether he is worthy of so high a calling and capable of performing its manifold duties.

Christian Character. — Character may be defined as the sum total of a person's qualities and attributes, which, functioning in his life, manifest themselves in certain traits or characteristics. Every one has his own individual character, which is the expression of what he is by nature and of what education has made of him. The character of man therefore is not a fixed and immutable entity; on the contrary, it can be modified and fashioned.

Every Christian has a Christian character. "If any man be in Christ, he is a new creature" (2 Cor. 5, 17). In his life and being he will show the traits and characteristics of a Christian, which are tokens of his new nature. But this character must be cultivated and developed, which is done by constant self-discipline and training. This means, in the first place, that by daily contrition and repentance the Old Adam be drowned and die with all his sins and evil lusts, that evil qualities and attributes be suppressed and evil habits broken. It means furthermore that those natural qualities and endowments which are not essentially evil be hallowed and sanctified by being used in the service of God. Finally it means that a Christian earnestly covet and cultivate those virtues which are the fruit of the Spirit, until they become permanent attributes and habits, traits of the nature reborn. In short, the new man must come forth and be strengthened, who lives before God in righteousness and purity forever. It is this Christian character Paul has in mind when he says that the Scriptures are profitable for education in righteousness that the man of God may be perfect, throughly furnished unto all good works (2 Tim. 3, 17).

Such a Christian character is a necessary qualification for every teacher of Christian children. He himself must be what he would lead his pupils to become. If he would train them, he must continue to train himself. Because of the Old Adam a perfect Christian character is not possible in this life; but the principal traits of such a character must be evident in a Christian pedagog. By self-discipline he must strengthen and augment them that he may ever more become what God wants him to be. Never content with what he is, he should always work on the improvement and perfecting of his character that he may come "unto the perfect man, unto the measure of the stature of the fulness of Christ" (Eph. 4, 13).

The Christian character of the teacher is a powerful factor in the training of children. They may forget many a lesson they have learned, but the impression of the personality and character of their teacher remains. The teacher is to his pupils the interpreter of divine truths, not only in this, that he explains Bible-texts to them, but principally also in this, that in his person and character he exemplifies the truths he has taught and thus becomes to them a living epistle, known and read and understood by all.

"To be a teacher of religion requires a particularly exalted personality. The teacher and the truth taught should always leave the impression of being of the same pattern. Whatever ideals we would impress upon others we must first have realized in ourselves. . . . The first and most difficult requirement of the teacher therefore is — himself, his personality. He must combine in himself the qualities of life and character he seeks to develop in his pupils. He must be the embodiment of what he would lead his pupils to become. He must live the religion he would teach them. He must possess the vital religious experience he would have them attain.

"He who would build a personality fitted to serve as the teacher of the child in his religion must constantly live in the presence of the best he can attain in God. There is no substitute for this. No fulness of intellectual power and grasp, no richness of knowledge gleaned, and no degree of skill in instruction can take the place of that vibrant, immediate, Spirit-filled consciousness of God in the heart. For religion is life, and the best definition of religion we can present to the child is the example and warmth of a life inspired and vivified by contact with the Source of all spiritual being." (*Betts.*)

Christian Life. — The character a person has, manifests itself in the life he leads. And a Christian character will show itself in a Christian life. Whoever would teach and train children to lead a Christian life must set before them the example of such a life.

Paul writes Phil. 3, 17: "Brethren, be followers together of me and mark them which walk so as ye have us for an ensample." And Titus is admonished: "In all things showing thyself a pattern of good works" (Titus 2, 7). And to Timothy the apostle writes: "Let no man despise thy youth; but be thou an example of the believers in conversation, in charity, in spirit, in faith, in purity" (1 Tim. 4, 12).

These words of the apostle apply especially to all who are called to train children. For these learn largely by observation. What they see their teacher do often makes a deeper impression on them than what he teaches and commands them to do. He must therefore not only be careful not to offend any of these little ones by allowing himself certain liberties in word and conduct, must not be content with leading an ordinary Christian life, but he must strive to be an *example* to his little flock. The life of their teacher is, and indeed should be, to children an interpretation and a practical illustration of what he teaches. And very often his example impresses and influences them far more than his precepts.

We know how readily children will copy the ways of their superiors, especially if they set a bad example, as this falls in with the evil imaginations of their own depraved nature. Therefore the teacher must scrupulously avoid whatever might lead the lambs of Christ astray and in his own conduct point out to them the way they should go. The shepherd is to lead his flock, and the sheep and the lambs are to follow him. Let every one, then, so walk and live that he may say to his pupils: Children, be followers of me and live so as you have us for an example.

Whoever would teach children sobriety must not himself be "given to wine" (1 Tim. 3, 2—9); whoever would warn them against evil company must not himself "sit in the seat of the scornful" (Ps. 1, 1); he who would train them in chastity and moral purity must avoid salacious jests and suggestive remarks. A teacher can hardly foster among his pupils the spirit of peacefulness if it is a notorious fact that he is quarreling with his colleagues or his pastor. He must also "rule well his own house, having his children in subjection with all gravity"; for if he cannot train his own children, how will he be able to train others? Moreover, the evil example of his own children will very much impair his influence in school.

The influence of the teacher's life must tend in a positive direction. He must be faithful in his duties, ready to serve where service is needed, chaste and pure in his talk, truthful, reliable, and trustworthy. He must show love and kindness to children and be fair in his dealings with them. He must love the Word of God, be regular

Spiritual Qualifications.

in attending public worship, and follow after those things which are honest, pure, lovely, etc. (Phil. 4, 8). Never should he think that in the presence of children he may behave in a manner that would otherwise not be tolerated; on the contrary, it is here that he must walk "circumspectly" (Eph. 5, 15) because of the influence his example will have on them.

While a teacher should earnestly strive to lead a truly Christian life, let him not try to make his pupils believe that he is a saint, that he never makes a mistake, and that all he does is right. They will discover his faults and shortcomings; they will know whether he practises what he preaches. And if they find or believe that he himself does not live according to the Word of God, they will consider him a hypocrite and lose confidence in him. It does not impair his standing, nor does it lessen his influence, if he admits a mistake or confesses a fault. On the contrary, if this is done in the right manner, the children will respect him all the more.

Let every teacher be warned against being like the scribes and Pharisees, who, sitting in Moses' seat, taught the Law of God, but of whom Christ said: "They say and do not" (Matt. 23, 2. 3). Teaching right and living wrong on the part of the teacher may have a most disastrous effect on his pupils. It trains them to become hypocrites, imagining it to be sufficient to know the will of God without also doing it (Matt. 7, 21).

The example of a Christian life is a tremendously important factor in the training of children. Example is better than precept. Wicked works paralyze the effect of godly words. Our teaching of religion will not be very effective if it is not supported by a truly religious life.

To cultivate true Christ-mindedness, to develop a Christian character, to live an exemplary Christian life, the teacher must constantly walk in the presence of his God and Savior. Christ must be his Prototype; to Him he must look for inspiration and guidance.

Speaking of the qualities of a Christian pedagog, we may, by way of contrast, call attention to a few things that should not be found in him.

Legalism. — Legalism in education is that attitude which endeavors to train by means of the Law. By nature all men are more or less inclined that way. Educators of this type will draw up many rules and regulations, insist on strict obedience, punish every transgression, and hope in this wise to train their pupils. To be sure, they do educate and apparently are quite successful. The product of their legalistic method is that, outwardly at least, the children conform to the letter of the Law. But while some do so from fear of punishment, others do so in hope of reward and recognition. But this is not the objective of Christian education, which aims to train children to avoid from fear and love of God what is evil and to do what is good. The legalistic teacher can never give his pupils a truly Christian training.

Some teachers, especially novices, are inclined to be predominantly legalistic in their methods. There may be different reasons for this. Perhaps they are spiritually dead. Theirs is an intellectual knowledge of the Word, but not a living faith in Jesus. More often it is lack of experience. They wish a child to behave a certain way, and the simplest thing to do is to command him to behave and enforce the command, forgetting, however, that they must also provide a proper motive for such behavior. Again, it may be a fault of temperament. They are quick and hasty, speaking and acting without thinking of the possible effect on the child. It may also be an error of judgment. They believe that such legalistic measures are the very thing to train children. Indeed, the Law also must be used in the training of children, but it must be used rightly.

Indifference. — Fully as harmful as this legalistic trend in education is total indifference on the part of the teacher. He instructs his pupils, and he tries to do this fairly well, but beyond this he is not interested in them. They may do as they please, right or wrong; he does not encourage them, nor does he curb them. It concerns him little what moral effect the lesson he teaches and the example he sets may have on the children, as long as they get their lesson and he gets his salary.

But the teacher should bear in mind that children do not attend school for his sake, but that he is in school for the sake of the children. And the success of his work is measured not chiefly by the knowledge he is able to impart, but by the influence he exerts. His influence on his pupils and their consequent training must therefore be a matter of chief concern to him. And it is inconceivable how any teacher worthy of the name can be indifferent in this respect.

Worldly-Mindedness. — The worldly-minded teacher exerts a negative influence upon his pupils. He cannot hide his worldly-mindedness, though he may try to do so. His influence will be for evil. Children will follow his example and stumble in their faith. "Whoso shall offend one of these little ones which believe in Me, it were better for him that a millstone were hanged about his neck and that he were drowned in the depth of the sea. Woe unto the world because of offenses! For it needs be that offenses come; but woe to that man by whom the offense cometh!" (Matt. 18, 6. 7.) Those to whom the care of children is committed should well ponder these words. It is a bad thing to permit children to grow up as they please, but it is far worse if he to whom they look for instruction and guidance corrupts their character by his evil influence. Children must not be entrusted to him, and he must be removed from office at once.

Besides the natural and the spiritual qualifications spoken of in the last two chapters, the educator has need of professional and pedagogical knowledge and accomplishments. He must know the child, he must know the aim and the means of Christian training, he must be able so to use these means as to accomplish his end, namely, the Christian training of the child. But these matters shall be treated in the subsequent chapters of the book.

Part III. THE CHILD.

VII. The Psychic Nature of the Child.

Knowledge of Children Is Necessary. — The child, not the lesson, is the chief objective of both teaching and training. Any one of fair intelligence can master a given amount of subject-matter and present it to a class, but it is far more difficult to teach this lesson to children and thereby so to influence them that the lesson learned also functions in their lives. This requires the mastery of the "inner secrets of the mind, the heart, and the springs of action of the learner."

"The child comes into school with much potential and very little actual capital. The powers of the mind and soul at first lie dormant, waiting for the awakening that comes through the touch of the world about and for the enlightenment that comes through instruction" (*Betts*) and, we add, for development and training that comes through education. Therefore the teacher should not presuppose too much, neither of knowledge nor of ability nor of character in his pupils. They do not know as much as he does, their mental powers are not yet fully developed; he may not expect them to behave as well-trained adults behave. They are still children, children in knowledge, in understanding, in experience, and in character. He must not expect them to know what he is to teach them nor to be what, with the help of God, he is to make of them.

To make sure advance in the education of the child, we must find a point of contact in his previous knowledge and experience from which we may proceed to teach the new lesson. For it is by means of what the child knows that he is able to understand what he is to learn; the mind content helps to apperceive and interpret the new idea and the new experience. For this reason it is so important that the teacher learns to know the child in order that he may connect what he would impart with what the child knows.

Luther says: *"Weil wir Kindern predigen, muessen wir mit ihnen lallen";* because we are teaching children, we must also prattle with them. He means to say, both the content and the presentation of what we would teach children must be sufficiently simple and plain for them to grasp without great difficulty. Hence the teacher must seek to understand the psychology of the child. At every step of either teaching or training he must watch the intellectual reaction and the emotional response of the child; for it is this that will determine his next step. The educator must therefore enter into the soul life of the child and learn to understand how he thinks, how he feels, and why he wills and acts. Any educational scheme, no matter how well planned, which does not respect the reaction of the child is bound to fail. Luther says: *"Sollen wir Kinder ziehen, so muessen wir auch Kinder mit ihnen werden";* if we are to train children, we must become children with them.

"It is more difficult to learn and to know the pupil than any other factor in the whole school situation. But it must not be forgotten that it is more important for the beginning teacher to know the pupil than to be the master of other educational factors. — Know more than their names. Know their minds, their souls, their dispositions, their home environment, their health, their bodily defects, their strong points, their weak points, wherein they need help and wherein they can help others. You will learn this if you enter largely into the lives of the children and veritably live with the children. This personal relation will secure you knowledge of the pupils that will enrich your own soul." (*Avent.*)

"How shall the teacher come to know the child? Prof. George Herbert Palmer sets forth a great truth when he says that the first quality of a great teacher is the quality of *vicariousness*. By this he means the ability on the part of the teacher to step over in his imagination and to take the place of the child. To look at the task with the child's mind and understanding, to feel the appeal of the lesson or story through the child's emotions, to confront the temptation with the child's power of will and self-control, — this ability is the beginning of the wisdom for those who would understand childhood. The teacher must first of all therefore be a sympathetic investigator in the laboratory of child life. Not only in the Sunday-school, but daily he must observe, study, and seek to interpret children." (*Betts*.)

Such study of the child will help the teacher in various ways. It will help him to understand what he is to do and how he is to do it and how the child is likely to react. It will prevent him from expecting immediate and permanent results; for he knows that a child does not yet possess that firmness, determination, and perseverance which he may reasonably expect to find in mature characters. He will not be disappointed to find reverses and new departures, nor will he suspect intention and malice where there is but weakness and thoughtlessness. And while he discovers that each child presents distinct problems, he will also find that certain fundamental laws apply to all childhood.

Children Are Creatures of God. — Whoever believes the child to be the product of evolution, the descendant of anthropoid apes, will hardly have a proper regard for his pupils nor a high conception of his calling as an educator of children. Quite different will be the attitude of him who believes that God has made them, has given them "body and soul, eyes, ears, and all their members, their reason and all their senses."

One outstanding difference between the vocation of a Christian pedagog and that of many others in the world is this, that, while they are dealing with inanimate things or irrational brutes or, at best, are concerned about the physical well-being or the economic progress of man, his is the privilege to educate human beings, who in the beginning were created in the image of God, which was restored in Holy Baptism, and to help them walk after the new man, in righteousness and true holiness. Children, even the poorest of them, are of high degree and nobility, and by the grace of God the Christian educator is to develop in them a still greater nobility of character, that, being God's children by faith in Jesus, they may also "glorify God in body and soul" (1 Cor. 6, 20). Let no one therefore despise one of these little ones (Matt. 18, 10).

Children Have a Body that is "Wonderfully" Made (Ps. 139, 14). — The Christian educator is not primarily a physical director, whose business it is by gymnastics and sports to develop the body and to keep it fit and healthy, but his object is to influence the soul of the child and to mold a good Christian character. However, the physical conditions of the body very strongly affect the psychological conditions of the soul. A child who is hungry, tired, or ailing will not respond to educative influences in the same manner as a child whose health is in prime condition.

In order, then, to obtain the best results the teacher should have a due regard also for the bodily well-being of his pupils. To this end he should have a fair knowledge of the principles of hygiene, so that he may be able to help in preserving and promoting the bodily health of his pupils. Proper ventilation and temperature in the schoolroom, correct posture in sitting and standing, in writing and reading, bodily cleanliness, clean hands, clean teeth, physical drills, relaxation, and outdoor plays, sanitary condition of outhouses, lavatories, etc., all these things the teacher should look after in the interest of the bodily well-being of the children. If he discovers that a child is sick and ailing, he should inform the parents that they may secure professional aid.

Mens sana in corpore sano has always been recognized to be a sound axiom in education. In the interest of effectual teaching and training the educator therefore should see that the children entrusted to his care have and keep a sound and healthy body.

Children Have a Soul. — "The Lord formed man of the dust of the ground and breathed into his nostrils the breath of life; and man became a living soul" (Gen. 2, 7). Here the Bible plainly teaches that man has not only life, like the beast of the field, but that he has also a soul. And it is this soul, this spiritual, rational, immortal being, which really constitutes man's conscious personality.

As the essence of life, so also the essence of the soul is not susceptible to scientific investigation and analysis. While no reputable scientist denies the reality of life, many psychologists either ignore or deny the existence of the human soul and speak only of states and processes of consciousness. But it is putting a heavy strain on the intelligence of man to speak of states and processes of which he is conscious and to deny that he has a soul. For how can there possibly be such consciousness unless there be a subject factor which is conscious? Consciousness does not exist for and by itself, there must be something which is conscious; nor can there be states and processes of consciousness unless there be something real to which they attach. "This necessity for a subject of our states of consciousness has constituted one of the strongest rational considerations adducible in support of the belief in a soul." (*Angell.*) This subject factor which is conscious, which perceives, thinks, knows, feels, and wills is none other than the soul of man, his real ego. And it is this soul in which the educator is chiefly interested. He should therefore know something of the soul life of the child.

Generally speaking, we distinguish three phases of soul activity — the rational, the emotional, the volitional.

The Rational, or Cognitive, Activity of the Soul. — This activity includes all those mental processes by which we acquire knowledge. It cannot be our object here to discuss in detail the several stages of cognition, from its first conscious appearance in sensation through various mental processes to clearly defined knowledge. But in general they are about as follows. Our sense organs receive a definite stimulation, as in touching an object, seeing a thing, hearing a sound. This is purely physical. The nervous system at once carries and reports these sensations to the mind. This may be regarded as the physiological process. The mind receives, interprets, and apperceives these sensations, linking up the new impressions with ideas and percepts already stored in the mind, which modify them and are modified by them. This is a psychic process.

While this process may be regarded as chiefly intellectual, it is not purely so. Also the heart and the will, yea, the entire soul and psychic constitution of man is active in giving shape and form to the new idea, in determining its importance, and in assigning to it its proper place.

The exact nature of the neural excitement is not known nor the manner in which the sensation is carried to the mind, and least of all do we understand how the mind transforms the report of the nerves into concepts, ideas, and thoughts. We know that these things happen, but we cannot explain how they happen.

Not only the physical organism, but also the mental activities of man must convince every sane and unprejudiced person that man cannot be the product of blind chance and evolution, but that there must be a God who has so wonderfully made him.

This cognitive ability of the soul is engaged in the acquisition of knowledge, and as it is being exercised, it is trained and developed. But also for the purpose of education we must make use of this phase of soul life. We cannot make an impression on the heart except by way of the mind. What the child does not know cannot affect him emotionally, cannot incite him to action, cannot determine his conduct. What the child has not learned he cannot observe. If, then, we would train and educate him, we must needs instruct him. Via cognition we produce affection.

The Emotional, or Affective, Activity of the Soul. — The child has not only a mind, which learns and knows, but also a "heart," which feels and is moved and affected.

We hear a message which concerns us very closely. We receive it not merely intellectually, but it affects us; not only do we know what the words mean, but we feel that they mean something to us personally. Evidently there is something more than a mere mental reception of the content of the message; there is also an emotional response.

We see a person doing something. Our mind not merely registers the facts we observe, but whatever the person does may strike us in a particular way, as clever or foolish, interesting or dull, fair or foul, right or wrong. Again there is more than mere intellectual knowledge; there is an emotional reaction caused by such knowledge.

We become acquainted with a man. But whatever we learn to know of him makes some kind of impression on us. It may inspire us with trust and confidence or with the very opposite. We may be drawn to him in friendship and love, or we may be repulsed, or we remain indifferent. Whatever we know of the man we do not merely know, but this knowledge affects us in some way. "Thus an act of memory or of reasoning is cognitive in so far as it involves knowledge processes. It is feeling in so far as it is *my* knowledge experienced in a certain way, with a certain tone." (*Angell.*)

All these personal impressions, whether they come to us directly through our senses or through ideas and thoughts, are called feelings, or emotions. They may be superficial and transient or deep and lasting. Whenever these feelings become more permanent and established, they may be called emotional attitudes.

Thoughts and ideas possess potential power to affect the heart and thus to produce emotions, each after its kind. The reason that they do not always do so is because other and more forceful thoughts dominate our consciousness. The new thought that has entered the mind receives no attention; it is crowded out and perhaps soon forgotten. It may also be that other considerations exert an inhibitory influence, counteracting any possible impression the new idea may make. Such is often the case in persons that are prejudiced.

As long as any idea or thought remains purely intellectual, making no impression on the heart, it is "dead." However, it does not always remain dead; it may stand by for a time and at some opportune moment exert its influence on the heart. Thus important truths but mechanically learned in youth may become a determining power in later life.

By our affections we assume a personal attitude towards the things we know and experience. Our feelings, taking the term in its psychological connotation, indicate what these things mean to us, how they affect and impress us personally. They are therefore the most subjective experience of man; they constitute the real personal element, the core and center, the very heart of his soul life. While the mind and its cognitive activities may be called the receiving-station and the storehouse of what enters our consciousness, the heart and its affective processes link up our real ego with these thoughts and establish a personal contact with them.

It is quite apparent that the affective phase of soul life is eminently important in the education of man. Indeed, we must instruct him and enrich his mind with knowledge. But this knowledge must mean something to him; it must touch his heart, must affect him, if ever it is to influence him. To be educationally effective, instruction must be affective.

Man is capable of an endless number and variety of feelings or affections. As to their origin they may be distinguished as sensuous and ideational feelings. Sensuous feelings are those which arise from sensations experienced in the body, such as pain, cold, bodily well-being, sickness, etc. Ideational feelings are those which are produced by, and concomitant with, ideas and thoughts that control the mind, such as sorrow, gladness, anger, surprise, love, hatred, trust, distrust, etc. Another classification, which regards the objects that affect us and our particular viewpoint of them, is esthetic feelings, feelings of beauty and its opposite; ethical feelings, feelings of right and wrong, of duty, of responsibility; personal feelings, which arise in respect to oneself, such as pride, shame, conceit, remorse, self-satisfaction; religious feelings, such as reverence for what is sacred and holy, fear and love of God and trust in Him. Perhaps other groups might be mentioned. But whatever their origin and whatever their peculiar shading, all feelings may be classified as affecting us either agreeably or disagreeably, positively or negatively. They may be strong, they may be weak; they may be passing, they may be more permanent. There is no qualitative difference between feelings and emotions, the latter being feelings plus a general or a restricted excitation.

The educator is interested chiefly in ideational emotions. While these can indeed be distinguished from the ideas or thoughts which produce them, they cannot be separated from them. The relation between the thought and its resulting emotion is very much like the relation between the voice and its echo, between cause and effect. A definite ideational emotion is produced by, and based on, a definite knowledge. Where there is no idea, no knowledge, there can be no corresponding emotion.

Also the Scriptures recognize the importance of knowledge. "How shall they believe in Him of whom they have not heard?" "So, then, faith cometh by hearing and hearing by the Word of God" (Rom. 10, 14. 17). According to these words, faith in God is impossible where there is no knowledge of God.

We must, however, also distinguish between knowledge and faith. "And that from a child thou hast known the Holy Scriptures, which are able to make thee wise unto salvation through faith which is in Christ Jesus (2 Tim. 3, 15). It is possible for a person to know the Scriptures, and to know them well, and still not to be made wise by them unto salvation. For his knowledge of the doctrines of the Bible may be purely intellectual, it is a knowledge of the head, *Kopferkenntnis*. And as long as it remains such, it is dead knowledge, which may be found even in unbelievers and devils (Jas. 2, 17. 19). Such a dead knowledge does not affect us, it does not impress and influence us. Aside from having learned it intellectually, it does not mean anything to us personally. There is no reaction of the heart to the knowledge of the mind.

Such dead intellectual knowledge may by the operation of the Holy Ghost at any time become alive. It is then that it touches and affects the heart, creating therein a definite emotion. Thus a person may have a knowledge of his sins. But as long as this knowledge is purely intellectual, it is dead and does not affect him. But as soon as this knowledge becomes alive, it means something to him that he is a sinner, and his heart is filled with remorse and contrition, perhaps with despair. In the same manner a person may have learned to know the work of the Savior and the promises of the Gospel. But as long as this knowledge is purely intellectual, it is dead and means nothing to him. The very moment, however, this knowledge becomes alive, it creates in the heart an interest in, and a longing for, the promised grace and finally firm assurance and blissful confidence.

Whatever emotions the knowledge of the mind has produced in the heart, they, for the time being, indicate our personal and most subjective attitude towards the things our mind has learned. They are the echo and the response of the heart to the knowledge of the mind.

While a person may have an idea, a thought, in his mind without being moved and affected thereby in his heart, there can be no ideational emotion without an idea which produced it. Thus a man may also have an intellectual knowledge of the Gospel without having true faith in his heart. But he cannot have faith in his heart if he have not first a knowledge of the Gospel (Rom. 10, 14). It is well for us to remember this. We cannot reach the heart but by way of the mind. We cannot impress and influence man unless we first teach him. Clear and definite instruction is necessary for effectual training. However, instruction is only a means to an end, and also knowledge, intellectual knowledge, is only a means to an end. The ultimate end and objective of all knowledge we impart by our teaching is that this knowledge may mean something to the child personally and may move him in a certain direction. In other words, our teaching must not be merely informative, but educative, appeal not only to the mind and intellect, but to the heart and the emotions.

It is therefore of utmost importance what we teach the child. For as the echo is determined by the voice, so the emotions of the heart are determined by the thought content of the mind. Whether we speak well or evil about others, this will in a large measure determine the emotional attitude of those who hear us. Teach a child a wrong view of God, and this will, if it affect him at all, produce a wrong attitude toward God. As long as Luther looked upon Christ as the just and angry Judge of sinners, his heart was full of fear and hatred. But as soon as he learned to know Him as the Savior of sinners, his heart was filled with trust and confidence, with love and peace and joy. We must therefore insist on purity of Scripture doctrines not only with respect to God, because we tremble at His Word (Is. 66, 2), but also with respect to the children, who are to learn them. For only the right doctrine can work in the heart right attitude toward God, the right faith (John 8, 31. 32).

We cannot analyze the process how thoughts produce emotions, nor can we force thoughts to produce emotions. The power to affect the heart lies not with us, but with the thoughts and ideas we impart. Very often they will not have the desired effect because other considerations and conditions exert an inhibitory influence.

There is one other important point we should remember. Ideas and thoughts which pass quickly through the mind have less chance to work on the heart and to produce corresponding emotions than those which linger and occupy our attention for some time. "No idea can dominate our movements which does not catch and hold our attention. Indeed, volition as a strictly mental affair is neither more nor less than a matter of attention. When we can keep our attention firmly fixed upon a line of conduct, to the exclusion of all competitors, our decision is already made." (*Angell.*) There will be little emotional response if we quickly dismiss from our mind what we have heard, or if we allow other ideas to "crowd it out." Whatever might distract the thoughts must be kept away, and we must concentrate our attention on the matter before us. The more intently we do this, the longer a given thought dominates our consciousness, the more likely it will affect our hearts.

If, then, we would influence men, we must win their undivided attention, must have them eliminate, forget, every other consideration and have them see things our way. If it were possible that by desuggestion we could remove every obstruction of the mind and the will, so that the truths we present have free course and full sway, the emotional response would be bound to follow. For the thought which controls our mind to the exclusion of all others will affect and influence the heart. (See Meditation, p. 158.)

The Volitional Activity of the Soul. — Under this title we would group all those conscious tendencies and activities by which our feelings and emotions seek expression in conduct, word, and action. Man has longings, wishes, desires; he wants and wills to do things. These tendencies may be weak or strong, vague or determined. While there may be gradual differences, they all are essentially acts of volition by which the emotional attitude tends to express itself.

Strictly speaking, there is no freedom of the will, but every voluntary act is caused and motivated, even though the motivating cause may not always be clear to our consciousness. What, then, causes these volitional activities?

We read: "Keep thy heart with all diligence; for out of it are the issues of life" (Prov. 4, 23). The moral issues of life proceed from the heart. Man, as a rule, wills and acts as his heart prompts and moves him. For those feelings and emotions that were produced by thoughts and ideas of the mind are by no means idle, but they are dynamic.

"What the stream of the mill-race is to the water-wheel working complex machinery, the emotions are to man's will and partly to his intellect. They are the moving power of action and, in some respects, of thought." (*Eclectic Dictionary.*)

"Feeling, emotion, and sentiment are tremendously important determinants of volition. Strong feeling of every kind is distinctly motor in tendency. Emotion and feeling are dynamic, but they have a definite tendency." (*Angell.*)

While it is true that feeling and emotion are the real moving power in man, inciting and stimulating will activity in a certain direction, it must be remembered that these emotions are produced and determined by sensations and ideas, and should at all times be controlled and directed by them.

"It must not be forgotten that in so far as volition is a process in which we anticipate actions, it must involve perceptions and ideas. Every voluntary act involves the presence in the mind of sensory or ideational material in some way anticipatory to the act." (*Angell.*)

There is indeed a fine interrelation between the cognitive, the emotional, and the volitional activities of the soul, and none of these functions separately and independently of the others. In every conscious process of mind, heart, and will the whole soul is active.

The Psychological Process. — In bold outline the psychological process is about as follows: —

The mind, or intellect, is primarily receptive. It receives and stores up ideas, thoughts, and knowledge. It is the gateway through which the outside world enters our consciousness.

The heart is motive. Each thought content is experienced by us in a certain way. It has inherent power to affect us. Whenever it does so, it produces in our heart feelings, emotions, passions, which indicate for the time being our most subjective attitude towards the things our mind has learned, showing what they mean to us personally.

The will is expressive. The affections of the heart are essentially dynamic and motor in tendency. They create likes and dislikes, inclinations and aversions, longings, wishes, desires, and various other phases of volition, which underlie all conscious expression of ourselves in conduct, word, and deed.

The idea enters the mind of knowledge. This knowledge affects the heart and produces an emotion. This emotion, regulated and determined by the knowledge of the mind, moves the will and prompts action. There is no voluntary act which is not caused by some emotion, and there is no ideational emotion which is not produced by some perception or idea.

"Verschiedenheiten im Verhalten werden ausschliesslich durch Verschiedenheiten der Vorstellung und deren Gefuehlsbetontheit bedingt. Dabei spielen die Gefuehle der Lust und der Unlust gewissermassen die Rolle des Motors, die Empfindungen und Vorstellungen die des Steuers. Wo eine Vorstellung falsch ist, kann nicht nur, sondern muss unbedingt falsches Verhalten erfolgen." (*Dr. Truslit,* Berlin.) The difference in conduct is exclusively determined by the difference of the mental concept and its emotional tone. The pleasurable and the unpleasurable feelings act as the motor, the sensations and the ideas as the rudder. Where the idea is wrong, the consequent behavior will be wrong likewise.

If evil imaginations control the heart, the life will be evil. If pure and holy thoughts dominate the soul, they will influence the conduct in that direction. "For out of the heart are the issues of life." "One tends to become what he thinks. If the thought stimuli are high and noble, one's character tends to be formed in that direction; if they are mean and low, one's character tends in that direction." (*Avent.*) There is much truth in this. For thoughts lead to actions. Ideas which dominate one's mind produce corresponding emotions, and these prompt corresponding actions and thus, in a large measure, determine one's character.

"Thought, feeling, and action belong together, and to leave out one destroys the quality and significance of all. Religious growth and development involve the same mental powers that are used in the other affairs of life. The child's training in religion can advance no faster than the expansion of his grasp of thought and comprehension, the deepening of his emotions, and the strengthening of his will. It follows from this that religious instruction must call for, and use, the same activities of the mind that are called for in other phases of education. Religious teaching must therefore appeal to the whole mind. Besides appealing to the emotions and will, it must make use of, and train, the power of thought, of imigination, of memory, it must through their agency make truth vivid, real, and lasting and so lay the foundation for spiritual feeling and devotion." (*Betts.*)

It is quite apparent that knowledge of the fundamental psychic processes is of great help to the educator. His aim is to fashion the character and the conduct of the child. But this is impossible if he does not influence the heart; for "out of the heart are the issues of life." The "heart" is the center of soul life, it is that power which, indeed determined by the knowledge of the mind, incites volition and action. It is not the knowledge a man has acquired nor only the will-power he has developed that shows his real character, but chiefly the emotional attitude of his heart. *"Qualis cuiusque animi affectus, talis homo."* Cicero means to say that the quality of the affections of one's soul determine what manner of man one is. For it is the feelings and emotions of the heart that indicate how the knowledge of the mind has affected him personally, and it is this personal impression that tends to express itself in the various phases of volition, thus revealing his personal attitude. If, then, we would educate and train children, we must needs influence their hearts.

But the heart cannot be reached except through the mind. Hence the educator must indoctrinate his pupils. He must teach them such truths as are able to produce in their hearts the right kind of emotions. And as much as in him lies, he must make these truths so real and vivid and big that they also do produce these emotions, which, in turn, result in corresponding expressions of will in conduct, word, and deed.

In all his educative efforts the teacher should therefore ask himself, How is the child affected thereby, and how will he react? What will be the emotional impression and what the volitional expression? Also in education the words apply: *Quidquid agis, prudenter agas et respice finem.* Whatever you do, may you do it wisely and consider the end and aim. The end we wish to attain in the training of the child must determine our course of action; in particular, it must determine what we are to teach and how we are to do it. The success of our work is measured, not by what we do, but by what we accomplish, not by what we teach, but by the influence such teaching has on our pupils. "The only true test of learning a thing is whether the learner lives it. The only true test of the value of what one learns is the extent to which it affects his daily life." (*Betts.*)

Temperaments. — While the soul life of all men follows, in general, certain fundamental lines, there is a great difference in its manifestations because of the different temperaments in men.

"When we compare individuals with one another, one striking difference which we observe concerns their inherited susceptibilities and predispositions to certain forms of emotional response. This characteristic is one of the most important elements in the constitution of what we call temperament. Whereas mood indicates a relatively transitory disposition toward a certain emotional tone, temperament refers to a permanent tendency, contributing to the warp and woof of character. In the conception of temperament intellectual and volitional attributes are also included, but the emotional character is perhaps most significant." (*Angell.*)

Temperament, then, is a peculiar trait or disposition affecting the entire soul life of the individual, his intellect, his will, and particularly his emotions, and consequently also his behavior and his actions. It is based upon the nervous system, its reaction or susceptibility to external and internal stimuli and its tendency to combine the reactions in various ways. It is said to be expressed in certain bodily peculiarities. Temperaments are in themselves not sinful; they are a gift of God, and they account, in part, for the multiform difference in the physical and the mental character of individuals.

It is customary to distinguish four general types of temperament.

The choleric temperament has strong emotions, is passionate, active, energetic, daring, persevering. "A person of choleric temperament is quick to be impressed and is aroused to feel deeply. He is quick of wit, alert, impulsive, and emotional; hence, likely to lack inhibitory power. The will becomes thoroughly aroused and holds to its purpose until other impressions turn it in another direction." (*Wentzlaff: The Mental Man.*)

The melancholic temperament is not easily moved, has deep emotions, is pensive, dreamily and sadly thoughtful, slow of decision. "The melancholic person also has strong impressions, intense emotions, but they come slowly. He is tardy of action, meditative, and sentimental." (*Wentzlaff.*)

The sanguine temperament manifests a cheerful and hopeful, excitable, but flighty disposition. "The sanguine person is quickly aroused to action and emotion, but the impressions are shallow and soon give way to other experiences." (*Wentzlaff.*)

The phlegmatic temperament is slow in thought, emotion, and action, calm, cold, heavy, apathetic; it is "unemotional and sluggish in thought and action. In regard to the will the phlegmatic person resolves but slowly, but once resolved, he tenaciously clings to his purpose. He is thorough and conservative." (*Wentzlaff.*)

This classification of temperaments is somewhat ideal. The four types are the extremes, and each one may shade into the other. Hardly ever is one type found pure in any person, but they are mixed in various proportions, one or even two predominating.

In this connection we would call attention also to those temperamental tendencies designated as *optimistic* and *pessimistic* with their many intermediate shades. The first takes a more hopeful view of matters in general. The optimistic child sees no difficulties, or it underestimates them; he will readily attack a problem and perhaps fail. The pessimistic child imagines and magnifies difficulties, hesitates to enter upon a new venture; but doing so, he may succeed better than the other. He is easily discouraged by failure or even the anticipation of failure, while his optimistic partner will try and try again.

These temperamental differences account in a large measure for the difference in which children receive impressions and respond to influences. Hence in training the temperamental disposition of each child must be taken into consideration. The teacher's study of his pupils must therefore necessarily include the study of their peculiar personality traits. However, let him not draw conclusions hastily, but rather let him continue to observe the ways and manners of the individual child, watch how he reacts to impressions, how he works, etc. No teacher will ever learn to know his pupils so thoroughly that he has no need of learning more about them.

Natural Gifts. — Natural gifts God bestows on man in birth. Where they are lacking, education cannot supply them; where they are present, education must quicken, develop, and train them.

There is a great difference in children with respect to their gifts, since not all have received the same kind nor the same measure of gifts from their Creator. Some children are very intelligent and of quick comprehension; others are very slow to grasp and understand. Some have a tenacious memory, others forget easily. Some have sharp reasoning powers, others jump at conclusions. Some are strongly emotional, others predominantly intellectual. Some have a strong, iron will, others lack will-power. Some are bright, the majority is mediocre, some are dull. We also notice that some children at an early age show inclination and talent for certain professions and occupations. No two children are alike; each has his proper gift of God, one after this manner and another after that (1 Cor. 7, 7).

When teaching and training children, one must certainly take into account this diversity of gifts. The fact that a child does not know his lesson or cannot answer a question does not always prove that he was lazy or inattentive; perhaps he is not well gifted. On the other hand, a child that stands high in his class is not always the most diligent. He could perhaps accomplish much more if he used his larger talent as faithfully as the other child uses his small talent. "Unto whom much is given, of him shall be much required" (Luke 12, 48).

Man is endowed by his Creator with many and great possibilities, but they are still in embryonic form. It is for education to develop these potential powers into dynamic abilities, and it is to education that man is indebted for his intellectual and moral culture.

This susceptibility to education by experience or instruction shows the fundamental difference between rational man and the irrational brute. While instincts of animals may, in a measure, adapt themselves to climatic and other conditions and thus be modified, we cannot train and develop them as we can cultivate and direct the gifts and endowments of man, whose intelligence immediately comes in to transfer native reaction in accordance with the dictates of personal experience. The robins to-day do not build their nests very much different from the nests robins built at the beginning of time, and the habits of animals have, in the main, not changed since the fall of man. Trees grow as they ever grew, and monkeys act as they always acted. Though man has learned much of the flora and fauna, he has not discovered any noticeable evolution and cultural progress. Even though by careful selection and breeding, plants and animals may be improved, they will revert to type. Comparing this apparent stability in floral and faunal life with the progress in the cultural life of mankind in general and of the individual, one must needs be impressed with the truth that man is indeed a creature essentially different from others, that he is a rational being, capable of intellectual and moral culture.

VIII. The Sinful Depravity of the Child.

The Depravity of the Human Nature a Fact that Must be Recognized in Education. — The natural depravity of man is denied by many modern educators. Children, they say, are by nature morally neutral, neither good nor bad, and they will be what life and education make of them.

Says Betts in his book *How to Teach Religion,* pp. 32. 33: "We no longer insist with the older theologies that the child is completely under the curse of 'original sin,' nor do we believe with certain sentimentalists that he comes 'trailing clouds of glory.' We believe that he has infinite capacities for good and equally infinite capacities for evil, either of which may be developed. We know that at the beginning the child is sinless, pure of heart, his life undefiled. To know this is enough to show us our part. This is to lead the child aright until he is old enough to follow the right path of his own accord."

This optimistic view of the moral condition of natural man is an illusion, contrary to experience and observation and contrary to Scriptures. When comparing little children with grown and hardened sinners, we indeed sometimes speak of them as being innocent; but this does not mean that they are by nature "sinless and pure of heart." For why is it that we observe in children brought up under most favorable moral conditions and led aright from early infancy, manifestations of sinfulness? If they are sinless and pure of heart by birth, why is it impossible to keep them so even though they be closely shielded against every contaminating influence? The reason is that there is in every child born of woman an inherited inclination toward evil. Even as children inherit from their parents certain physical and mental traits, they also inherit that moral corruption which is so deeply ingrained in the soul of man. To be sure, children possess moral endowments, inasmuch as they are capable of moral training, which is not the case with the irrational brute; but they do not possess embryonic moral tendencies for good which, if properly nursed, will develop into a good moral character.

The Sinful Depravity of the Child.

Bible Proof. — The Bible is very explicit on this point. It teaches that man is conceived and born in sin (Ps. 51, 5); that, born of sinful parents, he needs must be a sinful child (John 3, 6); that, therefore, the imagination of his heart is evil from his youth (Gen. 8, 21); that in his flesh dwelleth no good thing (Rom. 7, 18); and that out of his heart proceed evil thoughts, murders, adulteries, etc. (Matt. 15, 19). While influence and environment cultivate and develop this natural depravity, they do not create it, for it is born with man; it is not acquired, it is congenital.

This total moral depravity, brought on by the fall of man, clings to us through life. There is no system of education and training whereby it can be totally eradicated. As little as the Ethiopian can change his skin or the leopard his spots (Jer. 13, 23), so little can sinful man become a perfect saint on earth (Phil. 3, 12). To the end of his life even the best of Christians will have to admit that in his flesh "dwelleth no good thing."

Observation and the Word of God teach us that there is indeed a moral tendency in man, but it is a tendency toward evil. And whoever ignores or denies this natural depravity in children cannot truly educate them; starting from a wrong premise, he is bound to fail.

The Body Imperfect. — When, on the sixth day, God formed man of the dust of the ground, man's body was absolutely perfect in all its parts and functions. But since the fall of man his body is subject to disease and pain and death. Its members are often deformed, its senses are weak, the muscles tire, the alimentary system fails to act properly, its beauty and strength fade and diminish with age. This apparent frailty of the body shows that the physical condition of man is not as perfect as it was in the beginning, when he issued from the hands of his Creator.

No evolution, but a decided deterioration, brought on by the fall of man into sin.

Beyond rendering first aid, the educator, lacking professional training and experience, should not undertake to treat the bodily ailments of his pupils. However, he should bear in mind that physiological conditions often affect the psychical conditions of children.

The Soul Depraved. — The soul, which God breathed into the body of man (Gen. 2, 7) and which he clothed with the divine image (Gen. 1, 27), is now weakened and corcupted in all its faculties and functions. The blissful knowledge of God is lost, and only a fragment, the natural knowledge of God, remains. The mind is weakened in every respect; it no longer possesses its former perfection to perceive, to understand, to remember, to imagine, and to think and reason. How difficult for children to learn what is good! But how quick they are to grasp what is sinful! The heart is devoid of true fear and love of God; it finds no pleasure in things that are good, but delights in things evil (Gen. 8, 21). The moral tendency of man gravitates toward evil. And there is nothing in him that could change his attitude and turn his will toward that which is good in the sight of God. Even though he may have learned to know the will of God intellectually, there is in him no motive power that would urge and prompt him to do this will of God gladly and joyfully. By nature every man is his own god. His religion is pure selfishness, which incites him to satisfy his personal desires, the lust of the flesh, the lust of the eyes, and the pride of life. There is no instinct, no tendency, no inclination which need only be roused to blossom out in a holy and godly life. Because of his sin, man fears the punishment of God, and for this reason he also hates God and is not at all inclined to serve Him in holiness of life. Though he attempt to do so outwardly, he is not actuated by the right motive; not love of God (John 5, 42), but selfish considerations move him.

While man, unlike the irrational brute, is capable of being converted to God and of being trained to lead a holy life, there is absolutely nothing in his natural make-up from which such a life may be developed. No child can be trained to lead a Christian life unless he first become a Christian by faith in the Savior.

Temperaments Vitiated; Natural Gifts Weakened. — The natural depravity shows itself also in the disposition, or temperament, of the child. The sanguine child is flighty, fickle, and his temper is quickly aroused; the choleric child is audacious, saucy, refractory, and displays a strong temper. In the melancholic child we find envy, sullenness, acrimony, peevishness; in the phlegmatic, laziness, slothfulness, dulness. Also the natural endowments and gifts are no longer as perfect as they would have been otherwise. They lie dormant and must be aroused and developed at the cost of much patient labor and exercise, and when quickened, they are often employed in the service of selfishness and sin.

Each Child Potentially Capable of All Sins. — While by sin the human nature is not destroyed, it is morally totally depraved. Like a contagion, which affects and vitiates every organ of the body, sin has corrupted the entire human nature. And because of this moral corruption every child is inclined to all sins and is capable of committing any and every sin if there be but a sufficiently strong incentive and provocation. It is folly for parents to think and say that their children would never do such and such a thing, that it is not in them to lie or to steal, etc. Most certainly it is in every child to do any and all of these things. For Jesus, who "knew what was in man" (John 2, 25), says: "Out of the heart proceed evil thoughts, murders, adulteries, fornications, thefts, false witness, blasphemies" (Matt. 15, 19). While from the heart of one proceed especially "murders" and from that of another "thefts," each heart is by nature so corrupt that it is capable of each and all of these sins.

Outwardly there was a great difference in the lives of the Pharisee and of the publican of whom we read Luke 18, 9—14, but potentially there was no difference at all. Except for his education and training the Pharisee might have been like the publican. Let us not look with contempt on the vilest of sinners, thinking that we could never sink to such depths of shame. If it were not for the sustaining grace of God, we might sink lower than he. The sinful depravity is the same in all men, but it manifests itself differently in different individuals.

This difference we observe also in children. Some are given to all forms of dishonesty, others to unchastity, others to vanity or stubbornness or irreverence or revengefulness, etc. But this does not mean that a child which is characteristically dishonest may not also be stubborn, vain, revengeful, etc. For every child possesses the capacity for all possible sins, while in actual life the natural depravity may assume a certain bend and manifest itself in a certain direction.

All this is very important for the educator to know. For while he must be clearly conscious of the goal toward which he would lead the child and be conversant with the means and the method whereby he would attain this end, he must also know where to start, must know what kind of child it is that he is to educate, lest, starting from a wrong premise, his efforts be bound to end in failure. Hence he will study the child, diagnose the causes, the symptoms, the phases of sin as it shows itself in this particular child, so that he may apply the proper corrective.

Education Begins in the Heart. — All sins as they appear in the outward life of man are but expressions of the sinful condition of the heart (Gen. 8, 21; Matt. 15, 19). It is therefore evident that there can be no true education if we correct only these outward manifestations, leaving the heart unchanged. It has been truly said: The heart of education is the education of the heart. The heart must be renewed if the life is to be reformed; the inner man must be changed if the outer man is to improve. Solomon says: "Keep thy heart with all diligence; for out of it are the issues of life" (Prov. 4, 23). He means to say that the life a man leads will be as his heart directs. In spite of rules and laws laid upon him, he will always gravitate towards what his heart loves and desires. To be effective, then, education must begin in the heart. Discipline and external measures are necessary, but true education must link up with those spiritual endowments and emotions that come with faith in Christ. This is exactly what Paul does Rom. 12, 1. He does not simply command Christians to present their bodies a living sacrifice unto God, but beseeching them by the mercies of God, he endeavors to arouse their gratitude and thus to touch and influence their hearts.

This important truth is often ignored by educators who believe that by passing and enforcing laws they can reform the evil-doers. They will draw up a set of rules and regulations, and if they succeed in getting their pupils to "toe the mark," they are quite satisfied with the result. It is true, much can be accomplished this way, and certain habits may be established. But true Christian education affects not a mere "outward form of godliness," but would so train the child that from the heart he walks in the ways of God. To accomplish this, a change of heart, regeneration by faith in the Savior, is necessary.

IX. The Regenerated Child.

The State of Grace. — No matter how deeply depraved a child is by nature or how much his previous education has been neglected, the educator may not despise him nor regard him as educationally hopeless. Two things he must bear in mind — one, that this child is by nature not any worse than he is himself; the other, that from eternity God loved also this neglected child and that Christ redeemed him with His precious blood.

While this is true of all children, we must differentiate between those children that are regenerated and those that are not. Children who were baptized or who, though not yet baptized, have from instruction in the Word of God learned to know and to love Christ, their Savior, are born again spiritually. By faith in Jesus they are not only justified and saved in the sight of God, but are also renewed in their hearts. Their attitude toward God is changed; morally they have become new creatures (2 Cor. 5, 17). Because of this change of heart there is a radical difference between the regenerated and the unregenerated child. This difference is of immense consequence in their respective training. On the basis of his faith the regenerated child can be trained to lead a Christian life, while the unregenerated child must first become a Christian by conversion before such a training is possible.

The State of Grace Must be Recognized in Education. — Children who "by the washing of regeneration and renewing of the Holy Ghost" have become Christians must be regarded as such as long as they have not proved themselves to be faith-less. It is true, they still have the Old Adam, who will show himself in all manner of sins and evil lusts. But for this reason we must not doubt their state of grace and rashly pronounce them unchristians. For if the child becomes obsessed with the idea that his teacher no longer regards him a Christian, this will be of serious consequence in his further training. It might chill and harden his heart to any constructive and positive influence the teacher may try to exert. The case is quite different when the child is manifestly impenitent. Then he must be told that as long as he remains so, he cannot be a child of God. This might help to lead the child to repentance.

Even grown people are influenced by the opinion others have of them; much more so children. One should therefore be very slow to judge and condemn the heart even of a child (Luke 6, 37). The educator should remember: "Charity believeth all things, hopeth all things, endureth all things" (1 Cor. 13, 7). Christian children must be treated so that they feel their teacher believes them to be God's children. This will aid in opening their hearts to his influence.

Regeneration Does Not Make Christian Training Superfluous. — The fact that a child by regeneration entered into the state of grace does not make his further training superfluous, on the supposition that faith, which is indeed a power for godliness, will by itself guide the child aright. This would be true if there were not another power, the Old Adam, active in the child. In heaven, where the just are made perfect (Heb. 12, 23) and the image of God is fully restored (Ps. 17, 15), we shall have no further need of Christian education. But while in this earthly life, even the best of Christians cannot rid himself of his "flesh" and must say with Paul: "I know that in me, that is, in my flesh, dwelleth no good thing; for to will is present with me, but how to perform that which is good I find not" (Rom. 7, 14—25).

This depraved nature, which we inherited from our parents, this "old man, which is corrupt according to the deceitful lusts" (Eph. 4, 22), makes Christian education both necessary and difficult. For Christian training consists essentially in that we help the child in subduing the Old Adam and encourage "the new man daily to come forth and arise, who shall live before God in righteousness and purity forever."

Regeneration Makes Christian Training Possible. — But for regeneration, sanctification of life and hence also Christian training are absolutely impossible. For while it is true that rational man is capable of conversion and a Christian education, there is in him, as long as he remains unconverted, no spiritual endowment or power that might be educed, drawn out, developed, and trained. There is no foundation, no starting-point for Christian training; there is no emotion, tendency, or attitude that might possibly develop into a godly life and a Christian character. An unbeliever may indeed affect "the form of godliness," but he denies the power thereof (2 Tim. 3, 5).

It is even so with children. We may possibly train them in the outward forms of a godly and pious life. But such is not Christian education. For with respect to the life one leads the words of Samuel apply: "Man looketh on the outward appearance, but the Lord looketh on the heart" (1 Sam. 16, 7). Christian education can never be satisfied if the child only outwardly walks in the ways of God; on the contrary, it would so train him that he does this from the heart, from love of God and from gratitude for His blessings. But the unregenerated child has a carnal mind, and the carnal mind is enmity against God (Rom. 8, 7); hence with such a child Christian training is not possible.

The case is quite different with Christian children. They have experienced a new birth. The Holy Ghost has enlightened them with His gifts, working in their hearts faith in Christ, the Savior. Thereby a new spiritual life was created in their souls, the like of which they never had before. Having become new creatures (2 Cor. 5, 17), they

The Regenerated Child.

have a new mind, which delights in the law of God, their attitude toward God is changed, and they are endowed with new spiritual powers, which enable them to overcome sin in their lives and to walk in the ways of God. The faith which justifies them in the sight of God by accepting the saving merits of Christ now also sanctifies them in their lives by prompting them to live as it becomes God's children. Therefore, as soon and as long as there is faith in the heart, Christian training is possible and effectual.

With Christian children we must never despair of success. There is present in their hearts a power for good and a starting-point for our educational efforts, a power which supports our influence and guarantees final success. And it is the business of education to draw out and develop this power, so that it functions in their daily lives. "One great purpose in religious instruction is to attach the stimulus and appeal of religion to the common round of daily life and experience of the child." (*Betts.*) Because of the obstruction of the Old Adam the degree of success will vary. But if there is faith, some success in Christian training is not only possible, but also sure. Only when faith is dead, will it be without works (Jas. 2, 20).

Every Christian Child Has a Twofold Moral Nature. Each Christian child presents a complex situation. By his natural birth he is "flesh born of the flesh"; by his new birth he is "spirit born of the Spirit" (John 3, 6). Both "flesh" and "spirit" are active, each striving for the mastery over the child. "For the flesh lusteth against the spirit and the spirit against the flesh; and these are contrary the one to the other, so that ye cannot do the things ye would" (Gal. 5, 17). Left to himself, the child will yield to the impulses of his flesh and the influences of the world, and as a result his faith and spiritual life will die.

It is here that Christian education must exert its influence. On the one hand, it must help the child to repress and subdue the "deceitful lusts" of the old man, to fight down temptation, and to overcome and avoid what is evil in the sight of God. On the other hand, it must encourage the new man by bringing such influence to bear on the heart of the child that from love of God he gladly and willingly lives as God would have him live. It is particularly this second phase that must be emphasized. The possibilities of a holy life, which, as in a root, are bound up in the child's faith, must be drawn out and exercised, until habits are established and a Christian character is developed.

From what has been said it is apparent that a person not familiar with the teachings of the Bible and with their purpose or ignorant of the soul life of a Christian child, is not competent to offer a truly Christian education. The blind cannot lead the blind.

Diagnosis. — The importance of proper diagnosis in therapeutics is generally admitted; it is equally important in education. For the effectual training of the child it is necessary for the teacher to know whether a certain behavior must be attributed to natural traits and qualities or whether it is premeditated wickedness or whether it is a fruit of faith. He must not confound an impulsive temperament with intentional sauciness and impertinence, inordinate ambition with praiseworthy diligence, laziness and indifference with piety. As far as this is possible, the educator must discern whether a certain behavior is but an expression of the child's peculiar nature or of its Old Adam or of the new man. This is difficult at times, but he must try his best to diagnose the case properly, for the treatment will be accordingly.

The Old Adam will surely show himself in the conduct also of Christian children. He must not be flattered, but reproved and subdued. Likewise the new man will show himself. He must be nursed and encouraged that he may become strong and be the dominating power in the child's life. Great damage may be done if the teacher, not understanding the child, misinterprets his actions. He praises where he should reprove and reproves where he should encourage. Because he does not recognize the first feeble "fruits of the Spirit," or because they are not as fully developed as he would have them, he overrides them, with the disastrous result that they wither. A child will often err in his judgment, but his motive and intention may be good. Let the teacher therefore be careful that in criticizing the external act he do not rashly judge the motive, that he do not ignore where he should recognize, not chide where he should commend, nor discourage where he should encourage, and *vice versa*.

The educator must be on his guard lest, being deceived by the winning ways or the bright gifts of some children, he make them his pets and favorites and, overlooking their shortcomings and faults, neglect their training. Many a promising child was spoiled and came to ruin because he was petted. The fact that some children are more likable than others must not blind the teacher as to their weaknesses and sins. Remember the sons of Eli, who were spoiled by an indulgent father (1 Sam. 3, 13).

One must not reprove and punish as sin what is no sin. This would confuse the child as to the true knowledge of sin. But whatever is clearly against the Word of God must not be covered and glossed over. The child must be so trained that in all cases he submits to the Word of God as to the infallible rule of conduct. In dealing with the child, we must take into consideration, however, also the circumstances which provoked the act, the knowledge of the child, and the spirit in which the deed was done. For the act itself may be plainly sinful, while there was no wicked intention on the part of the child, perhaps not even a knowledge of its sinfulness.

Let no one become discouraged when, after much painstaking instruction and training, gross sins crop out unexpectedly. This happens with grown and mature characters (2 Sam. 11 — David); we may expect it in children. In an unguarded moment their Old Adam will, in spite of all previous training, prompt them to do his will. There will be setbacks. Education is a slow process, and if permanent results are not at once evident, we should not give up hope, but continue patiently. In the end our efforts will not be in vain.

But let us not try to change what is unchangeable. Natural qualities can be developed and modified, but we cannot change stupidity to intelligence. Hence a child should never be reproved or punished because he is not so well gifted as others. Such a child requires special attention and patience. To abuse him by calling him names and by hurting his feeling by all manner of caustic and biting remarks will not further, but retard his training.

Part IV. THE AIM OF EDUCATION.

X. The Aim of Christian Education.

A Clear Understanding of the Aim of Education Necessary. — A traveler will hardly venture upon a journey without having in mind some destination he wishes to reach; nor will any one undertake a task without having a definite aim in view which he hopes to accomplish. This is especially true in education. The pedagog, whose business it is to lead children, must certainly know where he would lead them. There must be an aim toward which he is striving, and there must be direction in all his endeavors. For as the destination will determine the course of our journey, so the aim of education will determine the means and the methods that are to be employed and will affect the entire educative procedure. The teacher must therefore have a clear conception of the aim toward which he is striving, and in all his dealings with children this aim must be his directive. Whatever he may do or not do, he must always ask himself how it will affect the child. Will it further or will it hinder the progress of the child, or will it divert him from the right path?

Various aims or principles of education have been advocated. We mention but a few of them.

a. *The eudemonic principle* is based on the idea of happiness as the proper end of conduct. The determining and regulating motive for all one does or does not do is the maximum amount of personal contentment and happiness he may derive therefrom. Thus children are to be so trained that they are happy and content and that in life they seek, above all, personal well-being, avoiding what might disturb, and doing what might increase, their happiness. Actions are right in proportion as they tend to promote happiness, wrong as they tend to produce the reverse of happiness.

b. *Utilitarianism* is but another phase of this principle. It is based on the idea of utility either to oneself or to others. Virtue is founded on utility. Whatever is profitable is good; whatever is harmful is wrong. *"Denn nur vom Nutzen wird die Welt regiert,"* and *"Aller Ausgang ist ein Gottesurteil."* (*Schiller,* in *Wallenstein.*) If you succeed, you are right; if you fail, you are wrong.

c. *The rationalistic principle* is based on reason. Reasonableness is the determining factor for one's conduct. Children are to be trained so that they avoid what reason tells them to be wrong or bad and do those things their reason finds proper and good. Irrespective of whether it brings them joy or pain, profit or loss, they should do what reason recognizes to be right and good.

d. *The humanitarian principle* denies, with respect to moral conduct, the insufficiency of man and holds that man's nature is perfectible through its own efforts. Educators of this school hope by proper training, without recourse to divine influence, to develop a true and perfect man.

e. *The naturalistic principle* also denies the natural depravity of man and assumes that he is inherently good or at least neutral. The purpose of education is to quicken dormant moral tendencies, to allow them to develop freely, without the distorting influence of civilization. Let the child do what he pleases, until by many sorrowful experiences he learns to eschew what is harmful. Whatever is natural is right; to sin is to act contrary to one's own nature. *"Recht hat jeder eigene Charakter, der uebereinstimmt mit sich selbst; es gibt kein andres Unrecht als den Widerspruch."* (*Schiller.*)

f. *The social and national principle* aims to train the child and develop his faculties that he may become a useful member of the human family. Service to the community,

The Aim of Christian Education.

loyalty to the country, good citizenship, are the determining factors of this system.

It is not our intention to offer an exhaustive criticism of these educational principles. It will suffice to say that some of them are fundamentally wrong, and whatever may be good and acceptable we find in a higher degree of perfection in the Christian principle.

Goethe, who may not justly be charged with being a Christian and therefore prejudiced, says: *"Mag der menschliche Geist sich erweitern, wie er will, ueber die Hoheit und sittliche Kultur des Christentums, wie es in den Evangelien leuchtet, wird er nicht hinauskommen."* (May the mind of man expand as it will, it will never surpass the sublimity and moral culture as it beams from the gospels.) Again he says: *"Je hoeher die Jahrhunderte an Bildung steigen, desto mehr wird die Bibel zum Teil als Fundament, zum Teil als Werkzeug der Erziehung, freilich nicht von naseweisen, sondern wahrhaft weisen Menschen, genuetzt werden."* (As the centuries advance in culture, the Bible will ever more be utilized partly as the foundation, partly as the means of education, indeed not by conceited men, but by truly wise men. Quotations from Lindemann's *Schulpraxis*, p. 253.)

A fair examination of the teachings of the Bible will convince every open-minded person that, as compared with the teachings of any philosophical system, the Bible offers the most sane and rational and satisfactory *Weltanschauung* and that the Christian principle of education represents indeed the highest type of ethical training.

The Christian principle of education was not devised by the ingenuity of man, but is given us by divine revelation in the Bible. God is the Creator, and man is His workmanship. It is God, therefore, who may authoritatively fix the aim of man's education and life.

The most explicit statement regarding the complete education of man we have 2 Tim. 3, 15—17: "And that from a child thou hast known the Holy Scriptures, which are able to make thee wise unto salvation through faith which is in Christ Jesus. All Scripture is given by inspiration of God and is profitable for doctrine, for reproof, for correction, for instruction in righteousness, that the man of God may be perfect, throughly furnished unto all good works." Here we distinguish two outstanding objectives of all Bible-teaching: the one, that man may be made wise unto salvation through faith in Christ Jesus; the other, that the man of God may be perfect, throughly furnished unto all good works.

In the teaching of religion the *preliminary objective* indeed must be to impart knowledge. This is fundamental. Indoctrination must necessarily precede education. Unless children "know the Scriptures," these will profit them neither for salvation nor for sanctification. Since it is by means of knowledge that we educate, it must be our first concern and aim to impart to children a clear and definite knowledge of Bible-truths.

The First Major Objective Is Faith in Christ Jesus. An intellectual knowledge of Bible-truths is by no means the ultimate aim of Christian education. But by such knowledge our pupils are to be "made wise unto salvation through faith which is in Christ Jesus"; thereby they are to become disciples of Christ, knowing and acknowledging Him to be the Son of God and their Savior. It is this what the Lord means when He says that we should go into all the world and make disciples of all nations. Teachers must get away from the idea that the aim of Christian education is accomplished when they impart to their pupils but an intellectual knowledge of the Bible-story or of the Catechism, and they must ever bear in mind that by such knowledge their pupils are to be made wise unto salvation through faith in Christ.

A teacher may have children in his school who are no Christians as yet, because they were neither baptized nor previously instructed in the Word of God. These he ought not to turn away; on the contrary, he should seek to win them for Christ. Let him teach them the knowledge of their sins and their responsibility to God in order that he may thereby lead them to repentance. But above all let him teach them the love of God in Christ in order that through the operation of the Holy Ghost true faith may be wrought in their hearts. If this is done faithfully in our Christian schools, they will become truly missionary institutes, through which souls may be won for Christ.

The majority of children attending our schools, however, are baptized; they are Christians. As to them, the first aim and purpose of education must be to preserve them in the faith and to keep them Christians. As they grow in the knowledge of the Word, their faith must be more firmly grounded and strengthened and their spiritual life nursed and enlarged. Whoever neglects to do this fails in the prime purpose of Christian education. The strategic point in all our church-work is to retain what we have, rather than to reclaim what has been lost. We certainly must go after the one sheep that is lost; but let us be careful that not one be lost because of any neglect on our part. Let us gather all we can into the fold and let us keep in the fold those whom we have gathered.

The second major objective in the teaching of religion is to train children in godliness of life. It is this phase of the educational activity that is particularly emphasized in the chapters of this book.

Children that have become wise unto salvation through faith in Christ Jesus are not at once translated into the kingdom of heaven, but they continue in this earthly life, until the number of their days is accomplished. But while they do so, they should also live as the children of God. And to encourage and strengthen them, to direct and help them to lead such a godly life, is the real aim and purpose of their Christian training.

Bible Proof. — Christ tells us that we are not only to make disciples of all nations, but that we also should teach them to observe all things that He has commanded (Matt. 28, 20). Hence also children must be taught and trained to observe in their lives whatsoever Christ has commanded. And Paul writes that Scripture is profitable "for instruction in righteousness, that the man of God may be perfect, throughly furnished unto all good works" (2 Tim. 3, 16. 17). The Greek word rendered "instruction" is *paideia,* which primarily does not mean instruction or teaching, but, as Luther gives it, *Zuechtigung,* or as we would now say, *Erziehung,* which is education or training. The meaning is that the Word of God is profitable so to influence, direct, and train the child that he will lead a righteous life in this world. Titus 2, 12 we read that the grace of God is revealed to us not only for the purpose that it may bring salvation to all men, but that it may teach or *train* us "that, denying ungodliness and worldly lusts, we should live soberly, righteously, and godly in this present world." Thus God's purpose in the economy of grace is not merely to save our souls, so that we may go to heaven when we die, but also to sanctify us in our lives. For Christ redeemed us that even here on earth we might live under Him in His kingdom and serve Him without fear, in holiness and righteousness all the days of our lives (Luke 1, 75). "For we are His workmanship, created in Christ Jesus unto good works, which God hath before ordained that we should walk in them" (Eph. 2, 10).

According to the Bible, then, the aim of Christian training is a fuller sanctification of life, "till we all come in the unity of faith and of the knowledge of the Son of God, unto a perfect man, unto the measure of the stature of the fulness of Christ" (Eph. 4, 13). Because of the Old Adam we shall never attain such perfection in this life, but we must incessantly strive to come nearer to it ourselves and to bring our pupils nearer to it.

The relation between the first and the second major objective of Christian education is clearly indicated in the Bible. The child must first have become "wise unto salvation through faith which is in Christ Jesus" before he can be trained in righteousness and holiness of life. Because faith justifies him before God by accepting the saving merits of Christ, it also sanctifies him in his life by working in him a new mind and a new attitude toward God. The child now sees and judges the things of life from an entirely different viewpoint. Because he knows himself to be a child of God and an heir of heaven, his thoughts and desires are no longer earthward, but heavenward, not worldly, but spiritual. Because he is born again of the Spirit, he is also able to walk in the Spirit. Though we must therefore distinguish these two objectives of Christian education, they may not be separated. Faith in Christ is necessary if Christian training is to be possible and effectual.

The Proper Motive of a Christian Life. — There is a fundamental difference between a merely moral life and a truly Christian life. There may be little, if any, difference in outward appearance, but there is in the underlying motives and principles. Whatever may be the motives of a moral life, the principle of a Christian life and character is, as Paul expresses it, faith of the Son of God, who loved me and gave Himself for me (Gal. 2, 20); and this faith, naturally, is a faith "which worketh by love" (Gal. 5, 6). The moral man is honest perhaps because he holds that honesty is the best policy or because dishonesty is to him a most despicable thing. The Christian is honest for the Lord's sake, because, loving God, he would not do anything that might displease Him.

Let it be clearly understood that Christian training can never be content with an outward display of godliness or a life that springs from improper motives. The Pharisee in the Temple was a very respectable man as far as his outward life was concerned; still he found no favor with the Lord because of his self-righteousness (Luke 18, 9—14). But when the woman, a sinner, bathed Christ's feet with her tears and kissed and anointed them, He was much pleased with such service because it proceeded from a believing and loving heart (Luke 7, 36—50). "For man looketh on the outward appearance, but the Lord looketh on the heart" (1 Sam. 16, 7).

A child who avoids sin because he fears punishment or does what is good merely because he must or expects recognition or a reward for himself, praise, high grades, etc., is not yet truly educated in the Christian sense. We must therefore endeavor so to influence and train the child that he does the will of God from the heart, not from coercion nor from any selfish or mercenary motive, but willingly and gladly, from love of God.

To create this attitude in the heart of the child, we must teach him the love of God in Christ Jesus, that thereby the Holy Ghost may work in his soul a sincere appreciation of God's grace and loving-kindness. For this love of God kindles love toward God in the hearts of our pupils (1 John 4, 19) and prompts them to lead a holy and God-pleasing life. Because they fear, love, and trust in God, they will not offend and grieve Him with sins (Gen. 39, 9), but will be ready to consecrate their lives to His service.

It is the motive behind the deed that determines its

ethical value. And the right motive of a truly Christian life is faith in Christ and love of God. Therefore children must be so taught and trained that they walk in God's commandments, not for their own sake, nor for the sake of man, but for God's sake, from fear and love of their heavenly Father.

Leading a Christian Life Must Become a Habit. — The aim of Christian education is not attained when a child will only now and then, spasmodically, avoid what is evil and do what is good. Education aims at permanent results. It wishes so to train the child that Christian living becomes a habit, a second nature; in other words, it contemplates a Christian character.

"The rôle of habituation in the formation of character is a matter that teachers and parents cannot easily overestimate. From the start the child begins to form habits, not only those conducive to continued physical life, but also those suited to social, moral, and mental well-being. Moral character, which is the most valuable part of us, is a habit of willing. . . . Habituation in the scheme of education as well as in pedagogics needs a more prominent place than it is receiving at the present time." (*Wentzlaff*.)

"All this is to say that our first care in teaching the young child religion should be to lead him to form religious habits. For our lives are controlled by a great network of habits, which come to us as a result of acts often repeated, until they become a second nature. There are many things about the child's religion that should become second nature, that is, should become habits, and are not certain and secure until they have grown into habits." (*Betts*.)

A Christian character, then, is developed in this wise, that by proper influence the child is induced freely to will what God wills, that, constrained by the love of God, he suppresses the lusts of the Old Adam and observes the will of his heavenly Father. If in the various conditions and circumstances of life this is done again and again, if the child is trained and habituated in yielding to the will of his God, then these modes of willing become fixed, and this habit of willing constitutes character.

"From one point of view the development of character is never complete. But in a practical common-sense way most of our important habits of reaction become fixed at a fairly early and definite time of life." (*Angell.*) Also the Christian character of man, though in this life never perfect and complete (Phil. 3, 12), must, in the main, be fashioned in childhood and youth. "Habits grounded in early childhood are more easily formed and more deeply imbedded than those acquired at any later time, and they exert a stronger control over life." (*Betts.*) Christian education continues indeed through life, but it is in youth that the deepest impressions are made and lasting habits are established. "Train up a child in the way he should go, and when he is old, he will not depart from it" (Prov. 22, 6).

But for the "flesh, which lusteth against the spirit" (Gal. 5, 17), the Christian education of the child would be easy enough. We find, however, that because of the Old Adam the training of the child is at times extremely difficult. Laws and rules, threats and blows, may somewhat curb the old man, but they will never encourage the new man to come forth. By a wise use of the Law and the Gospel the educator must endeavor to keep alive and to strengthen in his pupils their spiritual life, so that "by daily contrition and repentance the Old Adam may be drowned and die with all sins and evil lusts and, again, a new man daily come forth and arise, who shall live before God in righteousness and purity forever."

He who would have the fruit must nurse the tree, and he who would see the fruits of a holy life in his pupils must needs nourish their faith; otherwise all his educative schemes and methods will fail. Religious instruction should not be merely intellectual; it must be edifying in order that it may be educative. Be sure that the foundation of faith does not crumble while you are busy erecting the structure of education; let not the lifespring run dry while you are digging the channel for its waters.

Quotations. — To summarize and to corroborate what has been said in the preceding paragraphs, we wish to append a few opinions of others on the aim of Christian education.

"The end of all education is for the child the knowledge of God in Christ and out of that knowledge to love Him, to imitate Him, and to grow like Him." (*John Milton.*)

"Education in the true sense must have as its aim the development not only of the mind, but also of the heart; not merely the acquisition of knowledge, but the formation of the character as well. The building of a Christian character, however, is not man's work, but God's. The heart of man is truly sanctified and cleansed only by the Word. There is no other means. Therefore religious training, inculcating upon the heart the truths of Scriptures, is essential in any God-pleasing system of education. When our children have been enriched in Christian knowledge and the tender plant of faith, nourished and strengthened by their Christian training, brings in ever-increasing measure its fruits of good works, then character is being formed, and one of the aims of our school is attained." (*Anon.*)

"The entire aim and scope of religious instruction cannot be summarized more happily than in the words of Reu, when he states that our object is Christian maturity, such as fits one for successful participation in the life of the Church and a control of the emotional and volitional life of all its members, so that their life is spent in agreement with the ideals set forth in Scriptures. Or, to quote his excellent summary: The aim of Christian education is: 1) faithfully to imbed and anchor in the intellect of the rising generation all the holy truths upon which the life of the mature congregation fundamentally is based and by which alone it is constantly renewed and without the knowledge of which there is no possibility of an all-sided participation in the life of the Church; 2) to stir their emotions to a vital interest in these truths; 3) to bend the will, so that it may run in the paths in which the Holy Spirit, turning to account those truths in His own time and hour, lifts them into personal faith and, as a corollary therto, into the life of the mature congregation." (*Kretzmann.*)

Having in previous chapters spoken of "fruitful knowledge" and "right attitudes" as the first two aims in teaching a child religion, Betts continues: "We have now come to the third of the great trio of aims in religious education — right living. This, of course, is *the* aim, to which the gathering of religious knowledge and the setting up of religious attitudes are but secondary; or rather, fruitful religious knowledge and right religious attitudes are the means by which to lead to skill in right living as the end. The great thing in religious education is to find immediate and natural outlet in expression, a way for the child to use what he learns; to get the child to do those things pointed out by the lessons we teach him."

The **reason** for giving such Christian training to children is the command of God. Prov. 22, 6 we are told: "Train up a child in the way he should go, and when he is old, he will not depart from it." Jesus tells us Matt. 28, 19: "Go ye therefore and make disciples of all nations by baptizing them in the name of the Father and of the Son and of the Holy Ghost and by teaching them to observe

The Aim of Christian Education.

all things whatsoever I have commanded you." And to the parents Paul says, Eph. 6, 4: "Ye fathers, provoke not your children to wrath, but bring them up in the nurture and admonition of the Lord." These words are plain enough, and they clearly express the will of God with respect to the training of children. And Christian parents and Christian congregations certainly will gladly comply with this will of their God to the best of their ability.

The **purpose** of such training is —

a. *The Glory of God.* — We read 1 Cor. 10, 31: "Whatsoever ye do, do it all to the glory of God." Also the training of our children must ultimately redound to the glory of Him who created them. By an ungodly life the name of our heavenly Father is dishonored and profaned (Rom. 2, 23. 24); by a holy life of His children it is hallowed and glorified (Matt. 5, 16; 1 Pet. 2, 12). That in the lives of our children and pupils the name of our God may be glorified should be the ultimate purpose of Christian education.

b. *The Welfare of Mankind.* — The safety, the peace, and the prosperity of a country do not depend upon its natural resources, not upon the wealth of its citizens nor upon their learning and intellectual culture, but upon their good moral character. Any institution which helps to train the rising generation to become industrious, honest, loyal, and law-abiding citizens renders a greater service to society and country than large armies and powerful navies.

Christian education aims to teach and train children that for God's sake they love their neighbor and that for conscience' sake they be "subject unto the higher powers." The Christian home and the Christian school are therefore the bulwarks of peace and prosperity and the moral backbone of the country. Any reform which is to improve the public morals cannot be a matter of legislation, but must be a matter of education. It must begin in the home, be continued in school, and be supported by the Church. And it consists in bringing up children in the nurture and admonition of the Lord.

"If the Church is hampered in its activity of raising a generation of well-indoctrinated, God-fearing, law-abiding citizens, the State itself will be the loser, and its institutions, including the public school itself, will be affected by the evil consequences. Not 'Americanism,' but Christianity is the safeguard for the prosperity and safety of our nation. If Christianity ever goes down, Americanism will not long survive. We do not hesitate to state emphatically that, if all churches established truly Christian parish-schools, the benefits and blessings issuing from them upon parents and children, homes and churches, communities and states, would be immeasurable." (*K. Kretzschmar.*)

c. *The Temporal and Eternal Happiness of the Child.* "Godliness is profitable unto all things, having the promise of the life that now is and of that which is to come" (1 Tim. 4, 8). By training a child in true godliness, we confer upon him the greatest blessing. Unalloyed happiness of life consists not in the possession of wealth and the enjoyment of pleasures, but rather in this, that man lives the life of God. "The kingdom of God is not meat and drink, but righteousness and peace and joy in the Holy Ghost. For he that in these things serveth Christ is acceptable to God and approved of men" (Rom. 14, 17).

But godliness has also a promise for the life to come. The degree of glory in heaven will be a reward of grace given to those who during their lives served God in righteousness and true holiness. To confer upon our children these blessings is the purpose of Christian training.

Part V. THE MEANS OF EDUCATION.

XI. A Criticism.

Human reason knows of various principal means of training, chief of which are the fear of punishment, the expectation of reward, the sense of right, and the love of mankind.

Fear of Punishment. — During the Middle Ages the rod and all manner of corporal punishment were believed to be the most effective means of training. The child must learn to fear, and he will learn to obey. And to this day there are parents and pedagogs who look upon the rod as the sure cure for all educational ailments and believe that a periodic and generous application thereof will make a real man out of the boy. Others prefer to flay the child with words, hoping by smarting reproach or ridicule to deter him from repeating the offense.

It is true, the sinning child must be reproved, and the refractory child must be punished (Prov. 13, 24; 22, 15). But let us beware of making fear of punishment the only or even the chief means of education. Punishment may serve as a restraining curb on the child, but positive and constructive results are not attained thereby; for as soon as the cause of fear is removed, the child is likely to do as he pleases. There are instances where parents were very "strict" with their children at home, and they were very much surprised to find that their boys and girls "went wrong" as soon as they left home. The education at home was perhaps one of fear, and as soon as the restraining influence of the rod was no longer felt, there was a rebound, and the children abused their new liberty.

The aim of Christian education is not to instil and to nurse "the spirit of bondage again to fear" (Rom. 8, 15). If merely from fear of punishment the child obeys his parents and teachers, if from external compulsion he avoids what is evil and does what is good, then surely his was not a Christian training. True Christian education aims to nurse "the spirit of adoption," by which the child knows and feels himself to be a child of God and for His sake will avoid whatever might displease Him and gladly and willingly do what He desires. But the rod will never accomplish this. We cannot beat willingness into the heart of the child. The fear of punishment may, for the time being, suppress the Old Adam and "drive foolishness away" from the child, but never can it instil true love for God and induce the "new man" to come forth, who lives before God in righteousness and purity.

Expectation of Reward. — Realizing that by the use of the rod one can perchance repress evil, but cannot produce positive values, some parents and educators go to the other extreme. They discountenance every kind of punishment and hope to achieve lasting results by holding out all manner of inducements, promises, and rewards. The expectation of gain, of success, of advancement, of enjoyment, of honor and distinction, all these and other selfish considerations are to supply the impetus, the prompting motive for the child to be good and to do what is right. Like Eli (1 Sam. 3, 13) they hardly dare frown upon the iniquity of their children, and if they must take them to task for anything they have done, it is done so gently that the children will hardly notice it. On the other hand, praise, flattery, rewards, and honors are heaped upon the child for just doing his plain duty. Thus emulation, the desire to be something and to make something of themselves, to excel others, or the selfish desire for gain, honor, and advancement is made the basic power in the conduct of the child.

Such training is built up on the selfish instincts of the child. For his own sake he tries to be good and to do what is right. But if the selfish interest of the child should demand that he lie or that he be dishonest, what is there to hinder him? If there is no prospect of praise or of gain, why should he curb his evil desires? Ignoring moral principles, expediency becomes the rule of conduct. He does not ask what is right or what is good, but what is expedient, what is profitable.

But Christian education supplies an entirely different motive. The child is taught and trained to avoid evil and to do good not in the expectation of any reward, but as an expression of love and gratitude to his Father in heaven, from whom he has received blessings without number. Christian education can never appeal to ambition and incite emulation to accomplish its end. As character must not be judged merely by outward appearance, but also by the motives underlying it, it is the business of education to instil the right motives and to exercise them until they function habitually. An educational system which in the last analysis appeals to the selfishness of the child is of a rather low type.

The Sense of Right. — Others would base education upon the sense of right. Teach the child to know what is right and good, and his sense for what is right and good will induce him to do and observe it. If the conscience is quickened and regulated, it will control the life of the child.

There is no doubt that conscience is a most powerful factor in the education of man. But conscience must be regulated. Man must learn what is right before his sense of right can in any way affect his conduct. The question, then, is, What is right, what is wrong, what is good, what is evil?

The consensus of opinion of men, no doubt, has much weight with the individual. But it may also happen that he will pit his opinion against that of others; he may be convinced that he is right and that all others are wrong. The moral views and convictions of the savage differ very much from those of civilized man. And even among civilized men we find that one regards as morally wrong and wicked what another believes to be permissible or even good. The opinions of men as to what is right and good not only differ, but at times contradict one another.

If, then, we are to teach the child what is right or wrong, good or evil, we needs must have an absolute authority, whose pronouncements are not affected by the vacillating opinions of men. And such an authority we have in the Word of God. "The Word of the Lord is right" (Ps. 33, 4). It is the infallible rule of conduct; it teaches man what is truly good and right and will ever remain so. "Thy Word is a lamp unto my feet and a light unto my path" (Ps. 119, 105).

Besides this there must be some moving power that impels the child also to do and to practise what he has learned. The mere sense of right will not always suffice. We know from personal experience that, moved by strong impulses, we at times do what we know to be wrong. Hence there must stand behind every moral precept an authority to which all must bow. There must be present to the consciousness of the child his responsibility to the Higher Power, to the Lord God. He is "the one Lawgiver, who is able to save and to destroy" (Jas. 4, 12). It is not enough for the child to know what he is to do, but there must also be an impelling motive that urges him to practise what he knows. And this power is faith, which worketh by love (Gal. 5, 6); it is the grateful appreciation of the mercies of God in Christ Jesus (Rom. 12, 1—3).

Though we would not by any means deny the educative value of the sense of right in a child, it is apparent that, if not sufficiently supported by other considerations, it is inadequate for effectual training.

"Nobody knows how to teach morality effectually without religion. Exclude religion from education, and you have no foundation upon which to build moral character." (*Charles W. Eliot of Harvard.*)

Love to Mankind. — To train a child properly, we must, it is said, impress upon him the great truth of the "brotherhood of man." He must learn to love his neighbor as he loves himself and therefore in his intercourse with others be guided by the Golden Rule: "All things whatsoever ye would that men should do to you, do ye even so to them" (Matt. 7, 12). In this manner we shall be able to develop a high type of moral character, which, actuated by love for mankind, will refrain from doing what might hurt or harm others and follow after those things which are good and right.

This sounds well enough. The only difficulty is that this theory does not function in practical life. For by nature man loves first and foremost himself. As there is in his heart no love for God, even so there is no love for his neighbor. And all prating about the brotherhood of man will not instil true love into any heart. Love is engendered by love that is experienced. At best, natural man will love those that love him (Matt. 5, 46). In the battle of life, where there is no altruistic love, but pure and unadulterated egotism, this fancy of the brotherhood of man soon crumbles away, and the Golden Rule is utterly forgotten.

If man is to love his neighbor, if this love is to extend also to his enemies (Matt. 5, 44), and is to endure even under adverse and trying circumstances, then this love must be rooted and grounded in the love of God. Because God loved us first, therefore we love Him and also our neighbor. There can be no true love of mankind in our hearts if the love of God is not there first; and we cannot love God if we have not experienced His love toward us (1 John 4, 16—21). But this love of God, which is able to work in us love toward God and towards our fellow-men, we cannot teach without the Word of God, which reveals this love.

In conclusion, we do not wish to say that it is always wrong to punish a child, that we must never offer a reward, that we need not develop his sense of right nor teach him to love his neighbor; on the contrary, these things are perfectly proper in their place. But in themselves and without the Word of God they are inadequate for a Christian education.

XII. The Word of God Is Profitable for Education.

The Word of God Is Efficacious. — As the aim of Christian education is to train the child to observe from fear and love of God what the Lord has commanded, it is evident that the Word of God is the only true and efficient means for such an end. For God only can tell us how we must live that our lives may please Him (Micah 6, 8; Ps. 119, 9. 105). But the Word of God not only points out the way, it also gives us strength and willingness of heart "to run the way of His commandments" (Ps. 119, 32).

There is a vast difference between the word of man and the Word of God. Man may err in his judgments, may fail in his promises, and whatever he may say is supported by his but little human authority. But behind every word of the Bible stands the authority of God, whose commandments no man may ignore with impunity (Hos. 4, 6). Behind every promise of the Gospel stands the truth and faithfulness of the heavenly Father, whose Word shall not be broken (2 Cor. 1, 20).

Of this the teacher himself must ever be conscious; he must "tremble at God's Word" (Is. 66, 2); he must implicitly believe every promise of his God. For his personal attitude toward the Word will certainly affect his manner of teaching it. But he must also impress on the children that in every doctrine, commandment, and promise of the Bible we have the authoritative statement of God. For the Bible will lose a good deal of its effectiveness to him who regards it merely as the word of man. Therefore children must be trained to hold the Word of God sacred and to receive it with reverence and confidence of heart (1 Thess. 2, 13). The fact that to the consciousness of the child the authority of God stands behind every commandment and promise makes these more impressive and effectual. The "Thus saith the Lord" gives authority and force to every statement of the Bible.

The Word of God is effectual not only because the child believes it to be the Word of God, but especially because the power of God operates through this Word. Paul says of the Gospel that it is "a power of God" (Rom. 1, 16), and Heb. 4, 12 we read: "The Word of God is quick and powerful and sharper than any two-edged sword, piercing even to the dividing asunder of soul and spirit and of the joints and the marrow and is a discerner of the thoughts and intents of the heart." Even the word of man is a power to impress and influence the heart. But this is much more true of the Word of God, because there is inherent in it and operating through its divine truths the mighty power of God. "Is not My Word like as a fire? saith the Lord, and like a hammer that breaketh the rock in pieces?" (Jer. 23, 29). Whoever, therefore, speaks the Word of God "faithfully" wields that mighty power of God which is able to convert the soul, to impress the heart, and to influence the conduct of men. This Word of God is always efficacious, always able to produce results; it is never dull and void of strength; and in those who are regenerated it also works effectually (1 Thess. 2, 13).

Christian educators should fully realize that, when teaching the Word of God, they are wielding the "power of God." Hence they should remember the injunction of the Lord: "He that hath My Word, let him speak My Word faithfully" (Jer. 23, 28), and: "My Word . . . shall not return unto Me void, but it shall accomplish that which I please, and it shall prosper in the thing whereto I sent it" (Is. 55, 11). Let him be faithful in the use of this Word and confident of success.

As the curative strength lies not in the physician who prescribes the medicine, but rather in the medicine itself, so also the power to influence the heart and to educate the child lies not with the person that teaches the Word of God, but it is inherent in the Word itself. Therefore Paul writes: "All Scripture is given by inspiration of God and is profitable for . . . instruction [education] in righteousness, that the man of God may be perfect, throughly furnished unto all good works" (2 Tim. 3, 16). The activity of the teacher is merely instrumental; he diagnoses the case and applies the proper spiritual medicine. But the cure is effected not by him, but by the Word of God and by the Holy Ghost, who operates through this Word.

The Law and the Gospel. — We distinguish two principal doctrines in the Bible, the Law and the Gospel. Both must be used in education. But each has a different content and serves a different purpose, and each will produce a different effect. This the educator must know and therefore be skilled in "rightly dividing the Word of Truth" (2 Tim. 2, 15).

The Law as a Curb. — In the training of children the Law must often be used as a curb to check, in a measure, the coarse outbursts of sin. Children must be led to feel that God demands strict obedience to His commandments and that He will surely punish the transgressor (Deut.

27, 26). Occasionally we must use the Law as a curb also with regenerate children because of their Old Adam, who, not being a whit better than the Old Adam of the unregenerate, will not yield to other treatment. Hence also regenerate children must learn that "God threatens to punish all that transgress these commandments; therefore we should fear His wrath and not act contrary to them."

Insufficiency of the Law. — Such use of the Law, though at times necessary, is by no means conducive to true Christian training, as a study of the effect of the Law on the heart will readily show. The Law of God is in itself good, perfect, and holy, but it is made weak and ineffective because of the total depravity of the human heart (Jer. 17, 9; Rom. 7, 9—14). By its stern commands and its terrifying curse it may produce the obedience of a slave and by its promises the selfish obedience of a Pharisee. But neither the fear of punishment nor the expectation of reward is the proper incentive of a truly Christian life, but rather filial reverence, love of God, and gratitude for mercies received. And this the Law cannot instil. It works wrath in the heart of man against God (Rom. 4, 15); it kills all true fear and love of God (2 Cor. 3, 6; Rom. 7, 11). Hence the Law, in that it is weak through the flesh (Rom. 8, 3), is not only unable to justify man in the sight of God, but is also insufficient to sanctify him in his life among men.

The Law points out the way man should go, but it does not make him able and willing to do so. It demands that he love God above all things, but it does not fill his heart with that love which is "the fulfilling of the Law" (Rom. 13, 10). This pure and unselfish love, which is the real motive power that incites man to render joyful obedience to the commandments, cannot be worked in the heart by the demands of the Law, but only by the promises of God's grace in the Gospel. Because God loved us first, as the

Gospel shows (John 3, 16), we also love Him (1 John 4, 19). If this love of God is in our hearts, we shall also keep His commandments, and then these commandments will not be grievous (1 John 5, 3). The Law has its place in the training of the child, as shall be more fully pointed out below, but let no one imagine that in itself it is sufficient to achieve a true Christian education.

The Law as a Mirror. — To prepare the heart for the sweet and life-giving message of the Gospel, the Law must be used as a mirror, from which the child may learn to know his sins and the wrath of God. No one will ever accept God's promise of grace and forgiveness who has not in his heart experienced the need of it. Hence the child must first learn to know his sins and realize that they are offenses whereby he has provoked the sore displeasure of God. Where there is no knowledge of sin and no sincere sorrow for it, there can be no desire for forgiveness of sin and no appreciation of the promise of it. The sweetest Gospel promise will make no impression on a heart that is not convinced of sin. If, therefore, the Gospel is to take effect, the Law must prepare the way. Thus the Law becomes a "schoolmaster to bring us unto Christ" (Gal. 3, 24).

In using the Law as a mirror, it is indeed necessary to impart to our pupils a clear and definite knowledge of its commandments and of their meaning. However, let us not imagine that the purpose of the Law is now accomplished. For this knowledge may, after all, be merely intellectual, leaving the heart untouched. Our aim must be by such knowledge to strike the conscience and to move the heart. Applying the various precepts of the Law to our pupils personally, we must endeavor to drive home their meaning in order that through a conscious realization of their shortcomings and offenses and of the wrath of God their hearts be affected and moved and the feeling of sorrow and remorse be produced. Any knowledge of the Law which does not do this is dead and ineffectual as far as educational results are concerned. Let us therefore never teach the Law in a cold and formal manner, as perhaps other subjects are taught where we intend to impart mere information; but let us teach the Law with the definite purpose of leading our pupils through the knowledge of the Law to a live knowledge of their sins.

Because of their Old Adam also baptized children must use the Law as a mirror, from which they may learn to realize the heinousness of their sins and the fierceness of God's wrath, so that ever and again they will be reminded of the fact that they are "carnal and sold under sin" (Rom. 7, 14), that they have need of the Savior and therefore humble themselves in true repentance before their God. It is the penitent heart that will cling to the promise of God's grace; and where true knowledge of sin ceases, faith in the forgiveness of sin will likewise cease.

The Content of the Gospel. — After the Law has accomplished its purpose in working knowledge of sin and contrition of heart, the Gospel must be used. The content of the Gospel is entirely different from that of the Law. It is the story of man's redemption, and it is infinitely more. It is the glad tidings of the grace of God in Christ Jesus. It is God's own proclamation of pardon to a sin-cursed world. Its promises are unconditional and free, and they offer plenary grace and forgiveness to every sin-sick soul (Matt. 9, 2). They bring to the ungodly the righteousness of Christ and to the lost the assurance of eternal salvation. It is important that children have a clear understanding of God's promise of grace in Christ.

Effect of the Gospel on the Heart. — Every promise requires faith for its acceptance on the part of him to whom it is made. However, the faith whereby a promise is accepted is wrought in the heart by this very promise. Thus it is with the Gospel. There can be no faith in the grace of God unless there first be a promise to that effect. This promise we have in the Gospel. It not only offers to the individual, freely and unconditionally, the forgiveness of his sins, but unless inhibitory influences, such as the love of sin or despair, etc., dominate man's consciousness, it will work in the heart also the acceptance of what it offers — it works faith. "So, then, faith cometh by hearing and hearing by the Word of God" (Rom. 10, 17). Through the preaching of the Gospel, people come to faith (John 17, 20). Even as man is able by his word to impress, influence, and move others, so it is God Himself who by His Word impresses, influences, and moves the souls of men, working faith in their hearts (Acts 16, 14). Thus it is not man who "makes up his mind" to believe, but it is God who changes the mind of man to believe. Men believe "according to the working of God's mighty power" (Eph. 1, 19). If, then, the Gospel has any positive effect on the heart at all, it is this, that it works faith in its promises.

Man cannot add to the efficacy of the Word of God, but he can hinder its efficacy in various ways. Light and jesting remarks, by which the teachings of the Bible are held up to ridicule and contempt, are very likely to set the hearts of children against these teachings and thus preclude their efficacy. Nor should the Word of God be taught in a formal, apathetic, and businesslike way. Being deeply convinced of its truths, the teacher should seek to convince his pupils; having himself "tasted the good Word of God" (Heb. 6, 4), he would have them taste it likewise; having himself found peace of conscience and joy of heart in the assurance of the forgiving grace of God, he will evince a sincere personal interest in applying God's promise of grace to the penitent child and will pray that God would by His Spirit touch and open his heart to believe.

Teachers of religion are "workers together with God" (1 Cor. 3, 9), and they should certainly feel responsible for the souls of their pupils. Hence they must avoid whatever might counteract or hinder the effectiveness of the Word of God and teach it sincerely and faithfully.

What Is Faith? — Knowledge of Christ is a necessary prerequisite of faith in Christ. Men cannot believe in their Savior if they know nothing of Him. "How shall they believe in Him of whom they have not heard?" (Rom. 10, 14.) Before the Scriptures can make our pupils wise unto salvation, they must be taught to know them (2 Tim. 3, 15). Knowledge is so essential to faith that sometimes faith is called knowledge outright. "And this is life eternal, that they might know Thee, the only true God, and Jesus Christ, whom Thou hast sent" (John 17, 3). However, the word knowledge is here used in a fuller sense. It means not merely a purely intellectual knowledge, such as also an unbelieving scoffer may have acquired by diligent study of the Bible, but it is a *nosse cum affectu,* a knowledge which has affected the heart and the will, working conviction and confidence. While knowledge must indeed be regarded as the necessary basis of faith, faith is not only knowledge, it is more; it is a live knowledge, which has touched the heart and the will; it is essentially assurance, confidence, and trust of the heart based on, and sustained by, the knowledge of the mind.

This is quite plain from the classical definition of faith which we find in Heb. 11, 1: "Faith is the substance of things hoped for, the evidence of things not seen." This rendition of the original is somewhat difficult to understand. Luther's translation expresses the sense more clearly: *"Der Glaube ist eine gewisse Zuversicht."* Faith is the assurance and confidence of the heart in those invisible and spiritual things we have learned to know from the Gospel.

To believe in Christ therefore does not simply mean to know what the Bible teaches concerning Christ and His work, as one might know facts of history, but it means that the knowledge of the mind has become alive, has moved the heart and incited the will. The believer not merely knows in his mind what the Gospel teaches, but he is persuaded in his heart that these promises are true; he longs and yearns for the promised gift and trusts in God and relies on Him, who is able and willing to perform what He has promised (Rom. 4, 21). "Faith is not only knowledge in the intellect, but also confidence in the will; *i. e.,* it is to wish and to desire and to receive that which is offered in the promise, namely, reconciliation and remission of sins." (*Triglot,* p. 205.)

While faith may indeed be defined as knowledge (John 17, 3), taking the word knowledge, however, in a fuller sense, it is essentially *fiducia cordis,* confidence of the heart, which confidence is an emotional attitude of the heart plus an act of the will. The believer not only knows the promises of his God, but there is in his heart also an emotional response; he wants them, lays hold of them, and applies them to his personal need. Thus it is that the three phases of soul life, cognition, emotion, and volition, are engaged in the act of believing.

The fact that in the teaching of religion the same soul activities and processes are called forth and the same psychic "machinery" is used as in other phases of education does not in the least militate against the truth that it is God who by the power of His Word works and preserves faith in our hearts (Eph. 1, 19; Phil. 2, 13; 1 Pet. 1, 5). Making use of the cognitive, the emotional, and the volitional activity of the human soul, God teaches man to know His Word, enlightens him with His gifts, and works in him to will and to do of His good pleasure.

Endeavoring to understand what faith is and how it is engendered is not an idle speculation, but may prove to be of practical value. It shows the teacher that he must not merely impart information by formal instruction, but there must be an appeal to the heart and the will of his pupils. In other words, he must not only teach them to know the Scriptures, but his aim must be that by such knowledge they become wise unto salvation through faith in Christ Jesus.

"Our teachers dare never lose sight of the spiritual aim of our school. They must constantly bear in mind that they are serving in a capacity differing widely from that of public-school teachers. They are in a special sense servants of God and of the Church. Hence they should in all their teaching concentrate their efforts on the child's soul and its salvation.

"This necessitates that the teaching of religion be conducted with thoroughness, sincerity, and a definite spiritual aim. We expect our teachers, especially in the teaching of religion, to give due attention to the three parts of the human mind: intellect, the emotions, and the will. They dare never be satisfied with having educated the intellect by imparting religious knowledge; for that would be mere mechanical instruction. They must educate also the emotions, by arousing them in favor of the good and contrary to the evil, and finally concentrate upon the will of the pupil with the purpose of bringing him, by the grace of God, to a definite decision to be and to do what the Bible demands of him. In short, our teachers are called not merely to teach certain facts and principles in an abstract manner, but, above all, to cultivate the spiritual life of their pupils and to mold their character and conduct. They are to develop Christian personalities." (Quoted from *A Draft of Regulations for the Teachers of Our [Lutheran] School.*)

The Functions of Faith. — Faith has a double function. The first is its *justifying power*. Trusting in God's promise of grace, the believing child accepts the promised gift and thus stands justified before God (Rom. 3, 28). The very moment that by faith he lays hold of the promise he has what the promise offers, namely, the forgiveness of all his sins. Though at first this faith be very weak, it nevertheless has and holds the full grace of God and the complete forgiveness of sin. Thus by faith the child is justified in the sight of God, not partially, but perfectly.

The other function of faith is that it *sanctifies* the believer in his life on earth. While the justifying power and the sanctifying power of faith are not identical, neither power can be separated from faith. The faith that justifies man before God will also sanctify him in his life among men, for faith worketh by love (Gal. 5, 6). And any faith which does not sanctify man in his life does not justify him before God; for faith, if it has not works, is dead, being alone (Jas. 2, 17).

Faith, however, does not justify man in the sight of God because it sanctifies him in his life. The sanctifying power of faith is not its saving power; rather, because by faith man is assured of the forgiving grace of God, this faith will make him willing to lead a holy and righteous life, well pleasing to his Father in heaven.

This sanctifying power of faith is of paramount importance in the Christian training of adults and of children. The heart, which by nature is dead in trespasses and sins, now is quickened; a new, a spiritual, life is engendered (Eph. 2, 1). Having been void of true fear and love of God and full of enmity against Him (Rom. 8, 7), it is by faith morally renewed, and a new attitude toward God is created, so that morally the believer has become a new creature (2 Cor. 5, 17). The assurance of the pardoning grace of God will serve to intensify his abhorrence of sin and fill his heart with sincere love and gratitude toward God, which makes him able and willing to struggle against, and overcome, Satan, the world, and his own flesh and to walk in godliness and good works. Living in the Spirit, he will also walk in the Spirit (Gal. 5, 25). This renewing of the heart is not a thing which man can bring about by any effort of his own, but is the fruit of that faith which the Holy Ghost works through the Gospel.

This new spiritual life, this new man (Eph. 4, 24), is the basis and starting-point for all true Christian training. Because the child is sanctified in the faith, he can now be trained in holiness of life. For this is the very essence of Christian education, that we draw out, develop, and train this new, God-given endowment, so that the child in his life no longer conforms to the ways of the world, but, being transformed by the renewing of his mind, earnestly tries to observe the good and acceptable and perfect will of God (Rom. 12, 2).

The Gospel the Only Effectual Means for Positive Christian Education.—While there are indeed other means that must be used in the training of the child, as shall be pointed out in a subsequent chapter, we must bear in mind that to effect a Christian education, the Gospel is the only means. Its gracious promises not only quicken the heart with faith in Christ for the salvation of the soul, but they also instil true filial love of God and a sincere appreciation of His manifold blessings and thus supply that basic power which is absolutely necessary for a Christian life. The believer being sure of the grace of God and of eternal bliss, the fear of punishment or the expectation of reward can no longer be the driving force and innermost motive of his obedience to God, but it is simple, plain gratitude that constrains him to do his Father's will.

When Paul therefore admonishes the Christians not to be conformed to the world, but to be transformed to know and do the good will of God, he does not remind them of the stern commands of the Law and of its curse, nor does he hold out inducements to them that might appeal to their selfishness, but he beseeches them "by the mercies of God" (Rom. 12, 1). Because of the mercies they had received, they should willingly present their bodies a living sacrifice unto God. And Titus 2, 11—14 we read: "The grace of God, that bringeth salvation to all men, hath appeared," and of this grace the apostle says, "teaching," — *paideuousa* (Greek), *zuechtiget* (German), — training, educating, "us that, denying ungodliness and worldly lusts, we should live soberly, righteously, and godly in this present world, looking for that blessed hope and the glorious appearing of the great God and our Savior Jesus Christ, who gave Himself for us that He might redeem us from iniquity and purify unto Himself a peculiar people, zealous of good works." Here we are plainly told that, if we would train adults and children that they deny ungodliness in their lives and be zealous of good works, then this can be done only by means of the Gospel, by impressing upon them the blessings of God's grace, the redemption of Jesus, and the blessed hope of eternal salvation. All these things are not earned by leading a holy life, but Christians have them by faith, and because they have them without any merit or worthiness on their part, their gratitude will impel and incite them to lead a life that is well pleasing in the sight of God.

Children, too, must always be taught these blessings from God's Word, so that thereby God may work in them "both to will and to do of His good pleasure" (Phil. 2, 13). Knowledge that is forgotten or of which one is not conscious does not move the heart and exerts no educative influence, while the thoughts that occupy us most and dominate our consciousness are most likely to affect our hearts and to control our lives. If, then, we would accomplish anything in the way of Christian training, we must not fail to impress again and again on the consciousness of our pupils the promises of God's grace. These possess power to work not only faith in the forgiveness of sins, but also love of God and gratitude for His blessings and hence willingness and strength to do what is pleasing to Him. No machine will run if there be no power to drive it. The driving power of a Christian life is faith, and this faith must be nursed and strengthened by means of the Gospel.

The Law as a Guide and Rule of Conduct. — The sanctifying power of faith makes one willing and able to walk in the ways of God. But one may not always know which these ways are. The child should not be left to his own fancy in this matter, lest his service be but a vain worship (Matt. 15, 9). Here we must again make use of the Law and "teach it diligently to the children" (Deut. 6, 7) in order to show them what is good and what the Lord requires of them (Micah 6, 8). However, the Law is now used for an entirely different purpose. It is no longer the "Law of commandments," which demand obedience by their stern "Thou shalt" and "Thou shalt not" and would enforce this obedience by threatening punishment to the transgressor (Deut. 27, 26). Christians are free from the bondage of the Law. They do the works of the Law, but they do them, not because they are *Law* to them, but because their faith makes them willing to do whatever may please their Father in heaven. It is this what Paul means Rom. 6, 14: "Sin shall have no dominion over you, for ye are not under the Law, but under grace."

According to the "new man" Christian children are willing to do what pleases God; they need not be commanded, they need only be shown what He would have them do. And here the Law is used as a guide which directs them and points out to them the way they should go (Ps. 119, 9), while their love of God incites them to walk in this way. "For this is the love of God that we keep His commandments; and His commandments are not grievous" (1 John 5, 3). This is the new obedience in which Christian education must train children, an obedience that springs from faith, which worketh by love, and that is regulated by the Law.

Thus, besides making man wise unto salvation through faith in the Savior, which is the chief purpose of the Scripture, it is also profitable "unto education in righteousness."

XIII. The Use of the Word of God.

To achieve the principal objectives of Christian education, namely, wisdom unto salvation and holiness of life, the Bible must according to 2 Tim. 3, 16, be used for —

Doctrine. — The Bible teaches us the promises and the commandments of God. And we should use the Bible for this purpose, that we may learn to know what God would have us believe and what He would have us do. This use of the Bible is fundamental to every other use we may make of it.

Reproof. — This refers particularly to the refutation of error and false doctrine. It is not with reason, science, history, etc., that we must combat false teachings, but with the Word of God. From the Bible we must "convince gainsayers," proving their doctrines to be unscriptural or even anti-Scriptural. In this way the Bible serves as a defense against the inroads of soul-destroying errors, protecting in our hearts the faith that was worked by its teachings.

Correction. — Over against the exalted opinion man has of himself, the Bible shows him his depraved condition; pointing out to him his faults and failings, his shortcomings and sins, which must be corrected and amended. There is no book in the world which so truly depicts the moral conditions of man, and, without respect of persons, convinces him of sin as the Bible does.

Instruction in Righteousness. — The Bible not only points out to man where he needs correction, but in a more positive way it instructs him in the paths of righteousness. But more than this. Working in the heart true faith in Christ and love of God, it supplies the proper stimulus that incites and moves man also to do and observe what the Lord requires. Thus it trains and educates man in righteousness.

Comfort. — According to Rom. 15, 4; Is. 40, 1; Jer. 15, 16 the Bible is to be used for the comfort of God's people. Of this all Christians stand in great need, partly because of the weakness of their flesh, partly because of the tribulations they must endure. In the hour of trial and sorrow the sympathy and condolence of men is agreeable, but it does not so touch the heart and cheer the soul as does the Word of God.

Whether the Word of God is to be used for doctrine, for reproof, for correction, for instruction in righteousness, or for comfort depends upon circumstances. But in all cases the Word of God must be taught.

The Word of God Must be Clearly Taught. — While the Word of God is indeed the only means of effecting a truly Christian education, it does not work like a charm or incantation, which, pronounced over the child, but not understood by him, will produce this wonderful result. It is not the sound of the words we speak, but the ideas and truths these words express that possess power to influence and move the heart. However, the heart can be reached only by way of the mind. Hence we must teach clearly that our pupils may understand correctly.

A discourse, lecture, or sermon, however important its message, is of no benefit to the hearers if they do not understand it, the profound erudition of the speaker notwithstanding. If his presentation of the subject is confused and his language is too difficult, he is like a man who "speaketh in an unknown tongue," which no one understands (1 Cor. 14, 2. 16. 19). It is not sufficient for a speaker to be clear in his own mind on what he would tell and teach others, but he must make it so clear to his hearers that they may take with them definite thoughts and ideas. It is right here that much of our teaching and preaching falls short of its purpose.

Any lesson which the child does not understand is of no educative value whatever. Therefore the teacher must, in the first place, clearly understand what he would teach his class. If he himself is in the dark, how can he bring light to his pupils? In the second place, he must so teach the lesson that the children also clearly understand it. Only clear and definite ideas are able to make definite and clear impressions on the heart of the child. The lesson should be well organized, the progress of thought plain and easy, the language sufficiently simple for children, the presentation not abstract, but concrete, elucidated with fitting illustration, and the topic of the lesson should be clearly set forth.

It is a serious pedagogical blunder for a teacher to expect his pupils to know what he has not taught them and to observe what they have never learned. Therefore let him teach the Word of God clearly. Religious life is intelligent; it must grasp, understand, and know how to use many great truths. To supply children with a definite knowledge of religious truths must be the first and immediate aim of teaching the Word of God.

In this connection we would call attention to the **selection of proper material.** Indeed, all Scripture is given by inspiration of God and is profitable for doctrine, etc. However, some portions and teachings of the Bible are more important than others. The stories of the fall and of the redemption of man, the doctrines of sin and of grace, are certainly more important for the child to know than the genealogy of the patriarchs and the wars of Israel. Peripheral matters may be discussed if time permits, but never at the expense of those fundamental doctrines which the child must know for his salvation and for his life on earth. Matters of prime importance must receive first and foremost consideration.

It would be folly to launch out on a deep theological discussion in the schoolroom. Children must be taught the "first principles of the oracles of God" (Heb. 5, 12); they have need of "the sincere milk of the Word" (1 Pet. 2, 2); and as they grow in knowledge, they may receive "meat."

Again, the teacher must inculcate a knowledge of things worth while, of truths that can sooner or later, be incorporated into the child's life. The child may not at once grasp the fuller meaning and application of text or story; he will learn to do so as he grows older. Still the lesson should always be of such a nature and should be so treated as to benefit the child spiritually. Knowledge which does not and cannot function at some time in the religious life of children is of no educative value to them.

Hence, the material selected must be adapted to the mental capacity and to the peculiar needs of children, and it must really serve the purpose of their Christian education. Such material we have in our Bible-stories and in our Catechism.

The Word of God Must be Taught in Its Purity. — Christ says: "Teaching them to observe all things whatsoever I have commanded you." Whoever, therefore, is called to teach the Word of God must scrupulously "continue" in the words of the Master (John 8, 31). He may not teach his own ideas nor the opinions of others, but must adhere closely to what Christ has commanded. "He that hath My Word, let him speak My Word faithfully" (Jer. 23, 28).

Purity of doctrine is necessary also for this reason, that only thereby we can achieve the objectives of Christian education. All knowledge of the mind possesses potential power to make an impression on the heart, producing emotions and inciting the will. If knowledge makes a positive impression on the heart at all, this impression will be in keeping with the knowledge that made it. The emotional reaction is the echo of the heart to the voice of knowledge.

This is true also of religious doctrines. "The kind and the quality of a man's religion will depend largely on the religious atmosphere he breathes and the religious ideas and concepts placed in his mind through instruction and training." Teach a child false doctrines, and these also may make an impression on his heart. But as the teaching is wrong, the impression is likewise. Thus also the heathen trusted in their idols, and this was real trust. Yet it was wrong and false because they did not know the true God and did not put their trust in Him. As long as Luther entertained the erroneous conception of Christ as of an angry Judge, his personal attitude toward Christ was entirely different from what it was when he learned to know Him as his Savior. A false doctrine can never produce a right faith, nor can false teaching direct us in the right way (Matt. 15, 9). The religious knowledge we impart to children determines the religion of their hearts. Only the right doctrine is able to work in their hearts the right faith and to lead them in the right way of life.

It is therefore by no means narrow-minded bigotry on the part of the Lutheran Church to insist on purity of Gospel-teaching. For besides "trembling" at God's Word (Is. 66, 2) and not daring to depart from its teachings, we know that we can accomplish the purpose of this Word only if we most conscientiously continue in its teachings. This is true not only with respect to the soul's salvation by faith in Jesus, but also with respect to the lives we are to lead in this world, hence also with respect to the Christian training of children. For Christian training is built up on the spiritual and religious life of the child, and if this is wrong because of erroneous teaching, the training is bound to be wrong likewise. There can be no truly Christian life if there be no truly Christian motives that prompt it and truly Christian knowledge that directs it. Hence we must teach children the right Christian doctrine in order that they may have the right Christian faith and lead the right Christian life.

Teach Bible Doctrines as Divine Truths. — In order that the teaching of Bible doctrines may be more effective, they must be taught as divine truths. It is important for the teacher to bear in mind the words of Peter: "If any man speak, let him speak as the oracles of God" (1 Pet. 4, 11). But it is equally important for the children to receive this instruction, not as the word of man, but, "as it is in truth, the Word of God" (1 Thess. 2, 13).

If the stories and the teachings of the Bible are presented to children as myths and fairy-tales, as unreliable records and opinions of uneducated and fallible men, then such teaching, however accurate, will make but little impression on their hearts. Children must be made to realize that it is not the teacher, not the Church, not any human authority, but God, their God, who speaks to them from these sacred pages. Here are the statutes of the one Lawgiver, who is able to save and to destroy (Jas. 4, 12); here are the promises of their heavenly Father, which in Him are yea and in Him Amen (2 Cor. 1, 20). To the consciousness of the child the august majesty of God must stand behind whatever he learns from the Bible.

This is of great educative value. The personality and the authority of the teacher do not always make so deep an impression on the child that also in later life he will observe what he was taught. But if the child realizes, "It is my God and Father in heaven who commands this or promises that," then the instruction will have much greater weight and effect. Hence the teacher must make sure that his admonition is really the "admonition of the Lord" (Eph. 6, 4), and the child must feel: "This is the will of God in Christ Jesus concerning me" (1 Thess. 5, 18).

Teach the Child to Know. — While in the teaching of religion the proper text material is important, which must be taught clearly, in all its purity, and with divine authority, the child that is being taught is equally important, or even more so. We are to teach the doctrines of the Bible not for their own sake, but that by such instruction the child may learn to know them, may be indoctrinated. Let no teacher therefore be content with having presented a given lesson to his own satisfaction, but rather let him ascertain whether he has really taught his pupils, whether they really grasped and learned what he was teaching. All his efforts are in vain if he does not "put the lesson across." As a result of his teaching the child must "know the Scriptures."

Teaching the child does not mean merely teaching him so many Biblical facts and doctrines or explaining to him the literal sense of so many Bible-texts. This is necessary, it is basic, but it is not enough. Scripture-texts and -truths must be so taught that the child also understands what they mean to him personally. The teacher must make it his business to point out that the lesson learned from the Bible really means something to the child. He must teach the child not only the lesson in the book, but also the lesson of the lesson, the personal lesson the child should learn from the lesson in the book.

This knowledge must be clear and definite. Ideas and thoughts which are clearest to the mind are likely to prove strongest also emotionally. Dominating the consciousness of the child to the exclusion of others, they will exert a controlling influence on the heart. Hazy and vague notions are of little value, both intellectually and educationally. The reason why religious instruction at times fails of its purpose is that it failed to impart clear and exact knowledge. The reason why in practical life Scripture is not always "profitable for education in righteousness" is that it was not properly used "for doctrine."

"Our teaching must be made to stick. None but lasting impressions possess permanent value. The sermons, the lectures, the lessons that we remember and later dwell upon are the ones that finally are built into our lives and that shape our thinking and acting. Impressions that touch only the outer surface of the mind are no more lasting than the writing traced on the sand. Truths that are but dimly felt or but partially grasped soon fade away, leaving little more effect than the shadows which are thrown on the picture screen. Especially do these facts hold for the teacher in the church-school class." (*Betts*.)

Teach to Convince the Child. — Of Apollos we read Acts 18, 28: "He mightily convinced the Jews, showing by the Scriptures that Jesus was the Christ." In like manner the teacher of religion must convince his pupils, showing by the Scriptures that the doctrines he teaches are in truth the doctrines of God.

Little children will accept a mere assertion on the part of parent or teacher as sufficient proof for the correctness of the statement. But as they grow older, they begin to think for themselves; they have experiences of their own; they wish to know the why and wherefore and are not quite so ready blindly to accept and do whatever they are told. Still, they will listen to reason and proofs.

In order that faith and religious life may not be based on the word of man, but on the Word of God, the teacher must convince his pupils from the Bible that he is really teaching them the Word of God. It is not his business to harmonize the doctrines of the Bible with the science of men or to justify them before the bar of human reason. On the contrary, children are to learn that they must bring into captivity every thought to the obedience of Christ (2 Cor. 10, 5); and the teacher must make sure that the knowledge of his pupils is rooted and grounded in the Word of God.

Children must learn to believe, not because of the teacher's saying, but because they are convinced by Holy Scriptures that these doctrines are true (John 4, 42; Acts 17, 11). They must feel that, if ever they depart from the teachings they have learned at school, they depart from the Word of God and that, continuing therein, they "know the truth." It is when knowledge becomes conviction, grounded on the infallible Word of God, that it exerts a powerful influence on the heart and carries over into the life of the child.

Teach to Impress and Move the Child. — Religious teaching must never be exclusively intellectual. It must touch and move the heart; it must arouse the emotions "in favor of the good and contrary to the evil." We are at times in danger of superintellectualizing religious instruction, treating Bible-truths very much as we do an ordinary lesson in arithmetic or grammar. We should, however, always bear in mind that we must not only teach the child to know, but also move him to do what he has learned.

"Along with the knowledge that guides our steps must be impulses that drive to right action. Besides knowing what to do there must be inner compelling forces that get things done." (*Betts.*)

In order that religious teaching may be impressive, it must take cognizance of the actual needs and conditions of the child and be applied to them. Teaching the Law or the Gospel, we must not deal in such generalities that our hearers will think of everybody else and not of themselves; but the entire sermon or lesson must be direct, and every one must be made to feel: This commandment points to me; this fits exactly my case; this promise of grace is intended for me personally. Much of our teaching and preaching fails to be impressive because it lacks this personal directness and human appeal.

Studying the sermons of our Lord and the epistles of His disciples, we find that they were not elaborate abstract dissertations and essays, which may be very impersonal, but that they were addressed to their respective hearers and readers and therefore evince that personal directness and appeal which touches the heart. Whatever we preach or teach must be so preached and taught that it is immediately linked up with the personal needs and interests of our hearers.

Indeed, we cannot by any device of our own increase or diminish the power of God's Word, which is in itself "quick and powerful and sharper than any two-edged sword" (Heb. 4, 12). However, the manner of our teaching and preaching this Word may exert an inhibitory influence on the hearers, perhaps even neutralize its efficacy. If our teaching of religion is to be impressive, it should certainly not be mechanical, cold, and indifferent, but it must express our personal conviction and our sincere interest in the spiritual and eternal welfare of our hearers. The divine truths we are teaching are important and of eternal consequence to our pupils; but we must also *believe* that they are important and that it is important for our pupils to learn and accept them. There must be evident in our manner of teaching that burning zeal for the salvation of these children that would have them clearly understand and firmly believe every word the Lord has spoken. If this conviction and zeal is in our hearts, we cannot help but teach God's Word in an impressive and convincing way. To be impressive, our teaching must be expressive.

Says J. G. Herder in an address delivered 1796: *"Es gibt einen Ton des Herzens, der unmittelbar zum Herzen dringt, einen Ton der Ueberzeugung und der gesunden Vernunft, der die ganze Seele ergreift und als Sieger einnimmt; dahingegen der falsche Ton, wenn er Gesinnung und Affekte ausdruecken will, die man weder hat noch kennt, dem Gemuete viel widriger und unausstehlicher ist als ein falscher Ton im Gesange, wenn er auch noch so arg heulte. Wahrheit, Wahrheit bilde unsern Ausdruck auch im Ton der Stimme; ex abundantia cordis; wessen das Herz voll ist, dessen gehet der Mund ueber."*

Herder means to say: Whatever we say or teach must be true, not only with respect to its content, but also with respect to expression and tone of voice, whereby we reveal our personal attitude toward that which our words express.

We all know the great difference between the printed and the spoken word. The one conveys merely the thought, the other conveys to us the thought plus the speaker's personal feeling as expressed by the emotional tone of his voice and therefore makes a more direct and a deeper impression upon us. For this reason the Gospel is to be not merely printed and read, but should be preached and heard. The *viva vox* of the speaker, as an expression of his innermost feeling, will appeal more directly to the hearts of his hearers than the cold, printed letter.

Thus the impressiveness of our instruction depends not only on what we say, but also on how we say it. The tonal expression of the voice must be adapted to the content of the words; it must be true, not feigned; the heart must feel what the mouth speaketh. Therefore, to speak and teach impressively and convincingly, the teacher must needs himself be impressed with, and convinced of, what he says.

One reason why religious teaching at times falls flat is that it does not manifest that personal conviction and that warm interest which so strongly appeals to the hearts of the hearers. The entire sermon or lesson is given in a cold and apathetic manner; it makes little impression on the congregation or the class because there is so little expression on the part of the preacher or teacher.

"An interested and enthusiastic teacher is seldom troubled by lack of interest and attention on the part of the class. Nor, on the other hand, will interest and attention continue if confronted by a mechanical and lifeless teacher." (*Betts*.)

Here again we may learn from our Savior, who taught not, as the scribes, mechanically, without an apparent interest in His hearers, but as one "having authority" and whose "words were with power" (Matt. 7, 29; Luke 4, 32). His words were expressive of a deep conviction and of a loving zeal for the salvation of men. Thus He made an impression on His hearers; "they were astonished," for "never man spoke like this man" (John 7, 46).

In this also Jesus must be our exemplar. Not only the subject-matter, not only the general plan and method of instruction, but also the manner and spirit of presentation must be educative. To accomplish this, the teacher must himself be a true disciple of Christ. He must have experienced the power of forgiving grace in his own heart; he must know that, teaching the infallible Word of God, he also can speak "with authority." He must ever be mindful of his purpose, which is not merely to enrich the mind of his pupils with knowledge of spiritual things, but rather with spiritual knowledge, and to touch and influence the heart so that they may willingly do and observe in their lives what Christ has commanded.

Teach to Train the Child. — For the successful Christian training of the child it is not sufficient that we have at one time clearly and impressively taught him the truth of God's Word, but as opportunity offers and circumstances demand, we must remind him of what he has learned and show him how the knowledge of the truth ought to function in his life. We must not only teach the child to know the will of God, but we must also train him to do it. Too often the things our pupils learned from the Bible and received with joy when they first heard them are forgotten. They were accepted as true and then stored away in the mind never again to see the light of day. They never engage their thoughts and hearts and therefore do not function in their daily lives.

Religious knowledge must not be theoretical and abstract, but it must be practical and must be practised. To this end the teacher must connect the lesson with the lives of his pupils, showing what it means to them and how they should react on it. Having instructed their minds and moved their hearts, he must concentrate on the will to bring them to a definite decision to be and do what the Bible demands of them. If we would train children by our teaching, we must not only give them a few practical illustrations and applications, but we must so influence them that they also practise what they have learned. Children must not only know what they should do, but must be trained to do it, to "translate it into action." For training consists not in the knowing, but in the doing of things.

But there must be an inner compelling force that gets things done. This, in the case of Christian training, cannot be the Law, but the Gospel. "I beseech you by the mercies of God that ye present your bodies a living sacrifice, holy, acceptable unto God, which is your reasonable service," says Paul, Rom. 12, 1. The grateful remembrance of God's blessings and His promise of greater things to come will incite the heart to render joyful obedience to His Word.

And because children so often forget, it is necessary that we frequently remind them of what the Lord requires of them and why they should willingly observe His commandments. This is the way God trains us. Reminding us of what He has done for us and what we are and what there is in store for us, He would prompt us to do His will gladly (1 Pet. 1, 18. 19; 2 Cor. 8, 9—12; 1 Cor. 3, 16; John 13, 17).

Thus the teaching of religion must never become speculative, separated from the needs of the child, but must at all times serve practical ends.

Because of the obvious importance of educative teaching we would subjoin a few **quotations.**

Speaking of the teaching of the Catechism, by which we must impart to the child a clear understanding and a definite knowledge of the truths of the Bible, Dr. Kretzmann continues: "This is followed by the earnest endeavor to implant the true spiritual understanding of the facts of salvation upon the hearts and minds of the children; and throughout the lesson we must connect the facts taught with the lives of our pupils, so that the object of sanctification is never lost sight of. We must get away more and more from both mechanical and abstract teaching, so that our work as teachers of the great wonders of God be concrete, vivid, charged with the power of the living Word to bring salvation and a life of sanctification to all who study under our direction." (*The Teaching of Religion,* p. 129.)

"There should be, of course, a theoretical training in religious life, the mind of the child being filled with stories from the Scripture dealing with the Savior and with all the saints of the Old and the New Testament. There should also be a practical training in the religious life; for a mere intellectual or mechanical knowledge of Bible facts is not sufficient for that complete and harmonious development of Christian character which the Bible requires. The will must be so trained that it shall work out in daily service, in daily deeds, for the love of God and of the neighbor, a code of activities in harmony with the information received. If the will of the child is not trained along the lines of true consecration; if the child is not enabled to select, deliberately to choose, what is good and right according to the Bible and to carry it into execution; if the life of the child does not testify to the witness of the soul reborn by the power of the Word, then our education is a failure." (*Kretzmann*, p. 58.)

"Let us never be proud nor satisfied that we have taught our class so much subject-matter, so many facts, maxims, or lessons of whatever kind. We shall need to teach them all these things and teach them well. But we must inquire further. We must ask, What have these things done for the boys and girls of my class? What has been the outcome of my teaching? How much effect has it had in life, character, conduct? . . . We must measure all our success in terms of the child's response to our efforts. We must realize that we have failed except as we have caused the child's spiritual nature to unfold and his character to grow toward the Christ ideal." (*Betts*.)

Meditation. — The importance of meditation for effectual training is not always sufficiently recognized. We must teach children the Word of God and impress it on their hearts. But we must also encourage them to keep it in their hearts, to think on, to meditate upon, and to ponder, what they have learned.

Speaking of the study of the Catechism, Luther stresses this very point, saying: "For though they should know and understand it perfectly (which, however, is impossible in this life), yet there are manifold benefits and fruits still to be obtained if it be daily read and practised in thought and speech; namely, that the Holy Ghost is present in such reading and repetition and meditation and bestows ever new and more light and devoutness, so that it is daily relished and appreciated better. Besides, it is an exceeding effectual help against the devil, the world, and the flesh and all evil thoughts to be occupied with the Word of God and to speak of it and meditate upon it, so that the First Psalm declares those blessed who meditate upon the Law of God day and night. Undoubtedly you will not start a stronger incense or other fumigation against the devil than by being engaged upon God's commandments and words and speaking, singing, or thinking of them." (*Triglot Concordia*, p. 569.)

Of Mary we read Luke 2, 19: "Mary kept all these things and pondered them in her heart." And Paul, speaking of all manner of Christian virtues, tells the Christians at Philippi: "Think on these things." There is sound pedagogical wisdom in these words of the apostle. If the teachings, admonitions, exhortations, commandments, and promises of the Bible are to make a lasting impression on the heart and to influence our lives, then we must reflect and meditate on them.

No matter how important a thought may be, if it passes quickly through the mind or, though it linger for a brief space, is soon dismissed, being "crowded out" by other things that engage our attention, it is not likely that such a thought will make a deep and lasting impression on the heart, and consequently it will not influence our conduct. Thoughts, on the other hand, that occupy our attention, that dominate our consciousness, that possess us, these are the ones that affect the heart, regulate the will, and control our lives. Thoughts lead to action, and the longer a given thought engages our attention, the more intently we muse and ponder over it, the more will it become the controlling power in our lives. It has therefore been said: "A man becomes what he thinks," and: "Ideas change and mold the character and the conduct of man."

In this connection the parable of the Sower is very instructive (Luke 8, 4—15). The seed is the Word of God, which is heard by four different groups of hearers. Those of the first group hear it, but it makes no impression on them at all because they quickly forget what they have heard. Those belonging to the second group receive the Word of God with joy, they are very enthusiastic; but because the truth is not deeply imbedded in their consciousness, they fall away in the time of temptation, after the first flurry has abated. The third group represents those who allow other thoughts and ideas to occupy their attention, which choke the truth they have learned, not allowing it to impress their hearts effectually and to function in their lives. "But that on the good ground are they which in an honest and good heart, having heard the Word, keep it and bring forth fruit with patience." These have not only heard the Word of God, but they keep it in an honest and good heart, they ponder and meditate upon it, it continues to engage their attention. And with them the Word of God is effective; they "bring forth fruit with patience."

In order to help children to keep the Word of God in their hearts, we must keep it before their eyes. When God commanded the Jews to teach His Word diligently to their children, He added: "And shalt talk of them when thou sittest in thine house and when thou walkest by the way and when thou liest down, and when thou risest up. And thou shalt bind them for a sign upon thine hand, and they shall be as frontlets between thine eyes. And thou shalt write them upon the posts of thy house and on thy gates" (Deut. 6, 7—9). The import of this divine injunction was that the Jews should not rest content with the fact that God revealed His Law to them or that they had once learned it, but they were to ponder it, meditate on it, and think about it. They were to have it constantly before their eyes that they might have it constantly in their minds.

This teaches us an important lesson for the training of children. It is not sufficient that we have once plainly and impressively taught them a divine truth, but we must again and again bring it to their attention; they must be repeatedly reminded of what they have learned. We must try to get the children to think about what they have learned and to ponder what it means to them. This may be difficult, as children are not ordinarily given to meditation; but it is not impossible. Let us tell the children that they should think about the lesson they have learned; let us repeat and review the lesson and ever and again put them in mind of it. Let us use every device that will help our pupils to keep the Word of God in their hearts. Much of the educational effect of our instruction is lost because it is not "followed up."

Memory Work. — Memorizing of Bible-verses, of the Catechism, of hymns, etc., constitutes an important part of the religious curriculum in our Lutheran schools, and it should not be neglected, the criticism of modern pedagogs notwithstanding. Luther placed a high value on exact memorizing. In the preface to his Small Catechism he writes: "Among the young adhere to one and the same fixed form and manner and teach them, first of all, the text of the Ten Commandments, the Creed, the Lord's Prayer, etc., so that they can say it after you word for word and commit it to memory." To Luther, instruction did not, however, mean mechanical memorizing, but conscious, personal, enduring, and applicable spiritual appropriation. Memorizing was to serve the understanding. Therefore he adds: "After they [the children] have well learned the text, then teach them the sense also, so that they know what it means." When the text is safely embedded, as it were, in the memory, its explanation is facilitated, and the process of mental assimilation may proceed all the more readily.

There are, no doubt, many truths of the Bible that should become a permanent part of the furnishing of the mind and should be recorded and faithfully preserved by the memory. Children may not be expected to grasp the full meaning of all they commit to memory; still they should have some idea as to what these things mean to them. Here, again, Luther points the way. His repeated questions "What does this mean?" are to help the child's understanding. Truths that have been explained and learned should be reduced to a brief and fixed form and memorized.

Still, children will not understand all they memorize; but as they advance in years and understanding, the richer meaning of these texts and verses will gradually unfold and become an educational power in their lives. The experiences of life may teach the man the practical significance of texts which the boy memorizes without grasping their full meaning. In the hour of temptation he remembers a word of warning, in the hour of sorrow a word of comfort. And thus there are many instances where prayers and texts a man committed to memory in childhood came back to him in later life and exerted a powerful influence over him. By having children commit to memory Bible-texts and -stories, the Catechism and prayers, we are storing up, as it were, potential power for future use.

XIV. Secondary Means.

Besides the Word of God directly applied for the purpose of Christian training there are other means which may also be profitably employed.

Praise. — Praise has an educative value. It is very discouraging for the child when his efforts and successes, small though they be, are never recognized. God acknowledged the obedience of the Rechabites (Jer. 35, 18); Paul praised the love of the Galatians (Gal. 4, 15). In like manner should we let the children know that we appreciate their good intentions and sincere efforts and that we recognize their progress and success. Praise, justly deserved, will very much encourage them to continue in the good way and to strive for greater achievement. It will also open their hearts to their teacher and render them more susceptible to his teaching and training.

Praise must not be overdone. Excessive praise is dangerous. It begets vainglory. It may create in the child an attitude of doing his duty only when there is reasonable prospect of proper recognition. Never should the educator stoop to flattery. This is ignoble in any man, and it will prove most disastrous in education. The child that was raised, so to speak, on flattery becomes conceited, will resent even just censure, and will not submit to correction. If, on the other hand, the child discovers that the praise bestowed is plain flattery, he will lose confidence in the teacher and discount everything he may say. "A lying tongue hateth those that are afflicted by it, and a flattering mouth worketh ruin" (Prov. 26, 28). Children are often ruined by excessive praise.

Whenever the conduct or the progress of a child is truly commendable, we should not hesitate to acknowledge it. The child, however, should be made to understand that only with the help of God he was able to accomplish what he did. "For it is God that worketh in you both to will and to do of His good pleasure" (Phil. 2, 13). This will teach the child to look upon his gifts, his progress, and his successes in a truly Christian way, not proudly claiming credit for himself, but giving thanks to God, who bestowed the gifts and blessed his efforts.

Exhortation and Admonition.—Exhortation has reference chiefly to good things; we exhort a diligent child to continue in his diligence. Admonition takes into consideration also evil thing from which we would free one; we admonish the lazy child to be diligent. In the education of children both are necessary.

We must exhort, incite, urge, and encourage them by word and example to do what is expected of them, and to do the best they can. The child must clearly understand what he is to do and why he is to do it glady. Exhortation aims at positive results; we exhort a child to be good, to do his duty, etc. Exhortation is necessary and must be repeated occasionally. For let us not imagine that children will always remember what they were told; they forget. And though they may know what is required of them, the proper incentive and will are not always present with them. If Paul, in his epistles, found it necessary again and again to exhort the Christians, we certainly should not deem it superfluous to exhort our pupils repeatedly to walk in the ways of God. A kind word of exhortation does much to encourage a child to continue and to grow in holiness of life.

At times it is necessary to admonish. By reason of the weakness of the flesh the Christian child not only becomes listless and slow in the pursuit of godliness, but is also in danger of yielding to evil influences. The child must then be cautioned against wrong practises, and if he has stepped aside, he must be admonished to repent. This is not always a pleasant task, but it is a plain duty. For we read 1 Thess. 5, 12 that those who are "over you in the Lord" should "admonish you," and Eph. 6, 4 we read that children are to be brought up "in the admonition of the Lord." By such admonition we would wean the child from evil and start him on the right way; by exhortation we would encourage him to continue in this way.

Exhortation and admonition should be both brief and to the point. Lengthy discourses cannot be remembered and hence fall short of their purpose. They should be clear, so that the child understands what is expected of him. They should proceed from a loving heart and be given in the right spirit and at the right time. They should be properly motivated; *i. e.*, they should be observed not for selfish or worldly considerations, but for the Lord's sake. They should be repeated when necessary.

Censure and Correction. — When, in spite of exhortation and admonition, the child continues in his perverse way, rebuke, censure, and correction are in place. We must point out to him his fault, his wrong, his sin, and express our displeasure at his conduct. But if such censure is to profit the child, we must not merely tell him that a certain conduct is reprehensible, but we must convict him of his sin. The child must be led to see the error of his way and must realize that he has provoked the wrath of God. Censure is to show the child where correction and improvement is needed if he would win the approbation of the teacher and of God.

While the teacher must beware of continually criticizing every little thing, straining gnats and perhaps swallowing camels (Matt. 23, 24), nothing should escape his attention, and at an opportune time he should reprove the child for his conduct. If, however, the child himself sees his mistake and improves, it is best not to say anything; for if the child corrects his error, there is no need of correction on the part of the teacher.

Censure and correction must be employed in the education of children, but must not be overdone, as is sometimes the case with well-meaning and conscientious parents and teachers, who find fault with almost everything a child may do. We must remember the child is still a child and not a mature adult. Continual faultfinding discourages the child and tends to develop an inferiority complex, which will be a serious handicap in his further progress. Whenever it is necessary to reprimand the child, he should be made to see clearly where and why his behavior is reprehensible and be made to feel that not chiefly the teacher nor the parent, but God, is displeased with his conduct. The child must learn to look upon his shortcomings and failings in the light of God's Word. Therefore also censure should as much as possible be based on Scripture, which "is profitable . . . for correction" (1 Tim. 3, 17). It should be administered in a Christian spirit, which does not seek to humiliate the child before his class, but rather before God, so that he may truly repent of the wrong he has done.

Censure has a real educative value, particularly if the child feels that the words of reproof proceed from a loving heart. But care must be taken lest we reprove as sin what cannot be proved to be such. And while we may find fault with the external act or behavior, let us not lightly charge the child with wicked and malicious intentions. To do what is wrong knowingly is not identical with doing it intentionally. To accuse a child of malicious intention when he had none such will very seriously affect our further influence on him. Be fair when you must censure and correct a child.

Warning. — It may at times be necessary to warn a child. This is done by pointing out the evil and painful consequences which are likely to ensue if the offense is repeated. Such warning may have a deterrent effect on the child. But here also it behooves us to be very careful; do not threaten punishment when it is not deserved on the part of the child nor intended on your part. Do not "bluff"; for if found out, you have lost your point. In spite of much scolding and warning some people accomplish very little as far as the training of their children is concerned. One reason is that they scold too much, with the result that the children become hardened against it. The other reason is that they do too little. Though warned, the children know from past experiences that nothing will come of it if they do not heed the warning. Think twice before you make any kind of promise, whether it be a promise of reward or of punishment; but having made it, keep it. If your words are to have any effect on the child, he must never have occasion to doubt them. If your words mean little to you, they mean less to the child.

A Christian pedagog, however, will also take to heart what God said to Ezekiel: "Thou shalt hear the word at My mouth and warn them *from Me*" (Ezek. 33, 7. 8). He must point out how a sinful life, wilfully persisted in, will affect the child's relation to his God. The child must understand that he cannot remain a child of God, cannot have the forgiveness of sin and the hope of salvation, if he will not depart from evil; yea, that also temporal punishments are likely to follow. "God threatens to punish all that transgress these commandments."

Christ warned Peter (Luke 22, 31—34); He warns those that transgress the Fifth Commandment (Matt. 5, 22), that offend little children (Mark 9, 42), that deny Him before men (Matt. 10, 32. 33).

Warning and threatening must not proceed from an angry heart, but from love for the child and should therefore not develop into scolding and calling of names, etc. "The wrath of man worketh not the righteousness of God" (Jas. 1, 20). "And, ye fathers, provoke not your children to wrath, but bring them up in the nurture and admonition of the Lord" (Eph. 6, 4). Indeed, we cannot smile when warning and rebuking the child, — this would take the edge off our words, — but we must guard against anger and control our temper. Be serious, but keep calm and make an end of it. Do not continue to growl for some time; but after the case is settled, be kind and friendly, as usual.

XV. Punishment.

Scriptural Basis. — Notwithstanding the disregard into which punishment, especially corporal punishment, has fallen with many ultrahumane pedagogs, the Bible recognizes punishment as a legitimate means to be employed in the training of children. "Withhold not correction from the child; for if thou beatest him with the rod, he shall not die" (Prov. 23, 13); and again we read: "Foolishness is bound in the heart of a child, but the rod of correction shall drive it far from him" (Prov. 22, 15). "He that spareth the rod hateth his son; but he that loveth him chasteneth him betimes" (Prov. 13, 24). Over against the effeminate sentimentalism of our age, which would "spare the rod and spoil the child," these texts of Scripture have stood the test of time and are approved by all sensible educators.

The Purpose of Punishment. — While sparing the rod where it is needed will spoil the child, a liberal, indiscriminate, and cruel use of it will not improve him. According to the Bible the rod is to "drive foolishness away from the child," but it cannot implant Christian virtues. It is one thing to suppress sin and to curb the Old Adam, but quite another thing to bring forth the new man, who lives before God in righteousness and purity. Punishment helps to drive away "foolishness," but it will never produce true holiness of life.

Says Luther: "What must only be forced with rods

and blows will not be productive of good results; under such treatment they [children] will at best remain godly no longer than the rod comes down upon their backs." The adage *Schlaege bessern nicht* (blows do not mend) expresses the same truth. Walter von der Vogelweide (1170—1229) writes in his *Jugendlehren:* —

> *Nieman kan mit gerten*
> *kindes zuht beherten;*
> *den man z'eren bringen mac,*
> *dem ist ein wort als ein slac.*

He means to say, no one can with the rod force the education of a child; whoever may be brought to honors, to him a word is as a blow.

Punishment has a deterrent effect, but no constructive influence. The fear of it may result in an outward obedience, but it cannot work in the heart of the child joyful willingness to be good and to do what is right. Positive results in Christian training can be achieved only by means of the Gospel.

Punishment is indicated where words, admonitions, and warnings have failed. If the child persists in his "foolishness," it is proper that he should experience the degrading and perhaps painful consequences thereof. Also others will profit thereby and will avoid what is likely to bring shame and pain.

The right to punish children rests primarily with their parents. But if these entrust the training of their children to some one else, as to the teacher in school, they delegate to him also the right to punish whenever punishment is necessary.

As it is always a serious matter to mete out any kind of punishment, parents and teachers should be very slow in doing so. They should well consider whether punishment is really indicated and whether it will accomplish its purpose. Hasty, indiscriminate, unjust, and cruel punishments are detrimental to the training of the child. While the pedagog should think twice before he punishes, he should not hesitate to do so when punishment is necessary.

Punishment, to Be Effectual, Must Be Individual. — The individual offense and the individual child is punished. To punish on general principles is absurd and cruel. If the punishment is to mean anything to the child, he must know that he receives it for a definite offense, otherwise his heart will be embittered. In order that he may be able to amend, the child must link up the punishment he receives with a definite wrong he committed.

Punishment meted out on a large scale to groups of children or to an entire class is likely to become a farce, and children make light of it. Also frequent punishing falls short of its purpose. For while the child may not exactly enjoy it, he becomes hardened to it and will not amend. It is certainly most reprehensible to punish a group of suspects for the offense of one who cannot be detected. The guilty one may be among them, but the others will resent the treatment they received, and justly so.

With regard to all punishment we must bear in mind that we are dealing with the individual child and the individual offense. The guilt must be manifest to the teacher and to the child, and the child must feel that he is being punished for his own misdemeanor.

Punishment Must Be Corrective. — There is an essential difference between the spirit and purpose of punishment meted out by the civil government and that of an educator of children. That of the former is primarily punitive, in order to satisfy the demands of justice. That of the latter, however, should also be corrective; the punishment should "drive foolishness away" from the child; it should wean from evil. The chief purpose, therefore, must not be to punish the offense, but to correct the child. That this may be done, it is necessary that the child should know his offense and understand that he is punished for this offense. In order that punishment may be corrective, the child must connect the punishment he receives with the offense he committed. The child must know that the teacher does not want to punish anybody, but that, if pupils do certain things, they inevitably bring upon themselves a certain penalty. To the mind of the child the punishment must be associated with the offense and not with the teacher.

The nature of the punishment should, as far as possible, be in keeping with the nature of the offense, so that it may serve as a corrective. *"Womit man suendigt, damit wird man auch gestraft";* one is punished with those things in which one has sinned. A child should never be asked to copy a number of Bible-texts, to study a list of words, to solve problems in arithmetic, etc., as punishment for an offense which has absolutely nothing to do with any of these subjects. Punishment is never a pleasant experience for the child, and to use school tasks as punishment will set the child against them.

If the child has been flighty and careless in writing his lesson, he should be asked to rewrite it. If he has neglected to study and prepare his lesson at home, he may be asked to do so in recess or after school. If he has thrown paper on the floor, he may be asked to keep the floor clean that day. If he comes late to school without good excuse, he may be asked to come a little earlier for a few mornings. If the nature of the punishment fits in with the nature of the offense, it is more likely to be corrective.

The Measure of Punishment. — It is neither just nor wise to punish all offenses alike; there may be mitigating or aggravating circumstances. Minor offenses must be treated more leniently than gross transgressions, the first offense more leniently than repeated infractions. Sins that are committed with malice aforethought must be dealt with more severely than sins done in ignorance or thoughtlessness (Luke 12, 47. 48). Age and sex of children must be taken into account; small children must never be punished so severely as older ones, girls less than boys. The measure of punishment must also be determined by the effect it has on the child. Words go as far with some as blows with others. Never should the punishment be more severe than is needed to accomplish its purpose.

Kinds of Punishment. — There are certain forms of punishment which may be very effective for the moment, but in the end their outcome is most undesirable and should therefore be avoided. Sarcasm, ridicule, satire, calling of names, nagging, etc., are tongue weapons, which inflict smarting wounds. Never should a teacher use them on his pupils. To do so is not only a degradation of his dignity and authority, but with respect to the effect it has on children it is most reprehensible and inexcusable. "It is unjust, unfair, and wrong to make the child the butt of your ridicule or the victim of your satire." (*Avent.*) Sarcasm, ridicule, calling of names, etc., is a very successful way of destroying respect, confidence, and love in your pupils and in closing their hearts to the influence you should wield upon them.

There are other kinds of punishment which are educationally of doubtful merit, and the teacher should well consider whether the punishment he inflicts will really serve its purpose.

Before resorting to more severe forms of punishment, the teacher may deny his pupils privileges which others enjoy. They may be made to stand while others are comfortably seated. They may be required to stay in during recess or after school while other children are playing outside. In this case the teacher also must stay and see that the children are usefully employed. They may be asked to pick up the paper in the yard or to sweep the room; and the teacher must see that it is done properly. However, let us remember that children need recreation and exercise available at recess periods, and it is not wise to deprive them of it too often. They may be permitted to go out after the other children have returned to their work in school.

Corporal punishment should be used with utmost discretion and resorted to only in extreme cases, when all other means of curbing "the foolishness" of the child have proved futile, or when he has sinned wilfully, is plainly refractory, stubborn, rebellious, and is setting a bad example to others.

It is self-evident that the teacher will warn the children beforehand, telling them that, if such and such a thing happens again, he shall have to use the rod, that this is very unpleasant for him to do and also unpleasant for them to suffer, that therefore he would rather not use it, unless they force him to do so. The teacher will warn the children kindly and gently, yet in a manner that cannot be mistaken. Often this will suffice. If in spite of this the offense is repeated, the children must find out that the teacher meant what he said. To become lax would undermine his authority and jeorpardize the discipline of the school.

If in a grave case the guilty one goes unpunished, it will have a detrimental effect on the offender and on all that know of his transgression. The fact that he "got by" with his "foolishness" this time will encourage him to try again, and by frequent repetition habits are formed which are hard to break. *Principiis obsta,* "Resist the beginnings," expresses a truth that must be observed also in the training of children. Do not let evil tendencies grow and develop in the child, but curb them in the start. If the "foolish" child is permitted to have his way, others will follow his evil example. But punishment, and, if need be, corporal punishment, will make the guilty one feel the personal discomfort resulting from his sin and will "drive foolishness far from him," and it will also neutralize the evil effect of his example in others. But corporal punishment should not be administered when a child has sinned in ignorance.

The teacher should never punish in anger, while he is still wrought up over the matter. "Keep cool," think it over. "The wrath of man worketh not the righteousness of God" (James 1, 20), nor will the incensed teacher do what is conducive to the Christian training of the child. Especially must he not "take out" on his pupil a personal grievance. Even corporal punishment must proceed from a loving heart. The child must feel that in using "the rod of correction" the teacher is not actuated by personal motives, spite, anger, revenge, etc., or that it is a joy for him to inflict pain, but that also in this case he is doing the will of God (Prov. 19, 18). Behind the painful rod there must be a loving heart (Heb. 12, 6), which would save the child from ruin. Punishment should be meted out in such a manner and spirit that it does not estrange the child and leave resentment and rancor in his heart.

In punishing children, the teacher must be scrupulously careful not to injure them in their bodies. This would be a sin against the Fifth Commandment. Do not hit the child on the head, the hands, the arms, or the legs; "the rod is for the back" (Prov. 10, 13). Be not cruel when you must use the rod. *"Gott gebe uns barmherzige Schul-*

meister!" If severe punishment must be inflicted, it is often advisable to defer it and to talk matters over with a colleague or the pastor or the parents of the child.

The educational value of punishment lies not in the punishment itself, but rather in the fear of punishment. The boy who was punished for an offense will hesitate to repeat it. Though the fear of punishment is not the proper Christian motive for avoiding evil, it nevertheless serves as a check for the Old Adam and prevents many a child from yielding to sin and temptation.

While the teacher should be slow to punish, the children should not be made to feel that he will never do so; for they would soon take advantage of this and do what they please. If, however, they know that, doing things "worthy of stripes," they shall not escape, they will hesitate to do them. As the penalties affixed to the laws of the state indicate, the fear of punishment is recognized the world over as a powerful preventive of crime. And as a preventive measure it serves also in the scheme of education. "God threatens to punish all that transgress these commandments; therefore we should fear His wrath and not act contrary to them." Thus the fear of punishment is to keep the child from doing what would render him liable to punishment. In order that this may be so, punishment must be administered when it is justly deserved.

With respect to all kinds of punishment it is well to observe the following points:—

Do not try to punish every little infraction of the rules; it is impossible to do so. *Man muss nicht nach jeder Fliege schlagen.* The teacher will see many things that it is wise to overlook. In many cases a word of reproof is sufficient. Punishment is an extreme measure and should therefore be resorted to only in grievous and extreme cases.

Do not be quick to punish. Ascertain the facts and make sure of your case. Whoever is hasty in punishing children may often have to apologize for the injustice he has done them. Examine whether you yourself are perhaps to blame for the unruliness of the class.

Be just and fair. Convince the child that he has deserved punishment. The measure of punishment should be in keeping with the offense. Do not shield some and pick on others.

Public sins should be publicly reproved and punished (1 Tim. 5, 20); but if the offense is not generally known, the teacher should deal with the child privately.

Distinguish between sins of weakness and sins of malice, between sins against the Word of God and offenses against the rules of men. They must not be treated alike nor punished alike. The child must feel that it is far more grievous to sin against God than to transgress the rules of the school.

Take into account the individuality of the child, his age, sex, temperament, gifts, home conditions.

Before you punish (or praise), seek to understand what moved the child to act as he did. His motive may have been good while he erred in his judgment. On the other hand, the deed may appear praiseworthy while its motive deserves censure.

Do not loose your temper, no matter how irritating the offense may be, but control yourself. Do not yell and roar, but remain calm; speak in a natural tone, though with great earnestness. Do not let your language become abusive.

Be not resentful; do not nag and growl after the case has been settled. When the storm has passed, the sky should be bright and clear also in the schoolroom.

Der Apfel muss bei der Rute sein, says Luther; the

apple should be beside the rod. While the guilty child may have to experience the severity of the rod, the penitent child should feel the sincerity of our love.

Expulsion. — The extreme punishment is expulsion from school. However, no child may be expelled because he has sinned, even though the sin be very grievous or because the child is apparently impenitent. For it is the very aim of the Christian school to win such a child for Christ and to train him to walk in His ways. But if by continued and wilful stubbornness, disobedience, and wickedness on the part of the child the purpose of the school is jeopardized or frustrated; if the child's influence is such as to draw other children away from Christ and to seduce them into sin; if all other means of correction have proved futile, then expulsion must follow.

Expulsion may at first be temporary, and if the child repents and promises to amend, he may be received again. However, his confession, promise, and request should be made known to the other children. But if he will still not submit to Christian discipline and training, but rather continues in his former ways, disrupting the discipline of the school and hindering the training of the other children, he must be definitely removed. For while we should have a sincere interest in each individual child and do our best to win him for Christ and to teach him to walk in His ways, our concern for the other children demands that those who frustrate the very purpose of the school be expelled. *Salus populi suprema lex esto,* applies also here; the welfare of the school is the supreme law.

In a case of expulsion the teacher should never act by himself, but consult with his colleagues, the pastor, and the school board. The parents of the child also should be advised of the state of affairs and be requested not to send their child to school any longer.

XVI. Other Means of Education.

We have, for obvious reasons, dwelt at some length on punishment. But we would have it distinctly understood that all manner of punishment has only a deterrent effect on children and can never produce positive results. The most liberal application of punishment will not make the child truly good. Only positive influences can produce positive results. The most forceful and effectual means at our command for positive and constructive training of children is the Word of God, particularly the Gospel of Jesus Christ, our Savior. But in the training of children we must make use of every available means that might be of some service. In this chapter we would mention a few others.

Prayer. — The power to cure lies in the medicine we take; the power to move the heart and to educate lies in what one knows. Knowledge is power. This is true in things both secular and spiritual. It is possible for us to impart knowledge of spiritual things to the mind, but it is impossible for us to make this knowledge function so that it affects the heart. By our teaching we indeed aim to touch the heart, but it is beyond our power to open the heart to the influence of the truths we teach. This is the work of God (Acts 16, 14). It is God who through the Word of Truth sanctifies the heart and educates and trains us by the power of His grace that we deny ungodliness and live righteously in this present world (Titus 2, 12). Without His blessing all our labor and educative efforts are in vain (1 Cor. 3, 6. 7).

To secure this blessing of God, we must pray that He would enlighten us always to say and to do the right thing at the right time, that His Spirit would work effectually on the hearts of our pupils to impress and to influence them and to train them in the way they should go. "The effectual fervent prayer of the righteous man availeth much" (Jas. 5, 16). Many of our efforts in the training of children fall short of their purpose because they are not supported by prayer. "Ye have not because ye ask not" (Jas. 4, 2).

The Christian education of children is a momentous task, and it is presumptuous for any one to imagine that he can accomplish aught by his own wisdom and skill, without the assistance of God. We need more praying fathers, more praying mothers, more praying teachers and educators for the successful carrying on of this great work. Whoever has had any experience in the training of children realizes how little he was able to do and how much God had to do. Let us pray often, and let us pray sincerely, for the education of our children.

The Christian pedagog should pray *for his pupils,* for all in general, and for some specially. He should ask God that He would keep them from sin, help them to overcome temptation, make their hearts receptive for the word of instruction, and grant them strength and perseverance to follow the narrow path of righteousness. Some children are in need of special intercession, and the teacher or the parent should pray for them, as Jesus prayed for Peter (Luke 22, 32). As 1 Tim 2, 1 we are exhorted to pray for all men, a Christian teacher will, no doubt, pray daily for his pupils.

The Christian pedagog will pray also *with the children.* This is done in the daily devotional exercise, where teacher and pupils join in prayer. But let him guard against vain repetitions (Matt. 6, 7) and teach the children to call upon God "in truth" (Ps. 145, 18). It is advisable for the teacher to speak a short prayer *ex corde* in which he invokes the blessing of God upon the school, etc. Let him vary the wording and the content of the prayer, referring to the special needs of the children or to the lesson of the day. He may also speak a short prayer at the close of the religious lesson, thus setting it aside from the other lessons of the day and emphasizing its devotional character. Let him do all he can to make his Bible-history and Catechism lessons impressive and effectual. These prayers should be short, to the point, and sufficiently plain and simple for the children to understand and to hold their attention.

There are occasions when the teacher should pray *with the child privately*. Let him not simply tell the penitent child to pray to God for forgiveness, but right then and there let him pray with and for the child. Putting himself in the child's place, let him in simple and childlike language confess the sin to God and ask for grace. Again, a child is troubled and afflicted; perhaps he cannot get his lessons, though he tried ever so hard; perhaps there is some other trouble weighing on his mind. The teacher may then pray with the child and make his requests known to God, asking Him for comfort and help. Such a prayer is heard in heaven and makes a deep impression on the child. When visiting sick children, the teacher should not merely inquire as to their physical well-being or talk about irrelevant matters, but let him comfort the child with what he has learned from the Word of God and pray with him.

"Teach us to pray" (Luke 11, 1), the disciples asked of the Master. And He taught them that incomparable prayer "Our Father who art in heaven." The same request comes to us from our pupils; they know not what to say and how to express themselves in prayer. Let us teach them to pray. This may be done in two ways. We may have them commit to memory the Lord's Prayer, the General Confession, and other little prayers, explaining their meaning to them. But children should also be taught to express their personal requests in their own words. Excepting the prayers learned at school, many a grown person does not know how and what to pray. Children

Other Means of Education.

may therefore occasionally be asked to make, write, their own prayers, in which they express their own thoughts in their own language. Such a prayer, if approved by the teacher, may also be spoken by the child in the devotional opening exercise of the school. Thus children may be taught that prayer and devotion are not a matter which some one else performs for them, but in which they themselves participate. To pray must become a habit (1 Thess. 5, 17), and this habit must be formed in childhood.

If Luther was right in saying: *Fleiszig gebetet, ist ueber die Haelfte studiert,* praying diligently means more than half of the lesson studied, we may truly say: *Fleiszig gebetet, ist ueber die Haelfte erzogen,* praying diligently means more than half of the work of education done.

Example. — In a previous chapter we pointed out that a godly life is a necessary qualifications of a Christian teacher. Because of its signal importance in the training of children we are justified in classing the example set by parents and teachers under the means of education.

We train and educate children by the influence we exert on them. The type of training depends upon the character and the direction of this influence. The success of training depends upon the strength and consistency of the influence.

One of the most forceful and effectual means of influencing children is the example we set before them in our lives. The imitative instinct, present in every human being, is especially prominent in children. They learn by observation, they copy the ways and manners of others.

The example of their superiors and elders, whom they respect, has a particularly strong and determining influence on children. If such example be evil, they will so much more readily yield to it, as it falls in with their own natural inclination toward evil. For because of original sin the child is more easily influenced by one evil example than by many good examples. Hence there devolves upon every educator a double duty. The one is conscientiously and scrupulously to avoid giving any offense to the child in word or in deed, knowing that because of his position such evil example may prove doubly harmful; the other, incessantly to strive to set before his pupils a good example for their emulation, so that at all times he may say with Paul: "Be followers together of me and mark them which walk as ye have us for an ensample" (Phil. 3, 17). Let him not destroy by his example in life what he has taught the children by precept in school, but rather let his conduct be a practical illustration and an object-lesson of his teaching.

From the lives of those to whom they look for instruction and guidance, children must learn that religion is not merely a matter of intellectual knowledge, but that it is a power which fills the soul and manifests itself in daily conduct. The godly example of parents and teachers must demonstrate to children how they are to live their religion.

School Discipline. — School discipline, which pertains chiefly to external matters and management, must be distinguished from education proper, which aims to build up a character in children. But the very fact that in school the child is under constant supervision and is held to observe certain rules is also of educative value. The order which must be enforced in every school has a restraining effect on the mischievousness of the child. He learns that he must behave, may not yield to momentary impulses, may not do what he pleases, but must control himself and submit to the powers that be. All this, little by little, helps in the training of the child. Discipline must be maintained for the sake of school management in general, but also for the sake of the training the individual pupil derives therefrom.

But submitting to such discipline does not in itself prove that the child does this from the right motive.

Under the Fourth Commandment he must be taught to do this from fear and love of God. "Obey them that have the rule over you and submit yourselves" (Heb. 13, 17) is meant also for children in school.

The work in school has educative value. Idleness is the mother of all vice. Whatever keeps children usefully employed will also keep them out of mischief. Thus the regular routine of work in school serves as a preventive of evil. Their mind is occupied, their attention is engaged, they must think, solve problems, study their lessons, all which requires application and exertion on their part. Being thus required to work, though at times they are little inclined to do so, they are gradually trained to work. And this is a valuable lesson each child must learn — he must acquire the habit of working and of doing the best he can. The example of the industrious and faithful teacher will also make an impression on the pupil. Thus the purposive work at school has a definite value for the child. Heretofore he was given to play, now he learns to be usefully employed.

But in order that their work and diligence may be properly motivated, children must learn to do their work "not with eye-service, as men-pleasers, but as the servants of Christ, doing the will of God from the heart; with good will doing service as to the Lord and not to men" (Eph. 6, 67). Children who have learned to do their work in this spirit will do it also when no one is watching and driving them; they will be faithful in performing their duties also when they are no longer attending school.

Music and Singing. — We would call attention also to the restraining, soothing, and inspiring effect of good music and good singing. "David took an harp and played with his hand, so Saul was refreshed and was well, and the evil spirit departed from him" (1 Sam. 16, 23). There is no doubt that music of any kind makes a direct and deep impression on man. There is a kind of music that rouses his passions; there is another that stirs his baser lusts; but there is also a music which soothes and calms, one that elevates and edifies. As we keep away from our children evil influences, so we should keep away "wicked" music and teach them to know and love good music.

In like manner the singing of good secular songs, but especially of spiritual hymns, is to be strongly recommended because of the educative, elevating, and edifying influence of both tune and text. It is to be deplored that the daily schedule in our schools is often so heavily loaded down with other studies that little time and attention are given to singing. However, music and singing should be an essential part of the curriculum of religious education.

"No other form of expression can take the place of music in creating a spirit of reverence and devotion or in inducing an attitude of worship and inspiring religious feeling and emotion. Children ought to sing much both in the church-school and in their worship at home. . . . Ragtime hymns, which find a place in many Sunday-school exercises, need only to be mentioned to be condemned. . . . Care should be used to select hymns for children's singing which possess as fully as may be three requisites: 1) music adapted to the child's capacity, 2) music that is worthy, interesting, and devotional, and 3) words within the child's understanding and interest and suitable in sentiment." (*Betts.*)

By all means let us develop in our pupils the love for singing. Let them study the text and the tune; let them sing often and encourage them to sing. If the text is plain, pure, and full of meaning, if the melody is pleasing and inspiring, those songs and hymns will be sung also in later life and continue to exert their influence upon the heart. Let us have more singing that we may have fewer sinning children.

Part VI. THE EDUCATIONAL METHOD.

XVII. How to Preserve the Child from Sin.

Having in previous chapters spoken of the educator and of the child, of the aims and the means of education, there still remains one important question, What must we do and how must we proceed to accomplish the purpose of education? It is this that must now engage our attention.

We have learned that to educate does not mean merely to instruct and to impart knowledge; it means to influence and to train a child in a certain direction for the purpose of thereby creating permanent attitudes and developing a definite character. To accomplish this, our influence must be persistent, not spasmodic; it must be definitely directed and consistent, not vacillating, not shifting its aim and objective. Our aim must be to build up permanent habits and to mold a character which is habitually controlled by morally sound principles and not fitfully swayed by momentary impulses.

The educative pressure is not always at the high mark. Children are so different. Some are more tractable than others. A frown may suffice in one case, while a sharp rebuke is needed in another. Even the same child may at times be treated more leniently than at other times. It all depends upon circumstances and conditions and upon the reaction of the child. If mild means suffice, it would be folly to employ sterner ones. *Suaviter in modo, fortiter in re;* in the matter itself we should be firm, consistent, unyielding, but in the mode and method we should be suave and as gentle and mild as conditions permit. The educational influence must be constant and firm, but its pressure varies and must adapt itself to the individual case requiring treatment.

Generally speaking, this pressure is strongest and most

pronounced in childhood. As the child grows up and his previous training has taken effect, the correcting, regulating, and habituating influence will diminish until he is able "to stand on his own feet." For while it is true that the education of a person continues through life, it is likewise true that the premeditated and purposive efforts on the part of parents and teachers to train children gradually diminish as these grow up and become more independent. We teach the infant to walk until he can do so without our help. Thus we train children morally and religiously until they can walk in the ways of righteousness without our constant assistance and guidance. With some this will require more time and effort than with others, but with regard to all our final goal must be to develop in them a Christian personality, Christian manliness and womanliness, until they all come "in the unity of faith and the knowledge of the Son of God unto a perfect man, unto the measure of the stature of the fulness of Christ" (Eph. 4, 13), "that the man of God may be perfect, throughly furnished unto all good works" (2 Tim. 3, 17).

To facilitate a better understanding of the entire educational activity, it may be advisable to discuss the subject under the following three principal headings: —

I. *Preserve the child from sin and help him to overcome temptation.*

II. *Save the child from sin into which he has fallen.*

III. *Induce and encourage him to do what is good and to continue and to grow in holiness of life.*

Prevention. — "An ounce of prevention is better than a pound of cure." This is true, not only with respect to the physical well-being of man, but also with respect to his moral education. We are very solicitous to protect our children against infectious diseases; we ought to be more so in shielding them against moral contagion. Every temptation is dangerously infectious, not only because it suggests the thought of sin, but also because man is by nature not immune against its seductive fascination. And such evil thoughts increase in strength and motive power as they continue to occupy and dominate his consciousness. They stir the wicked desires of the flesh and are thus experienced as real temptations. Every time a person yields to these temptations, his strength to resist grows weaker, until finally he becomes a slave of sin.

It is even so with children. The first sin paves the way for the next one. Any sin repeated over and over again will become a habit, which it is far more difficult to break and to cure than it is to prevent. The training of the child therefore must begin not after he has fallen into sin and developed evil habits, but before this happens; he must be preserved from sin and trained so as to be able to overcome temptation. If we would lead a child to walk in the ways of God, we must do all we can to keep him from walking in the ways of the devil.

We must keep temptation away from the child. The moral atmosphere of the home and the school must be pure. No conditions and associations should be tolerated that might lead the child astray. We must eliminate as much as possible every opportunity to sin and avoid in word and deed whatever might suggest to them the thought of sin. "Woe to that man by whom the offense cometh" (Matt. 18, 7)!

Children must not be permitted to read books on crime and adultery nor to see shows and moving pictures which suggest impure and criminal thoughts. For though in many of them virtue is supposed to triumph over vice, still the seductive presentation of vice will make a deeper impression on the corrupt imagination of children than the moral lesson the book or the film is to teach. Such experiences do not immunize and fortify them against similar temptations in life; they rather pave the way for them.

Children must not be tempted to dishonesty by making it possible and easy for them to cheat in an examination or to steal or to lie, etc. As much as in him lies, the teacher must remove whatever might possibly lead children into sin. Since they are taught to pray, "Lead us not into temptation," those engaged in their training must certainly not tempt them to evil, but keep temptation away from them.

Preparation. — In spite of all precautions, temptation will come. "For it needs must be that offenses come" (Matt. 18, 7). Because the world is as it is and because the children we are training are still living in this world, they are exposed to its manifold temptations. Hence it must be the concern of parents and teachers so to prepare them "that they may be able to withstand in the evil day and, having done all, to stand" (Eph. 6, 13).

The first thing necessary is proper instruction and warning. Not knowing any better, children will often yield to temptation and do what is sinful and wrong. Therefore we must show them clearly what they are to avoid. While children are small, we may simply forbid them to do certain things, and the will of the parents or the teacher must be a sufficient law unto them. But as they grow older, they would like to know the reason why. It is not always necessary to state these reasons, nor does obedience depend upon whether or not they are sufficiently convincing to the child. Still, if he is to act intelligently, it is well for him to know why he must not yield to temptations and why it is wrong to do a certain thing. Hence we must not only forbid, but must also show from the Word of God that the forbidden thing is sinful, so that the conscience of the child may be trained to submit to divine authority.

All this, however, will help the child but little if we do not enable him to overcome sin. By his own reason and strength he is unable to resist sin and temptation, nor will an appeal to the will-power of the child avail anything. For the will does not function unless there is a sufficiently strong motive to actuate it.

Speaking of the temptations of the devil, Peter admonishes us: "Whom resist steadfast in the faith" (1 Pet. 5, 9), and John writes: "This is the victory that overcometh the world, even our faith" (1 John 5, 4). To fortify children against temptation and to help them to overcome sin, we must strengthen their faith in Christ. Lead them to understand and appreciate the mercies and blessings of God, and they will not conform to the ways of the world (Rom. 12, 1. 2). Have them realize that they were bought with a price, and they will keep themselves pure and blameless (1 Cor. 6, 20; 1 Pet. 1, 18. 19). Let them know that they are buried with Christ by Baptism into death, that therefore they are dead to sin and should not let sin reign in their mortal bodies (Rom. 6, 1—14).

The most powerful preventive of sin therefore is faith in Christ and a life in this faith. By faith in Christ the Holy Spirit lives in the hearts of children; and He prompts them not only to do the works of the Spirit, but also to avoid the works of the flesh. Let us by all means nurse in our pupils that spiritual life whose cleansing, purifying, and sanctifying power will enable them to overcome sin and temptation. "The cure lies ultimately not in mere human force of will, but in the cleansing stream of spiritual life that follows upon genuine conversion. It is what Paul means when he writes: 'Walk in the Spirit, and ye shall not fulfil the lust of the flesh' (Gal. 5, 16). It is what a great psychologist has called 'the expulsive power of a higher affection.'" Yes, the love of noble things will drive out the love of baser things; the love of the Savior will cleanse us from the love of sin, as a continuous stream of pure water will wash away filth and impurity (1 John 2, 15; 3, 3. 9).

To prepare children "that they may be able to withstand in the evil day," when they must wrestle against "spiritual wickedness in high places," we would call attention also to the "whole armor of God," of which Paul speaks Eph. 6, 10—18. This armor consists of the following pieces: —

a) We must be blameless and righteous in our lives, so as not to lay ourselves open to any attack of the enemy (vv. 14. 15).

b) We must be firm in our faith in the forgiveness of our sins in order to be able to quench those fiery darts, accusations of sin, which the devil may hurl into our conscience (v. 16).

c) We must be sure in the hope of our salvation and of our final victory (v. 17).

d) Taking the offensive, we must with the sword of the Spirit, which is the Word of God, attack the enemy and fight down his temptation (v. 17).

e) We must pray that God give us strength and endurance and grant us the victory (v. 18; Matt. 26, 41).

The story of the temptation of Christ in the wilderness offers excellent opportunity to show how Christ fought down temptation. Let the children know that Christ conquered the devil for them and that in the strength of faith they also can beat back the assaults of Satan. Indeed, a mechanical quoting of Scripture-texts will avail nothing, — the devil will laugh at that, — the texts must be believed from the heart. When the Word of God controls the soul, the Tempter has no power over us.

While children must understand that "with might of ours naught can be done, soon were our loss effected," still we must guard against their developing an inferiority complex in this matter, which would cause them to think that they cannot resist and therefore might just as well yield to temptation. By faith in Christ and with the Word of God they *are* able to withstand in the evil day of temptation. This Word inclines their will to conquer and gives them the assurance of victory, inspires them with the determination to fight and to win. "For sin *shall* not have dominion over you; for ye are not under the Law, but under grace" (Rom. 6, 11—18).

While included in what has been said above, the fear of God and the abhorrence of sin are of sufficient importance in the education of children to merit special consideration.

The Fear of God. — To preserve children from sin, we must teach them the true fear of God. Inasmuch as Christian children are controlled by faith, they do avoid sin, not from fear of punishment and painful consequences, but from reverence and awe of the Lord. It is this profound respect of God that prompts them to eschew whatever might displease Him. "The fear of the Lord is to hate evil" (Prov. 8, 13), and: "By the fear of the Lord men depart from evil" (Prov. 16, 6). Hence the Christian pedagog must say: "Come, ye children, hearken unto me; I will teach you the fear of the Lord" (Ps. 34, 11), and must so train them that, like Nehemiah, they walk in the fear of God, not doing those things that are offensive to Him (Neh. 5, 9. 15).

How is this done?

There are many Bible-stories and Bible-texts that give the teacher excellent opportunity to explain to, and impress upon, his pupils that God is holy and pure, that He hates all works of iniquity (Ps. 45, 7; 5, 4), that He is omnipresent and omniscient and therefore sees and knows all they do, say, and think (Jer. 23, 23. 24; Ps. 139, 1—4). We ought not to operate chiefly with the fear of punishment, — though also the wrath and punishment of God must be pointed out to children, — but with the fear of God. We must try to get the children to realize the perfect purity and holiness of the great, almighty, and ever-present God, so that they stand in awe of Him and would not dare do anything that might displease Him. "How, then, can I do this great wickedness and sin against God?" (Gen. 39, 9.) Hold up to them the examples of men who lived in the fear of God: Abraham, Joseph, Samuel, Daniel, and others.

In order that these impressions may not be forgotten, it is well to have children commit to memory such Bible-texts as enjoin the fear of the Lord. If these texts and the thoughts they contain dominate the consciousness of the children, they will produce in their hearts a feeling of respect, reverence, and awe that will induce them "to depart from evil."

Abhorrence of Sin. — Children by nature love sin and are inclined to all manner of evil. If, then, we would keep them from sin, we must teach them to abhor it.

How is this done?

Children must be made to understand that sin is by no means a small matter, but a most serious and dangerous thing.

Show from the Bible that God hates sin. "The way of the wicked is an abomination to the Lord" (Prov. 15, 9). "Oh, do not this abominable thing that I hate!... Behold, I will set my face against you for evil" (Jer. 44, 4. 11). If children have learned that their heavenly Father, who loves them, who blesses them with temporal and spiritual blessings every day, and who promises them still greater and more glorious things for the future, abhors sin, they will learn to detest it for His sake and avoid whatever might grieve and provoke Him.

How to Preserve the Child from Sin.

Children must be made to realize that sin is a transgression of God's holy Law and not merely an infraction of some man-made rule. "Whosoever committeth sin transgresseth also the Law; for sin is the transgression of the Law" (1 John 3, 4). Again we read: "He that committeth sin is of the devil; for the devil sinneth from the beginning" (1 John 3, 8). To commit sin is to do a devilish work and to become like the devil. Sin is rebellion against God. Speaking to the children of Israel in the wilderness, who had provoked God to wrath, Moses says: "Ye have been rebellious against the Lord" (Deut. 9, 7). Sin defiles man in the sight of God and brings shame and reproach upon its servants. "For your hands are defiled with blood and your fingers with iniquity; your lips have spoken lies; your tongue hath muttered perverseness" (Is. 59, 3). "Sin is a reproach to any people" (Prov. 14, 34). But more than this, sin brings temporal and eternal unhappiness, misery, and death. "The soul that sinneth, it shall die" (Ezek. 18, 20). "The wages of sin is death" (Rom. 6, 23). "Cursed be he that confirmeth not all the words of this Law to do them! And all people shall say, Amen" (Deut. 27, 26).

The dire consequences of sin may be depicted also in the treatment of Bible-stories, such as the fall of man, the Deluge, the destruction of Sodom and Gomorrah, the idolatry of the children of Israel at Mount Sinai; the sin and the punishment of Absalom, of Ahab, of Saul, of Judas, etc. In these and many other stories we have practical illustrations of the truth that God will in some way visit the iniquity on those who hate Him and persist in their evil ways. Having such examples set before them, children will hesitate to "walk in the counsel of the ungodly or to stand in the way of sinners or to sit in the seat of the scornful" (Ps. 1, 1).

But it should be especially impressed upon children that our sins brought suffering and death upon our beloved Savior, who was wounded for our transgressions. "Thou hast made Me to serve with thy sins; thou hast wearied Me with thine iniquities" (Is. 43, 24). Our sins pressed the crown of thorns upon His brow, our transgressions nailed Him to the cross. Are we, then, to continue in a life of sin? Are we to crucify to ourselves the Son of God afresh and put Him to an open shame (Heb. 6, 6)? If this is properly brought home to children, it will not fail to fill their hearts with an abhorrence of sin.

While it is true that God will graciously forgive sins to every penitent sinner, children must also learn that the love of sin will separate them from God. By wilfully continuing in sin, they "grieve the Holy Spirit, whereby they are sealed unto the day of redemption" (Eph. 4, 30), and drive Him from their hearts and the guardian angels from their side; thereby they cease to be children of God and forfeit the hope of eternal salvation.

To create in children an abhorrence of sin, it is advisable to contrast, at times, the ugliness of sin and vice, as in drunkards, liars, thieves, and murderers, with the beauty of holiness and virtue. Though the service of sin may please for a moment, it does not satisfy. "There is no peace, saith the Lord, unto the wicked" (Is. 48, 22); the end is misery and shame and ruin. "I was envious at the foolish when I saw the prosperity of the wicked, . . . until I went into the sanctuary; then I understood their end" (Ps. 73, 3. 17). The prodigal son is a fit illustration.

In our day, when many have lost the proper sense for what sin really is, it is doubly important for us not only to teach children that sin is the transgression of the Law, but that we also seek to impress upon them what sin will mean to them personally in order that they "learn to look with terror at their sins and to regard them as great indeed."

If the child understands that behind the alluring appearance of sin there lurks ruin and despair in the end, he will hesitate to yield to its temptations.

Conscience. — Conscience is congenital with man. While it is, indeed, a powerful determinant of conduct, it is not the infallible norm of what is morally right or wrong. It rather "denotes the consciousness which one has within himself of his conduct as related to moral obligation." It is that personal sense or feeling which agrees and consents to some moral rule regarded as authoritative and divine and obligates and urges the individual to conform to this rule.

In a wider sense some speak of conscience with reference to things that are neither moral nor immoral, such as matters of conventional propriety, the manner and method of doing a thing, etc. Indeed, also in this case we have essentially the same functions; there is the internal urge to behave and to act according to some accepted rule or standard and the feeling of satisfaction or dissatisfaction when we have done so or failed to do so.

Ordinarily, however, we speak of conscience with reference to our moral conduct. Conscience is "the moral sense, the internal monitor, which signifies approval when we do well and inflicts more or less lasting pain when we act sinfully. This suggests that conscience is not a simple, but a complex part of our nature. In its decisions there mingles first an operation of fallible intellect judging of conduct; then follows an emotional part, generating the satisfaction or the dissatisfaction produced by that judgment."

If conscience is to judge our actions, there must be some law or rule that we regard as binding upon us. If this law is wrong, the conduct will be likewise, as we see in the case of Saul (Acts 26, 9). It is the Law of God, written in the heart of man, but more fully revealed in His

Word, that definitely determines what is to be regarded morally right or wrong. And it is this Law that must control the conscience of man. Conscience, in return, will bear witness to this Law, obligating man to conform to its demands. It is also the arbiter of his thoughts, words, and deeds; it rates them according to the Law; it excuses or accuses; it justifies or condemns (Rom. 2, 15).

The voice of conscience must never be disregarded; to do so is sin. Paul writes Rom. 14, 23: "He that doubteth is damned if he eat because he eateth not of faith; for whatsoever is not of faith is sin." The word "faith" here does not mean faith in the Savior, but, being set in opposition to doubt, it signifies the personal conviction that the thing one is about to do is right. Especially in moral matters the words apply. First be sure that you are right and then go ahead. We must never do what our conscience disapproves and never leave undone what it urges us to do. If any one believes it is sinful for him to eat meat that was offered in sacrifice unto idols, it really is a sin for him to eat thereof (1 Cor. 8, 7). Thus things which are otherwise allowed become sinful to him who does them against his conscience (Rom. 14, 22).

While the witness of conscience must never be ignored, it is not infallible; but controlled by a wrong norm, it will err in its judgments. Some have a conscience in matters which are allowed, others even in such things as are plainly against the revealed Law of God. Thus Saul verily thought with himself that he ought to do many things contrary to the name of Jesus (Acts 26, 9). Thus it may happen that a person sins, no matter whether he acts according to, or contrary to, his conscience; he sins either against the Law of God or against his conscience. In this case we must not force or urge him to act against his conscience, but we must instruct him and set his conscience right, so that its witness agrees with the Law of God. Since conscience is the personal assent to some authoritative norm or rule, it is important to impress upon the child the divine authority of God's Word, by which his conscience must be regulated and controlled.

Conscience is a very powerful factor in the education and in the life of the child. It will warn him not to do what he knows to be wrong and urge him to observe what he believes to be right (Rom. 13, 5). The personal influence of the teacher may vanish with his presence, but conscience, regulated by the Word of God, will remain with the child and continue to influence and control his conduct.

How are we to treat the conscience of children?

Teaching and learning must not be a merely intellectual process, but whatever children learn from the Bible as the will of God concerning them must become a matter of personal conviction and of conscience to them. To this end the teacher should not only explain the sense and meaning of the commandments and the doctrines of the Bible, but he should drive them home, impressing upon his pupils their responsibility to God for whatever they do or fail to do (Matt. 12, 36). They should be made to feel that it is not at all optional with them whether or not they do what God requires of them, but that it is a sacred duty, which they should gladly perform for the Lord's sake. "If ye know these things, happy are ye if ye do them" (John 13, 17). A well-regulated and responsive conscience is a valuable educational asset.

The weak conscience must be respected (1 Cor. 8, 12). The teacher must ascertain whether a certain faulty conduct is based on an erring conscience or whether it is sheer carelessnes, ignorance, or wickedness. If it is a matter of conscience, the child must be set right by patient instruction; such thoughts and ideas must be instilled into his mind as are in agreement with the Word of God, which will then control his conscience.

When conscience has become dull and callous because its warnings were systematically ignored and its reproofs stifled, it will finally cease to function. This is a very serious condition, and we must do all we can to quicken and rouse the conscience by impressing upon the child his responsibility to God.

When a child has sinned and his conscience accuses, judges, and condemns him, the teacher must seek to restore peace to the troubled and guilty conscience of the child by assuring him of the grace of God in Christ Jesus (Heb. 10, 22; 1 Pet. 3, 21).

Children must be warned not to sin against their conscience and again and again be reminded to keep their conscience pure and undefiled (Acts 24, 16; 1 Tim. 1, 19).

If we succeed in quickening and regulating the consciences of our pupils, we have indeed done much towards their education; for conscience will continue to exert its influence on them even when our personal influence ceases to operate.

"Labor to keep alive that little spark of celestial fire called conscience." (*Washington*.)

XVIII. How to Preserve the Child from Sin.
(*Continued.*)

While thus in a general way, as outlined in the previous chapter, the educator will try to keep his pupils from sin, he will find it necessary to help them in overcoming special sins which beset them.

Self-Will. — The will is indeed a wonderful gift of God, and the exercise of it is in itself not sinful. The purpose of education therefore is not to suppress independent will activity in the child, but rather to direct it into the right channels. And this is necessary, for because of original sin the will is perverted and inclined to evil. This bent of the will shows itself particularly in the self-will of children. Opposing their will to that of others, they want what is forbidden to them and insist on having their own way and on doing whatsoever they please. Hence they are independent, disrespectful, quarrelsome, contrary, disobedient, obstinate, mischievous, etc.

Such self-will, when out of harmony with the will of God, is sin and, if allowed to go on unrestrained and undirected, will be a source of much trouble and unhappiness to the child in later life. The child is to be pitied who was always permitted to have his own way, whose every wish and whim was gratified, who never learned to deny himself and to submit to those that have the rule over him, but was allowed to follow his fancy and inclination in all things. He will have to learn in later years what he did not learn in his youth, and learning this will be far less pleasant then. However, this does not mean that a child should never have his own way; on the contrary, whenever he has set his mind on things that are good and praiseworthy, he should be encouraged to go ahead and to persevere in spite of obstacles, so that his will-power may be developed and strengthened.

How is the self-willed child to be treated?

At times it is possible to anticipate his inclinations and by advance suggestions to direct his will. A hint or a question will often suffice. Keep the child busy, and you will keep him out of mischief. Forestall as much as possible every opportunity for ill-directed wilfulness. In matters of small consequence children may, if they will not be warned, be permitted to have their own way in order that they may learn by sad experience. If the matter is plainly sinful, we must convince the child of this fact; often this will suffice to change his mind. But if he insists in his perverse way, we must hinder him to do his will by force, if need be. In case of such obstinacy we must subdue the self-will of the child and make him submit to authority.

All this is more difficult the first time when, so to speak, the trail must be blazed, than the second and the third time, after the child has learned from previous experiences. The outcome of the first encounter between the will of the child and the will of his trainer is of great consequence for the latter's further influence. For if the child once learned that he can carry his point, and have his way contrary to the wish and will of parent or teacher, it will be rather difficult to train him in the way he should go. If, on the other hand, he learned to know his master, he will in the future more readily submit to his authority.

Such training must begin in early childhood, it must begin in the home. But, alas! many parents neglect this. Little "Johnny" has his own way about the house; mother is delighted because "he is so cute"; father is quite proud of his boy, who is so self-assertive, etc. Nothing is done to curb his self-will. Result: insubordination as "Johnny" grows up to be "John." The teacher at school is then expected to retrieve what the carelessness of parents permitted to develop.

The neglect of parents will not excuse any neglect on the part of the teacher; on the contrary, he must try his best in the training of this self-willed child. And the case is by no means hopeless. He is a stranger to the child, who looks up to him with a certain respect and fear. From the very outset he must gently, but firmly, insist on obedience and submission, teaching the child that he cannot always have his own way, that he must at times relinquish a wish and deny himself. The child must learn to mind, to submit to authority, especially to the authority of God.

Christian education aims to train children so that readily and willingly they subordinate their will to the will of God and of those whom He has placed over them as His representatives, and that they do so, not because it is expedient, but for conscience' sake. For to be self-willed is a sin, which God reproves (2 Pet. 2, 10) and which Christian children will avoid.

Curbing the self-will of children is by no means an easy matter, and on the part of the teacher it requires a goodly portion of wisdom and patience. He must be consistent and persistent, must himself not be self-willed and capricious, and must not forget to pray for divine guidance.

Pride. — It was pride that induced man to eat of the forbidden fruit in the garden of Eden. He desired to be like God. And pride is in the hearts of all men to this day, for the Savior tells us that pride is one of the evil things that come from within and defile man (Mark 7, 22. 23).

This proud spirit is evident also in children, who do not yet know how to control their emotions and in whom it was perhaps fostered by foolish parents. Having a very favorable opinion of themselves, of their gifts, their attainments, their strength, etc., children like to "show off"; they wish to be heard and seen and want to be "smarter" than all the rest. They covet recognition and praise, are arrogant, envious, jealous, overbearing, and strive to excel others in study and in play for the honor it might bring them. Like the Pharisees in the Temple, they despise others and believe themselvs to be far better than they. This pride of the heart reveals itself in words and deeds, in features and gestures.

What must the teacher do to counteract these sinful tendencies and to instil true humility into the hearts of his pupils?

He must teach them the sinfulness of pride. "Every one that is proud in his heart is an abomination to the Lord" (Prov. 16, 5), and "God resisteth the proud, but giveth grace unto the humble" (Jas. 4, 6). These texts should be explained to the children, illustrated, and committed to memory.

Pride is the source of many other sins, such as envy, jealousy, haughtiness, insubordination, rebellion. Korah, Dathan, and Abiram were desirous of vainglory and rebelled against God's chosen leader of Israel (Num. 16). A proud person is very apt to despise God (Ps. 10, 4; Jer. 43, 2) and his neighbor (Luke 18, 9) and will fall into many a temptation and a snare, which drown him in destruction and perdition.

Pride is not only exceedingly foolish, but it brings shame (Ps. 11, 2) and destruction; for "pride goeth before destruction and a haughty spirit before a fall" (Prov. 16, 18). Point to the examples of proud men, such as Nebuchadnezzar (Dan. 4, 30; 5, 20), Belshazzar (Dan. 5, 22), Sennacherib (2 Kings 19, 8—13), Herod (Acts 12, 20—23), and show how distasteful and repugnant their pride was and how the Lord punished them.

It may at times be expedient to humble or even to humiliate the child whose pride is plainly manifest by rebuking him before others.

While we must in every way counteract the spirit of pride and vainglory, we must, on the other hand, set forth the beauty of true Christian humility. Such humility is rooted in the knowledge of our utter unworthiness in the sight of God. The centurion said to Jesus: "Lord, I am not worthy that Thou shouldest come under my roof" (Matt. 8, 8), and Jacob said: "I am not worthy of the least of all the mercies and of all the truth which Thou hast showed unto Thy servant" (Gen. 32, 10). Thus it behooves the most gifted of children to be most humble.

It is the will of God that Christians be meek and humble. "Let nothing be done through strife or vainglory, but in lowliness of mind let each esteem other better than themselves" (Phil. 2, 3). And to children God says:

"Likewise ye younger, submit yourselves unto the elder; yea, all of you be subject one to another and be clothed with humility, for God resisteth the proud and giveth grace to the humble" (1 Pet. 5, 5). For "though the Lord be high, yet hath He respect unto the lowly" (Ps. 138, 6) and will in due time exalt him that humbleth himself (Luke 14, 11). Therefore, "whosoever will be chief among you, let him be your servant; even as the Son of Man came not to be ministered unto, but to minister and to give His life a ransom for many" (Matt. 20, 27. 28).

To illustrate what humility is and to incite the children to emulate this virtue, the teacher may hold up to them the examples of Abraham (Gen. 18, 27), of Paul (Acts 20, 19), and especially of our Lord Jesus (Matt. 11, 29; Phil. 2, 5—8). The teacher himself should set a good example. Fighting against his own pride and cultivating true humbleness of mind, he will, with the help of God, be able to train his pupils also in this respect.

Dishonesty. — God made man upright and true. With a lie Satan seduced man to sin; and having sinned, man tried to deceive God and is now inclined to all forms of dishonesty. "All men are liars" (Ps. 116, 11), and children are no exception to this. Because they fear to be punished for what they have done, they will try to "lie out of it"; because they wish to gain favor, they deceive; because they wish to make their mark in class, they are tempted to cheat; because they covet what is not theirs, they steal. Thus in various forms of dishonesty will the Old Adam of children manifest himself.

What is to be done?

In the first plase, children must be instructed as to the nature of what they have done. The little child does not know what it is to lie, to deceive, to cheat, or to steal. There is no sense in reprimanding him for any of these things as long as he does not understand what he has done. Before the child may be told that lying is a sin, he must learn to know what it means to lie, etc.

Lying. — We must show the child that all manner of dishonesty originated with the devil. "When he speaketh a lie, he speaketh of his own; for he is a liar and the father of it" (John 8, 44). God hates lies. "He that worketh deceit shall not dwell within my house; he that telleth lies shall not tarry in my sight" (Ps. 101, 7). Impress upon the child that, though he may deceive man, he cannot deceive God, who understands his every thought (Ps. 139, 2), and that "he who speaketh lies shall not escape" (Prov. 19, 5). Therefore "lie not one to another" (Col. 3, 9). As the members of our body do not lie to one another, even so Christians must put away lying and speak the truth with their neighbors; "for we are members one of another" (Eph. 4, 25). The teacher may also point out how cowardly and despicable it is to lie and that a liar is distrusted and despised even among men.

The teacher should, however, not from the outset doubt the veracity and honesty of his pupils, but rather show that he trusts and believes them. This often makes a deep impression on the child. If there is reason for warranted doubt, let him ascertain the facts and then deal with the child accordingly. If the child has spoken the truth, well and good; if not, he must learn that "he that speaketh lies shall not escape."

"One feature must be watched with particular care during this age, namely, the lying proclivity of children.... Unless properly handled, this may become a real menace in the life of the child; for many a statement is immediately branded a lie, when in reality it is a matter of false understanding, coupled with an imaginative interpretation. Teachers must learn to distinguish between the various kinds of falsehoods, so that they will not confuse the deliberate and wicked lie with the foolish exaggeration and the imaginative overstatement." (*Kretzmann.*)

Children sometimes lie and dissemble from fear of punishment. The teacher must be careful lest by his severity in punishing even small offenses he cause them to try "to lie out of it."

The teacher must himself also be truthful in all his utterances; for it has a most harmful effect on his pupils if they discover any prevarication and dishonesty in him. "It is essential that adults deal with children of this age with all openness and sincerity. Every question must be met with the utmost frankness. If there is reason why the teacher thinks it best not to impart a certain bit of information, this fact must be plainly stated and a reason given to the child. Every kind of prevarication, whether it deals with the secrets of the home or with sex matters, will be resented by the growing child, the result being, as a rule, the withdrawal of confidence." (*Kretzmann.*)

Deceiving. — Under the caption of dishonesty belong also all forms of duplicity and hypocrisy, which consists in "the practise of feigning to be what one is not or to feel what one does not feel"; it is "the false assumption of the appearance of virtue or religion." Also children dissemble, either to avoid reproof or to win praise and favor. For selfish reasons they "put on appearances," and their conduct is not the true expression of their heart. In the presence of their superiors they are very assiduous in the practise of Christian virtues, but among their equals or when by themselves, they show their "true color." Such dishonesty in conduct clings to many a one throughout life who would not exactly tell a plain lie, but whose entire life is a lie.

Though it is extremely difficult to establish a definite case, the teacher must do all he can to counteract the very tendency of this type of dishonesty. Christ upbraids the Pharisees for their hypocrisy, saying: "Ye are like unto whited sepulchers, which indeed appear beautiful outward, but are within full of dead men's bones and of all uncleanness. Even so ye also outwardly appear righteous unto men, but within ye are full of hypocrisy and iniquity" (Matt. 23, 27. 28). And Timothy is advised to turn away from such as have "a form of godliness, denying the power thereof" (2 Tim. 3, 5). In like manner children must be warned not to dissemble and exhorted to be true and honest, not only in words, but also in their conduct. No one should try to appear what he has not the will to be.

Nun, so woll' auch keiner scheinen,
Was keiner Kraft und Willen hat zu sein. (*Grillparzer.*)

Stealing. — Little children have no sense of property; they do not distinguish between what is theirs and what belongs to others; hence they take and appropriate to themselves whatever strikes their fancy and suits their taste, as every one has observed in infant children. This tendency, unless checked at an early age, may become a real menace to the child in later life. Parents must by all means counteract this stealing proclivity and teach the child that he must not take things that belong to brother or sister. In school also we often find that children will take from others a bright pencil, a colored picture, paper, fruit, and the like. They see others have things which they desire, and, unable to resist the temptation, they pilfer, they steal.

When treating the Seventh Commandment, the teacher has excellent opportunity to instruct children in this matter. He will show them what property is — things that belong to a person and which no one may take from him against his will and without his consent. It is God who gives to each what he should have (Prov. 22, 2), and it is He who says: "Thou shalt not steal." If, then, we fear and love God, we shall not take our neighbor's money or goods nor get them by false ware or dealing. Bible-stories, such as the stories of Achan (Josh. 7), of Gehazi (2 Kings 5), of the thieves who stripped the man that went down to Jericho (Luke 10, 30), may be profitably employed to explain, and to drive home, this point. Attention may also be called to the fact that, unless children with the help of God overcome the covetousness of their hearts, it will grow on them until they receive a thief's reward at the hands of the civil government.

Remove temptation from the child, and if temptation comes, help him to overcome it by proper instruction and admonition.

On the other hand, children should be taught and trained to help their neighbor to improve and protect his property and business.

Other Sins. — While self-will, pride, dishonesty, and whatever goes with these, are perhaps the most outstanding sins from which children must be preserved, there are numerous other sins against which they must be warned at the proper time.

We may not expect to find in children, or demand of them, that sober sedateness which is characteristic of riper age; still we must set our influence against levity, flightiness, giddiness, frivolity, etc. It is necessary to warn them against filthy language and uncleanness and sins against the Sixth Commandment. But in doing so, care must be taken not to acquaint them with sins of which they were ignorant before. The teacher must have his ears and eyes open to discover whether there is filthy talking and actual uncleanness among his pupils; he must inspect the lavatories of the school, occasionally also the books of the children. Let him speak to those in private who are guilty or whom he suspects, and by all means ask God for wisdom to say and do the right thing. He must warn the children against going to dances, theater, etc.; against games of chance, playing "for keeps," betting, etc.; against tattling and speaking evil of one another; against attending false churches and keeping company with unbelievers. Wherever he finds that his pupils do not walk according to the rule of God's Word, he must warn them and do all he can to preserve them from sin (Ezek. 33, 7).

Instruction Is Necessary. — In order that children may intelligently react to such warning, it is necessary to instruct them. For often they do a thing without knowing that it is wrong. While they are yet very small, we may simply forbid this or that, and the will of the parent or of the teacher should be a sufficient reason for them henceforth to avoid this thing. But as the child grows older, he will ask the reason why. Then he must be clearly shown what he is to avoid and why he is to do so. We often fail in this, that we do not clearly state just what is forbidden and what is enjoined. In every case we must refer to the Word of God, so as to train the conscience of the child to submit to divine authority.

If we would help the child in his battle against sin, we must remember that it is not sufficient merely to reprove sin or to tell him that he must fight down temptation by a determined effort of his will, but *we must strengthen his faith and thus fortify him against sin*. Faith in Jesus is the power that enables us to resist temptation. "Whom resist steadfast in the faith," says Peter (1 Pet. 5, 9). Lead children to appreciate the mercies and blessings of God and to consider well that therefore they should not conform to the world (Rom. 12, 1. 2). Tell them that they were bought with a price and that therefore they should glorify God in their bodies by keeping themselves pure and blameless (1 Cor. 6, 20; 1 Pet. 1, 18. 19); that because

How to Preserve the Child from Sin.

they fear and love God, they should not do anything that might displease Him (1 John 5, 4; John 8, 34; Rom. 6, 1. 2).

Children must be so trained that they do not lose courage in the fight against sin. They must understand that they *can* resist temptation and overcome sin (Rom. 6, 11—18); that God is faithful and will not suffer them to be tempted above that they are able; that if they pray (Mark 14, 38; Eph. 6, 12. 18), He will with the temptation also make a way of escape that they will be able to bear it (1 Cor. 10, 13). They must know that because of their weak and sinful flesh this battle against sin will continue as long as they live, but that by "daily contrition and repentance they must drown the Old Adam with all his sins and evil lusts" until by a death triumphant through faith in Jesus this body of sin shall be destroyed and the just shall be made perfect in their Father's home (Heb. 12, 23).

Watching. — "To everything there is a season and a time to every purpose under heaven" (Eccl. 3, 1). This is true also of instruction and reproof and warning. If overdone, it loses its force; if done at improper time, it will have little effect. But to watch the children is always in season. As the shepherd watches his flock, so the teacher must watch the lambs of Christ that are entrusted to his care (John 21, 15; Acts 20, 28). He must watch his pupils in the schoolroom, watch them in the school-yard, watch them, as far as this is possible, on the way to and from school and wherever he meets them. While he should especially watch them as long as they are under his immediate supervision, he should never feel that he is relieved of all responsibility and that it is no concern of his what his pupils do otherwise, just so they behave in school. Under Christ and within the limitations of his call he is the shepherd of these "lambs," and at all times he should take heed unto his flock.

As children should always be conscious of being under the eyes of God (Gen. 17, 1), they should, in a measure, also feel that the eye of their teacher, who is to them God's representative, is upon them. The very presence of the teacher, though he utter not a word, will have a strong restraining influence upon them, inasmuch as he represents to them what he taught them. Left to themselves, they will more readily yield to all manner of mischief and sin. They learned not to do these things, but they forget, or they do not mind, because "the teacher is not around." But the presence of the teacher serves as a check. It is furthermore a serious mistake merely to instruct, admonish, and warn, but never, to watch whether or not such instruction and warning are also heeded.

Such supervision, however, should not be like that of a stern master, but rather like that of a friend. Its purpose is not to spy on the children and to catch transgressors, but rather to hinder and forestall misdemeanor. If we keep a watchful eye on children, there will be little need of scolding.

To exercise such watch over children, the teacher should be the first one at school. Children should not be permitted to loaf about the school premises long before the lessons begin. During school hours he should keep them busy and watch not only the group or class he is teaching, but the entire school. During recess the presence of the teacher on the playground will be very effective in preventing mischief, quarrels, etc. Boys and girls should never be left together by themselves for any length of time.

But children should be so trained that they behave, not only while and because they are being watched by their teacher, but for conscience' sake. Even though the teacher may not see them, children should feel: "Thou, God, seest me" (Gen. 16, 13), and therefore for His sake "walk before Him and be perfect" (Gen. 17, 1).

A Word to the Teacher. — Let no teacher imagine that, after he has done all he can to keep and preserve children from sin, they will henceforth avoid it and overcome every temptation. They are living in a world that is full of offenses (Matt. 18, 7), and their own Old Adam is ever ready to yield to sin (Gen. 8, 21; Matt. 15, 19). In spite of all preventive measures, therefore, it will happen that children again and again fall into sin. This should neither surprise nor discourage the teacher, but he should feel that without his efforts to keep them from sin, matters would be much worse than they are. He may be assured that the Word of God, which he uses in the training of his pupils, will not return void, but will accomplish that which God pleases and prosper in the thing whereto He sent it (Is. 55, 11).

XIX. How to Save the Child from Sin.

"Brethren, if a man be overtaken in a fault, ye, which are spiritual, restore such an one in the spirit of meekness" (Gal. 6, 1). These words of the apostle the teacher must remember also with respect to his pupils. They will be overtaken in a fault and fall into sin. Then it is not for him to say, "What is this to me? I am not their pastor." Let him bear in mind that he is commanded to feed the lambs of Christ (John 21, 15), that he must watch for their souls as one that must give account (Heb. 13, 17), and that therefore he must do all he can to seek and save the lost.

Teach Children Clearly the Way of Salvation. — In order that a child may know how to be saved from sin, he needs must have a clear understanding of the way of salvation. This does not mean that he must have the detailed knowledge of a theologian, but it does mean that he must clearly understand the doctrines of sin and of grace.

The child that has sinned and transgressed the commandment of God must realize that thereby he has offended not merely man, his parents, his teacher, his neighbor, but God Almighty in heaven (Ps. 51, 4), that he has provoked His wrath and deserved His punishment (Deut. 27, 26). This thought must be deeply impressed on the consciousness of the child; for it is this knowledge which is capable of working in the heart true sorrow over sin. No man and no child can be saved from sin if he does not truly repent of the evil he has done.

Especially must the child learn: "God so loved the world that He gave His only-begotten Son, that whosoever believeth in Him should not perish, but have everlasting life" (John 3, 16). God hates and abhors sin, but His loving compassion goes out toward the sinner, and His love for the lost children of men was so great that He spared not His own Son, but delivered Him up for us all (Rom. 8, 32). Jesus died for all men, even the vilest of them, and redeemed, purchased, and won them from sin, from death, and from the power of the devil. No matter, how great the sin may be or may appear to the child, he must learn that the grace of God in Christ Jesus is still greater (Rom. 5, 20; Is. 1, 18).

The child must learn that this full forgiveness of sin is freely and unconditionally offered in the promises of the Gospel. Here God Himself assures every penitent sinner: "Be of good cheer, thy sins be forgiven thee" (Matt. 9, 2). Whoever believes this promise thereby receives and has what the promise offers, namely, the forgiveness of all his sins. Let us be sure to make this point very clear to our pupils: Jesus has not only procured for them full remission of sins, but He also freely offers it to them in His Gospel. It is this knowledge which can work saving faith in their hearts, and working and strengthening this faith, it supplies that power which makes for sanctification of life. Where there is no such faith in Jesus, the Savior, Christian education is impossible.

Children must also learn that such saving faith, which is not merely intellectual knowledge of Bible-truths and promises, but confident trust in the grace of God, cannot exist in an impenitent heart. To be wilfully impenitent in one sin kills faith in the forgiveness of all sins. Hence they must not only in a general way, perhaps even thoughtlessly, acknowledge themselves sinners before God, but in special cases where they have sinned, and where they know their sins to be sins, they must feel truly sorry for these very sins and then be assured that also these sins are forgiven by their Father in heaven.

Sins committed in ignorance do not kill faith in the heart because they do not affect and change the soul's attitude toward God and will be repented of as soon as they are understood; but sins which we commit knowingly and wilfully, sins, though they be ever so small, of which we will not repent, at once utterly destroy all saving faith, because wilful impenitence and faith cannot live in the same heart.

While faith in the forgiveness of sins is impossible as long as the heart remains impenitent, we may be sure of the forgiveness of sins as soon as we repent. Let children clearly understand that it is not sin itself that separates them from God, for Jesus has atoned for all of them, but it is the love of sin and impenitence that makes it impossible for them to love God and to trust in His mercy (1 John 2, 15).

If the child knows that the Savior procured forgiveness

of sins for all men, also for all children, and that by faith he may for his own person obtain this forgiveness, he knows how he can be saved from sin.

To Save the Child from the Power of Sin. — The object of Christian education is not only to save the child from sin before God by faith in Jesus, but also to save the child from the dominion of sin in his life. However, the latter is not possible without the former. An unregenerated child cannot but let "sin reign in his mortal body to obey the lusts thereof." But the case is quite different with the child that truly believes in his Savior. There is in his heart a new life, a new power, which enables him to overcome sin and temptation. When God admonishes His children to put off concerning the former conversation the old man (Eph. 4, 22), to crucify the flesh with the affections and lusts (Gal. 5, 24), and to resist the devil (1 Pet. 5, 8. 9), He does not send them out on a hopeless venture, but would have them feel sure of success, "knowing that our old man is crucified with Christ, that the body of sin might be destroyed, that henceforth we should not serve sin" (Rom. 6, 6).

Children often lack confidence in their ability to resist temptation and to break with an evil habit, and hence they take up the fight against sin in a rather faint-hearted way. While it is proper for them to realize their own weakness, they should know that by faith in Christ they are endowed with power "to wrestle against spiritual wickedness" and are thus divinely imbued with the will to conquer and with the assurance of ultimate success. This ability to combat sin is a product of faith, and the confidence of success is based upon the help of God. Hence it is absolutely necessary to nurse the spiritual life of our pupils, their faith in Christ, which will save them not only from the guilt of sin before God, but also from the dominion of sin in their lives.

The Penitent Child. — While the Christian teacher will earnestly try to save all his pupils from sin, he must at times deal with the individual child. What is he to do?

It is not necessary for the teacher to institute a thorough investigation and treatment in every case where a child has sinned. Sometimes a glance of the eye (Luke 22, 61) or a word of reproof is sufficient to recall the erring child. Grievous offenses, however, such as cursing, despising God's Word, manifest disobedience, theft, lying, and all sins that are likely to destroy the faith of the child and to disrupt the discipline of the school, must be a matter of grave concern to the educator.

In order to judge fairly, the teacher must be familiar with the home environments of the child; he must know whether there were special influences, provocations, temptations, etc., that induced the child to act as he did. Having established all the facts of the case, he must convince the child that his offense is a sin against God, whereby he has grieved Him and provoked His displeasure, thus leading him to true repentance.

A child is to be regarded as penitent when he acknowledges his sin, expresses his sorrow, and asks for forgiveness. Do not demand a certain degree of contrition, not a perfect repentance; but if indications point to a true repentance, then do not hesitate to forgive and make it easy for the child to reinstate himself. Assure him of the grace of God in Jesus, the Savior; point out God's great love, not only to mankind in general, but also to him. Remind him of his baptism, where a full and lifelong pardon is promised, so that he may be sure of the forgiveness of sins. Call attention to the comforting invitation of the Savior: "Come unto Me, all ye that labor and are heavy laden, and I will give you rest" (Matt. 11, 28; John 6, 37), and to His promise: "Son, be of good cheer; thy sins be forgiven thee" (Matt. 9, 2).

The teacher may at times be inclined to doubt the sincerity of the child's confession. But let him beware of judging the heart (Luke 6, 37), and let him by no means show his distrust. Unless there is positive proof to the contrary, the confession of the child must be accepted at its face value, "lest perhaps such a one should be swallowed up with overmuch sorrow" (2 Cor. 2, 7. 8) or be driven back into the service of sin, thinking that he might just as well continue in sin as his repentance is not accepted.

On the other hand, we must guard against training hypocrites, which is done by glossing over sins, by refraining to insist on true repentance, by comforting the impenitent child with the assurance of forgiveness. "Repent ye therefore and be converted that your sins may be blotted out" (Acts 3, 19). Such repentance is not a mere outward confession of the mouth, but it is essentially a change of the mind and a turning of the heart from sin to grace. "The sacrifices of God are a broken spirit; a broken and a contrite heart, O God, Thou wilt not despise" (Ps. 51, 17). Our aim must be by proper instruction to move the heart, which in this case means to lead the child to a deep realization of his sin. If we succeed in this, the child will confess, apologize, accept the promise of forgiveness, and amend.

If the offense of the child was public, he should be required to make also public confession (1 Tim. 5, 20). This matter should by no means be treated lightly. A word of admonition should be addressed to the school in which the children are warned to beware of similar and other sins. "Let him that thinketh he standeth take heed lest he fall" (1 Cor. 10, 12). Nor should they act like the elder brother of the prodigal son, despising the child that sinned and confessed, but rather, like the angels of God, rejoice over the sinner that repented and show him love and kindness (Luke 15, 10). If such cases are handled in the proper way; they will have a most salutary effect upon the whole school.

Whether the penitent child should still be punished, depends upon circumstances. If the sin is not generally known, punishment is not necessary, except where it was previously threatened. If the offense, however, is known also to other children, the wisdom of the teacher must decide whether the discipline of the school demands that even the penitent child should suffer the external consequences of his transgression or whether it is sufficient for him to make public confession and to apologize for the offense given. The teacher may then conclude with an exhortation to thank God for His pardoning grace and a warning to guard against future sins (John 5, 14; 8, 11).

The Impenitent Child. — Very often children deny their sins and try to "lie out of them." The teacher must then ascertain the facts and first convince the child of the act of sin. If this is utterly impossible, he must let the matter rest on the conscience of the child, calling attention to the text: "He that covereth his sins shall not prosper, but whoso confesseth and forsaketh them shall have mercy" (Prov. 28, 13). The teacher's conviction does not prove the guilt of the child.

At times, children will try to excuse themselves and justify their sins, as Adam and Eve did in Paradise. The teacher must then tell the child that before God there is no excuse for sin and that the child's own conscience holds him responsible for what he has done. The commission of the sinful act being admitted, the teacher must bring home to the consciousness of the child the guilt of his transgression.

However, though the child admit all this, he may not be ready to confess his fault, but harden his heart in impenitence. The teacher should then not regard the matter closed, as far as he is concerned, but must earnestly seek to save that which is lost (Luke 15, 4). While it is necessary to reprove and perhaps also to punish the impenitent child (Jer. 2, 19), he must not force a confession of sin and of repentance by intimidation. This will never win the heart of the child. Let the teacher pray for the child that God would touch and move the heart to true repentance; let him speak to the child in private and show that he is interested in his soul's welfare. He may have to speak to the child repeatedly and at different times. Let him do all he can to bring back the lamb that has been lost from the fold. It is in such cases that the teacher must prove himself a real pastor, a real shepherd of Christ's lambs, who in patience and in love will endeavor to reclaim the child that has gone astray. He must not be satisfied if the impenitent child but outwardly submits to certain demands and regulations, but he will try to win the heart. Only when the heart has been won for Christ, can there follow a true and God-pleasing reform of life.

The Backsliding Child. — Children, just as grown people, often relapse into their former sins. They received the Word with joy and sincerely intended to follow the narrow path, but, being weak in faith and character, they fall in time of temptation and go astray. Let the teacher not become discouraged nor lose patience when he finds that the very child which he saved from sin but a few days ago falls into the same or into some other sin. Because of the weakness of children this may be expected. The forbearance and long-suffering which God shows us, who sin daily, should teach us to practise the same towards our pupils.

What has been said about the treatment of sinning children applies, in general, also here. Reminding them of the repetition of their offense, it may be necessary to rebuke them sharply in order that they may more fully realize the seriousness of the situation; but we must not give them up as hopeless.

The training of a child is not accomplished in one treatment, nor can it be perfected in a month or two; prolonged activity is necessary, inurement and habituation. It requires much love and patience, steady and continuous influence and wise direction to break down an old habit and to establish a new one. We must do the same thing over and over again, often with the same child, until a more permanent impression is made and a definite attitude is achieved.

Children whose training is neglected at home or who are otherwise exposed to evil influences often relapse into their former sins or commit new ones. They cause the teacher a good deal of trouble. But he should not despise nor neglect them. They are in need of special attention and love. As it requires a more skilful instructor to teach pupils who are dull and stupid than it does to teach such as are bright, so it requires a good deal more of educational skill and patience to train a weak and wayward child than it does to train one that is tractable. However, the child which is most difficult to train is in greatest need of training. Let your Christian influence bear firmly, but lovingly, upon the spiritually weak and backsliding child, and your labor will not be in vain. You may not accomplish as much as you wish, but you will accomplish more than if you had simply neglected him.

Sins whose Perpetrators Cannot be Discovered. — At times sins are committed and tricks played the perpetrators of which are not known to the teacher. He will try to find the guilty one, and those who know of it should tell it when asked to do so by the teacher. This is not tattling, but a plain Christian duty. Joseph brought to his father the evil report of his brethren (Gen. 37, 2). "Whoso is a partner with a thief hateth his own soul; he heareth cursing and bewrayeth it not" (Prov. 29, 24).

If from the outset it appears that all efforts to find out the guilty one will prove futile, then it is not wise to start a searching investigation; for if it fails, the little culprit might laugh in his sleeve and try the same trick over just to vex his teacher. Do not hold the entire school responsible for what one child has done and do not reprove and scold all the children for a thing of which many of them may be ignorant. There is a way of handling such cases that will make matters worse.

Let the teacher, in a calm and objective manner, show how wicked it was to do such a thing. Let him express his sorrow that any one of his pupils would allow his Old Adam to lead him into sin. Let him impress upon the children that, though the guilty one may succeed in hiding himself and covering his sin before men, he cannot do so before God, that he therefore hopes and prays the guilty child will repent of his sin and seek forgiveness with God. Children must feel that it is not the prime object of the teacher to punish the offender, but rather to correct him. If the teacher will handle this matter in a calm and sane manner, he will make a deep impression on all children. Sometimes the guilty child will come and confess, though it may not always be advisable to demand this. Just as much is accomplished if the child confesses to God and amends his ways.

Such occurrences, however, should teach us to be more watchful lest the children play their pranks under our very nose. Be sure of your case and then deal prudently and fairly with the child. If children feel that sooner or later the teacher will find out, they will hesitate to do what they do not wish him to know.

At times children will do what is likely to vex the teacher personally. Then he must control himself and not let personal resentment dictate his actions. If it is a small matter, it is best to ignore it, as children will not continue to do what does not accomplish their purpose, *i. e.,* roiling the teacher. But let him watch whether the offense is repeated. If the matter is of a more serious nature, he must certainly speak to the children about it. But let him forget all about himself and think only of saving the child. The child should not be reproved or punished because the teacher is personally offended, but because the child has done what is wrong in the sight of God. The child must feel that the teacher harbors no personal ill will towards him for the offense which he penitently confessed. Forgive and forget. It is self-evident that the teacher will not speak to others about the sins of his pupils, especially not about those which are known to him only. To do so is not only a sin against the Eighth Commandment, but will also destroy the confidence children should have in their teacher.

Parents Not Agreeing with the Educational Procedure of the Teacher. — It sometimes happens that parents, because they were misinformed by their children and do not know the facts in the case, or because they have such a favorable opinion of their children that they do not believe they could ever misbehave, or because there is an honest difference of opinion as to how children should be treated, will call on the teacher and reproach him for being unfair to their children or for having mistreated them. Here it behooves the teacher to remain calm and courteous. Let him remember: "A soft answer turneth away wrath, but grievous words stir up anger" (Prov. 15, 1). Avoid discussing the matter before the whole school, but be ready to talk the matter over with the parents privately. Never put father or mother to shame or humiliate them in the presence of their children, for this may undermine the respect they owe their parents. Honor the parents of the children that they may profit by your example. In private let the parents speak their mind freely — it will be a relief to them — and then discuss the matter with them soberly and courteously. Wise parents will mostly agree with you after they have heard the facts in the case and will strengthen your authority over against their children. They may also show you a better way of handling such cases. For the practical experience of parents may at times teach the professional pedagog some sound pedagogy. The purpose of such discussions with parents should not be to find who is right and who is wrong, but what is good for the child and which is the best way to save him from sin.

Some parents ask special consideration for their children, either with respect to their lessons and promotions or with regard to their treatment and training. Let the teacher remember: "Thou shalt not respect persons neither take a gift; for a gift doth blind the eyes of the wise and pervert the words of the righteous. That which is altogether just thou shalt follow" (Deut. 16, 19. 20).

Unwarranted favors and privileges to some are unfair to other children and detrimental to the training of that particular child which receives them. Unless plainly justified, such special favors will stir up envy in other children against the favored one, mistrust against the partial teacher, and in the child so favored they are likely to beget pride and the "better-than-thou" spirit. Even the personal liking the teacher may have for some children should not influence him to overlook their faults and to treat them with more consideration than others. "He that justifieth the wicked, and he that condemneth the just, even they both are abomination to the Lord" (Prov. 17, 15). If the teacher's efforts at saving children from sin are to be effective, the children must feel that he is fair and just, that he is actuated not by any personal considerations, but solely by the desire to help and save them.

XX. How to Train a Child in Christian Virtues.

The General Scope. — Whoever wishes to raise a crop of vegetables must not only keep his garden free from weeds, but must also sow good seed and water it and nurse the tiny plants till they grow strong and ripen unto the harvest. It is even so in the training of children. It is not sufficient to keep the child from walking in the way of the transgressor or to save him from sin into which he has fallen, but *education must strive for positive results;* it must direct the child in the way he should go, must encourage and strengthen him to practise godliness, to continue in it, and to grow therein. *Die Erziehung soll das Kind nicht allein vom Boesen abgewoehnen, sondern sie soll das Kind vornehmlich zum Guten gewoehnen.* Education must not only repress evil, break bad habits, correct faults, but it should preeminently be constructive; it should build up positive values, cultivate Christian virtues and godly habits, and mold a Christian character.

The Christian's sanctification of life consists not only in this, that he eschews evil, but also and especially in this, that he does and practises what is good in the sight of God and man. Christian education, which is but a method of helping the child to sanctify his life unto God, must therefore stress this positive influence, whereby the child is trained to love and observe the things which are good. Says Paul: "Whatsoever things are true, whatsoever things are honest, whatsoever things are just, whatsoever things are pure, whatsoever things are lovely, whatsoever things are of good report, if there be any virtue and if there be any praise, think on these things" (Phil. 4, 8). Christians are exhorted not only to "put off the old man," but also to "put on the new man, which after God is created in righteousness and true holiness" (Eph. 4, 22. 24; Col. 3,

12—14). In his explanations to the commandments Luther tells us not only what is forbidden, but also what is enjoined in them. While thus it is necessary to weed out sin, it is just as necessary that by proper training we implant and cultivate Christian virtues in our pupils.

Parents and educators often do not give sufficient attention to this phase of their work. They do all they can to repress and curb the Old Adam in children, but they forget to encourage and foster the new man. Thus the training becomes rather one-sided; children learn to avoid evil, but they never learn to do what is good. But the Scripture is profitable not only for "correction" of what is evil, but also for " instruction in righteousness that the man of God may be perfect, throughly furnished unto all good works" (2 Tim. 3, 15—17). It is this constructive phase of education that needs to be stressed more than it usually is, for it is this that makes for righteousness of life and molds a Christian character. Parents and teachers must therefore not only keep children from "going wrong," but exert every influence to train them in the way they should go. They must impress upon them not only what is forbidden in the commandments, but also what is enjoined therein. This should be done in the teaching of Bible-stories and of the Catechism, but also at other times, whenever an opportunity presents itself. At all times the predominating influence of education must be positive and constructive, tending towards the establishment of Christian virtues and the upbuilding of a Christian character.

The Fundamental Prerequisite. — To produce such positive results it is absolutely necessary to nourish and strengthen in children true faith in Christ by means of the Gospel. They can be trained to lead respectable lives also by means of the Law, as we may learn from the Pharisee in the Temple (Luke 18, 11. 12) and by being promised

How to Train a Child in Christian Virtues.

all manner of rewards and advantages. However, such is not a Christian education, and such an education will not be productive of lasting results. The type of character we must seek to develop in children is such that from love of God they consecrate themselves to His service and are zealous of good works.

Such unselfish love, which seeks no glory and reward for oneself, is the product of faith in Christ; for "faith worketh by love" (Gal. 5, 6). Where this faith is lacking, there can be no godliness of life. But where the light of faith is burning in the heart, it will shine forth in all manner of good works and Christian virtues. If, then, we would have the fruits of faith in the lives of our pupils, let us first nourish and cultivate true faith in their hearts.

How to Make Children Willing to Serve God in Good Works. — The Old Adam, who is still active also in Christian children, is never willing to do the works of God (Rom. 7, 17—23). We must therefore impress upon them that God indeed expects them to abound in every good work. "Exercise thyself unto godliness" (1 Tim. 4, 7). "But thou, O man of God, flee these things and follow after righteousness, godliness, faith, love, patience, meekness" (1 Tim. 6, 11). The fig-tree that does not bear fruit will ultimately be cut down and destroyed (Luke 13, 6—9).

But by commanding good works, we shall never make the child truly willing to do them, much less shall we succeed by scolding and by threatening punishment. To overcome the unwillingness of the Old Adam, we must strengthen the willingness of the new man (Rom. 7, 22. 23). This is not done by appealing to the selfish instincts of children, but by following the example of Paul, who beseeches us "by the mercies of God" to consecrate ourselves to His service. We must remind the children of the great love of God to them, of the blessings they have received in the past and are receiving every day and of the still greater things the heavenly Father has in store for them. If they begin to realize this, their hearts will be filled with gratitude and willingness to serve, and they will ask: "What shall I render unto the Lord for all His benefits toward me?" (Ps. 116, 12.)

We should point out to the children the beauty of holiness and the gratification it affords. The service of sin, though it please for a time, never truly satisfies the heart. "But godliness with contentment is great gain" (1 Tim. 6, 6), and "godliness is profitable unto all things, having the promise of the life that now is and of that which is to come" (1 Tim. 4, 8). A good deed done in the service of the Lord carries with it its own reward in this, that it satisfies the heart. Feeling that we have done something worth while, we experience in our hearts a certain joy and contentment. "It is more blessed to give than to receive" (Acts 20, 35). Living under Christ in His kingdom and serving Him in righteousness and true holiness, we shall also be happy and blessed in doing so. For a child of God it is a real joy to do the will of his heavenly Father.

But godliness has a promise also for the life which is to come. In the Day of Judgment the Lord Jesus will recognize our deeds of love and mercy: "Verily I say unto you, Inasmuch as ye have done it unto one of the least of these My brethren, ye have done it unto Me" (Matt. 25, 34—40). Then will He graciously reward with a crown of glory what we have done in His service here on earth. Therefore: "He which soweth sparingly shall reap also sparingly, and he which soweth bountifully shall reap also bountifully" (2 Cor. 9, 6).

These things we must impress on our pupils and thus make their hearts willing to do what is pleasing in the sight of God.

Teach Children to Know the Will of God. — Having made the children willing to serve God in good works, the teacher must also show them which such works are. For in this they must not be left to their own fancy and imagination, but both by instruction (Deut. 6, 6. 7) and by his own example (Phil. 3, 17) the teacher will show what the Lord requires of them (Micah 6, 8). He will be very careful to have the children understand that it is not only the teacher, but that it is principally God who would have them serve Him in these works. Thus children must be trained not to render mere eye-service as men-pleasers, but as the servants of Christ to do the will of God from the heart, with good will doing service as to the Lord and not to men; knowing that whatsoever good thing any man doeth, the same he shall receive of the Lord (Eph. 6, 6—8).

In order that children may well understand the will of God, it is necessary for the teacher not only to dwell upon those Bible-stories which show God's displeasure with the sins of men, but especially to stress those examples which exhibit positive godliness and to hold them up to his pupils for their emulation. He will have them commit to memory pertinent Bible-texts and the Ten Commandments with their explanations. Not only are they of immediate value in controlling the conduct of the child, but they will also serve as a directive later in life. Moral truths should not only be impressed upon the conscience of the child, but should, if possible, be reduced to brief and convenient forms that can easily be remembered. Bible-texts and rules of conduct that were well committed to memory in childhood may, like a seed, lie idle in the heart for many a year without bringing forth fruit, but at some time later in life they may, under the blessing of God, become alive and active and exert a determining influence.

Extolling the beauty of holiness, of consecrated service,

and of well-doing to his pupils and teaching them the way of righteousness, the educator will exert an edifying and constructive influence, one that builds up positive values.

Train Children to Observe the Will of God. — "The only true test of learning a thing is whether the learner lives it. The only true test of the value of what one learns is the extent to which it affects his daily life. The value of our teaching is therefore always to be measured by the degree to which it finds expression in the lives of our pupils." (*Betts.*)

It is not sufficient to teach the child to know what he should do, but he must also be trained to *observe* and *do* what he has learned. We would very much stress this point. Let the child learn to do, and let him learn by doing. "A good deed done is a more potent former of moral character than the learning of a rule of conduct." (*Avent.*) It is very easy for a child to learn that he must obey parents and teachers, but it is quite difficult for him to obey. Obedience must be learned by obeying. Thus it is with all matters in which the child is to be trained. He must do them, and do them again and again, until it becomes a habit to do them as they should be done. "*Erziehung ist zum groszen Teil eine richtig geleitete Gewoehnung zum Guten.*" Education is properly directed habituation. "*Gewoehnung ist die Mutter der Gewohnheit.*" Habituation is the mother of habit. Children, therefore, must not only be told which works are good and pleasing to God, they must not only be encouraged to do them, but they must also be given opportunity to practise them.

"Impractical theorizing about how to live and unintelligent practise are both ineffectual in producing the principles that constitute moral character. It is a combination of theory with practise, of impression with expression, that counts." (*Avent.*)

Tell children what they should do and why they ought to do it; have them do it and see that it is done. "Teach them to *observe*," the Master said, "whatsoever I have commanded you."

This is by no means an easy task, as every educator of some experience can testify. However, that is no reason why it may be neglected. On the contrary, this is the very aim and end of education, that we get children to live and practise what they have learned. At times they will do this quite readily, especially if the thing is new and interests them. But soon they tire of it, become careless, and are unwilling to continue the good work. At times they are from the very beginning opposed to what is required of them. Then the educator must act wisely and firmly and do all he can to get them to do what he requires. If he succeeds once, he is likely to succeed again. Having learned by their first experience, the children are more ready to yield to his influence the second time, until by frequent repetitions a habit is formed. "Activities and thoughts engaged in grow strong by their use." (*Avent.*) Thus a boy may at first obey rather reluctantly, perhaps obedience must be enforced, but by and by it comes easier to him, the habit is forming, and finally he is an obedient boy. In like manner, if the child is trained to practise godliness, the practise of godliness will become a habit that may cling to him through life. *Jung gewohnt, alt getan.* "Train up a child in the way he should go, and when he is old, he will not depart from it" (Prov. 22, 6).

"Provisions must be made for the application and doing of what is taught. Lead children to learn right living through doing righteousness. Much of the effects of moral and religious teaching is totally lost because of lack of provision and opportunity for giving immediate expression to the impressions received." (*Avent.*)

The wide-awake teacher will find many such opportunities in school as well as in the life of the child of which he will avail himself; and if there be none, he will make provisions for children to do and practise what they have learned.

"The wise teacher will therefore seize upon every opportunity to find something worth while for his pupils to do. He will have them help with the distribution of supplies in the classroom; he will see that they volunteer to help the superintendent or other officials (of the Sunday-school) who may need assistance; he will give them responsibility in decorating the church or the classroom for special occasions; he will leave to their cooperation as large a measure as possible of the work to be done in arranging and carrying out class and school picnics, excursions, social gatherings, and the like; he will arrange for special groups to visit the aged, sick, or shut-ins for the purpose of singing Gospel-songs, and will open the way for those who are qualified to do so to read the Bible or other matter to the blind or those whose sight is failing. In short, the devoted teacher who understands the laws of childhood will make his instruction as nearly as possible a laboratory course in religion, finding the material and the occasion in the human needs and opportunities for loving service which lie closest at hand." (*Betts.*)

It is the supreme test of one's educative ability if he not only teaches children to know, but also trains them to do what they have learned from the Word of God.

What Betts says of the Sunday-school applies also to the parochial school: "Nothing can take the place of whole-hearted, joyous participation in the real activities of the Sunday-school as a means of catching the interest of the members and securing their loyalty; for interest and loyalty finally attach to those activities in which we have a share. The school in which the child finds a chance to express the lessons and put into practise the maxims he is taught is the school which is building Christian character and providing for future religious leadership."

Recognize Every Effort and Improvement on the Part of the Child. — As the gardener will eagerly watch for the first tiny leaf that sprouts from the seed and take good care lest he crush it by rough handling, so also the Christian educator must watch for the first-fruits of faith and see that he does not destroy them. At first there will be but a timid effort and little progress. But it would have a blighting effect upon the tender buddings of faith if the teacher would severely criticize and reprimand the child because the fruits of faith are not so fully developed as he would like to see them. The child, conscious of his sincere intention and effort, will become utterly discouraged and may not try again. Unwise and untimely censure may stifle the first weak efforts for holy living. On the other hand, undue and untimely praise may cause the child to be satisfied with mediocre achievements and to become puffed up, even though he has not tried his best. Acknowledge every sincere effort, but also encourage the child to continue and to strive for still better results. When we must point out shortcomings, let us not forget to acknowledge what may be commended. Witness the messages to the angels of the seven churches, Rev. 2 and 3.

Strengthen the Child in His Efforts to Improve. — Christ said to His disciples: "The spirit indeed is willing, but the flesh is weak" (Matt. 26, 41), and Paul says: "To will is present with me, but how to perform that which is good I find not" (Rom. 7, 18). Such is the experience of all Christians, also of children whom we are training in holiness of life. After the inward man they delight in the Law of God and would gladly do what it enjoins. But often they find that they are not doing the good things they would, but rather the evil things which they would not (Rom. 7, 19). This experience very much discourages them, and they despair of ever making any progress.

It then becomes the duty of the teacher to strengthen them in their efforts. A word of recognition will greatly encourage them. He may remind them also of their baptism (see Questions 292—299 in the Catechism), which is to them an inexhaustible source of spiritual strength. The promise of God made to the child in Holy Baptism remains firm and unshaken (Rom. 3, 3; Is. 54, 10; Ezek. 16, 60). This assurance gives the child strength and inspires him with willingness to walk in the ways of God. Have children commit to memory such texts in which God promises them His help (2 Cor. 12, 9; Is. 41, 10; Ps. 145, 18. 19; 50, 15). Encourage them to pray (Matt. 26, 41) and pray with them. Hold out to them the glorious hope of salvation (1 Thess. 5, 9) and the reward of grace in heaven (Acts 14, 22; Rom. 8, 18). In every way let us "strengthen the weak hands and confirm the feeble knees" (Is. 35, 3) that our children may run the way of God's commandments (Ps. 119, 32).

XXI. How to Train a Child in Christian Virtues.

(Continued.)

The educator will strive to develop all manner of Christian virtues in the children entrusted to his care. But there are some which must be especially stressed.

Respectfulness.—Respectfulness is the quality or state of being respectful, of showing honor, esteem, and reverence to those who are entitled to it. There is much complaint that the rising generation does not show the proper respect to those who are placed over it for its guidance, training, and government. This condition is due to a lack of proper education. Ever since Adam and Eve set aside the respect and reverence they owed to their God, no man is by nature inclined to respect and honor his superiors. It is therefore the prime duty of all who are engaged in the education of children to teach and train them to honor and respect their parents and masters.

How is this done?

It is folly to assume that this can be done by punishment and intimidation or by a stern and severe manner of dealing with children. This may create fear in their hearts, perhaps even hatred, but never respect, esteem, and reverence. Children must be taught what it means to respect and honor some one. It means to think highly of a person, to regard him greater than oneself, to look upon him as one's superior. The word *honor* in the Fourth Commandment implies that father and mother are more than the children, that God has placed parents and masters over children and servants, that they are His representatives, that He has clothed them with divine authority, and that He therefore wants all children to look up to, respect and esteem them. While it is true that all men are created equal and that God is not a respecter of persons (Acts 10, 34), still the position and office God has given to some entitles them to the respect and honor of others.

Children must be told whom they should honor: in the first place, father and mother and all those who may take their place in the home; then their teachers and pastors (1 Tim. 5, 17; 1 Thess. 5, 13); also the officials of the civil government (Rom. 13, 5—7; 1 Pet. 2, 17). Servants, hired men, and laborers should honor their masters (Eph. 6, 5—8; Mal. 1, 6), and young people should honor and respect those who are their elders (Lev. 19, 32). It is a beautiful Christian virtue to show due respect and honor to all men (1 Pet. 2, 17), "in honor preferring one another" (Rom. 12, 10).

Children must be told why they should do this. The chief reason is that God expects it of them, and for His sake they should conduct themselves respectfully over against their superiors. They should follow the example of their Savior, who, though He was the Son of God, yet honored His foster-father and His mother (Luke 2, 51). Such respectfulness on the part of children commends them to the favor of all men.

In the teaching of Bible-stories and the Catechism one will find ample opportunity to impress this lesson on children. But let the teacher also in this be an example to his pupils, and let him so conduct himself that he holds and retains their respect.

It is not sufficient, however, merely to instruct children on this point; they must also be trained. They do not always know how to act and what to do. Whenever, therefore, in their conduct the teacher notices anything that does not reveal the proper respect, he must call their attention to it and show them what they should do and how they should act. "Thou shalt rise up before the hoary head and honor the face of the old man" (Lev. 19, 32). "Elihu had waited till Job had spoken because they were elder than he" (Job 32, 4). Meeting people whom they know, they should greet them politely; spoken to, they should pay attention; asked, they should make answer as best they can; called, they should come; if they desire information, they should not be afraid to ask, but should ask with all modesty; asked to do a favor, they should be ready at once to render service if it is in their power to do so. Thus there are many, apparently little, things in which children may be trained to honor and respect their parents and masters.

Obedience. — A child that has learned to honor his parents and masters will also obey them. By nature children are self-willed and not inclined to submit to authority.

Still, without obedience a godly life is impossible; for true godliness consists in this very thing, that from the heart we obey the will of our Father in heaven. However, we must distinguish between obedience from fear of punishment and obedience from love of God. At times, indeed, it is necessary to enforce obedience by means of punishment, for the stubborn Old Adam will not be subdued otherwise. But the obedience to be developed by Christian education is one that springs from faith and love of God, "doing the will of God from the heart" (Eph. 6, 5—8). Such obedience must become a habit, so that also in later years the child may willingly do what God requires in His Word.

In training children to be obedient, it is necessary to show them that God requires such obedience of them. "This thing I commanded them, saying, Obey My voice, and I will be your God, and ye shall be My people; walk ye in all the ways that I have commanded you that it may be well unto you" (Jer. 7, 23). Impress upon them that for the numerous blessings received they owe such obedience to their God; "for all which it is my duty to thank and praise, to serve and obey Him," and that it is well-pleasing to God if we gladly obey His commandments. "Behold, to obey is better than sacrifice" (1 Sam. 15, 22). And because God commanded: "Obey them that have the rule over you and submit yourselves" (Heb. 13, 17), children must for the Lord's sake obey those whom He has placed over them in home, school, church, and state. They must learn to do this willingly, not to please men, but as the children of God. In all this, children must be thoroughly instructed as opportunity presents itself.

But children must also be trained in obedience. This requires a goodly portion of prudence on the part of him who commands. Do not capriciously command anything that enters your mind, but weigh well what you ask the child to do and let it be worth while. Do not demand things that are foolish, useless, humiliating, or contrary to the conscience of the child and to the Word of God. Do not ask too much and not many different things at the same time. Beware of a multitude of rules and regulations which the child does not understand and cannot remember. Many laws bring many transgressions.

Let the child clearly understand what he is to do, even though he not always understands why he is to do it. Do not forget what you have commanded lest the child soon forget to obey. Do not take for granted that, because you have given an order, the child will also obey, but see that he does obey. The child must learn by actual experience that he may not ignore or circumvent the orders of his superiors. One case of actual obedience on the part of the child does more for his training than twenty orders he receives, but ignores. The child must learn to obey by obeying. Parents and teachers should not be too liberal in giving orders, but having given one, they should make sure that it is carried out. Such follow-up work may not always be pleasant, but it must be done if children are to be trained in obedience.

It is not always necessary, nor is it wise to give, especially to small children, a satisfactory explanation as to why they should do this or that. They must learn to obey also without asking questions. As they grow older, we may tell them why we ask them to do a certain thing. Still their obedience must not depend upon whether or not such explanations are satisfactory to them. A child that obeys only when he is personally satisfied as to the reasonableness of the command has not yet learned to obey. Least of all should children be coaxed by flattery and promises to obey their parents and masters. They must know that it is not at all optional with them whether or not they will mind, but that they must obey.

How to Train a Child in Christian Virtues.

Obedience is a lesson which it is necessary for every child to learn; for the further progress and the success of his training will largely depend upon to what extent he submits to authority and influence. It is extremely difficult to educate a disobedient child. One chief reason why many young people are not well trained is that they never learned to obey. Obedience on the part of the children is necessary for a pleasant and agreeable home life; it is a prerequisite for maintaining discipline in school; we must have it in Church and cannot do without it in the State. And this lesson is best learned in early youth. At the age of four years the child should know that he must mind his parents, and at school he must learn to obey his teachers, and thus he must be trained to submit to those whom God has placed over him.

Obedience is a lesson difficult for the child to learn and difficult for the pedagog to teach. The child must subdue his own will and submit to that of another. The teacher must prevail upon the child to forego that on which he has set his heart and to do what may not be to his liking. It is the will of the teacher against the will of the child. It may be that the first encounter runs off very smoothly, and much has been gained. If the child, however, at any time shows himself reluctant and obstinate, the teacher should by no means desist, but, using all his influence, insist that the child obey. Having thus succeeded once, it will be far easier the next time. However, a teacher must be consistent; not insist on strict obedience once in a while and at other times not even make an attempt to enforce his commands. To be successful, training must be continuous.

Truthfulness. — From early youth, children must be taught and trained to tell the truth, and to live it, too. Let no one take for granted that his children and pupils will do so, that they will not lie and deceive and hence have no need of training in this respect.

What are we to do?

In the first place, we must explain to the children what it means to tell the truth. When questioned about a certain matter, they must tell all they know about it, without intentionally misrepresenting or concealing anything. Under certain conditions they may, and even must, refuse to tell what they know (Prov. 11, 13); but they must never deceitfully belie their neighbor. When relating certain events and experiences, they must learn not to exaggerate, as they are often inclined to do, but to state things as they are, confining themselves to actual facts. When making a promise, they must have the sincere intention of keeping it and earnestly try to perform it to the best of their ability (Deut. 23, 23). If this is impossible, they must give an explanation to him to whom the promise was made and who is perhaps depending on its fulfilment. Teach children to be slow in making promises, but scrupulously conscientious in keeping them. If others are to take our words for what they express, we certainly must mean what we say.

And why should children be truthful? The Lord is a God of truth (Deut. 32, 4), who loves those that speak the truth in their hearts (Ps. 15, 2). Christian children, who love their God and Father in heaven, will certainly also love and speak the truth. This is what God expects of them. "Speak ye every man the truth to his neighbor" (Zech. 8, 16). This they also will do, for the "fruit of the Spirit is in all goodness and righteousness and truth" (Eph. 5, 9).

It may also be proper to call the children's attention to the fact that, though the liar may prosper for a while, he will finally come to grief. The truth, however, will win out in the end, and the truthful child is respected and trusted by men. As children expect others to tell them the truth, they should do likewise.

Also in their conduct the children must not simulate, but be true and without guile (John 1, 47), unfeigned in love (2 Cor. 6, 6). God desires truth, uprightness, and honesty in their lives. The psalmist says: "Behold, thou desirest truth in the inward parts, and in the hidden part thou shalt make me to know wisdom" (Ps. 51, 6). Paul writes: "Let us keep the feast, not with old leaven, neither with the leaven of malice and wickedness, but with the unleavened bread of sincerity and truth" (1 Cor. 5, 8). Therefore every Christian child should pray: "Teach me, O Lord, I will walk in thy truth; unite my heart to fear Thy name" (Ps. 86, 11).

Truthfulness in speech, faithfulness in promises, uprightness in conduct, these are the virtues we must seek to develop in our pupils. "Lord, who shall abide in Thy tabernacle? Who shall dwell in Thy holy hill? He that walketh uprightly and worketh righteousness and speaketh the truth in his heart" (Ps. 15, 1. 2). But it is not sufficient merely to tell children these things, we must train them therein. We must watch and insist that they speak and live the truth.

Diligence. — The child may be very busy at play or in doing things which he likes. But even at this he is often fitful and lacks perseverance. He is loath to perform duties, especially if they be irksome and unpleasant or if they must be done again and again. He is inclined to be idle or "to loaf on the job." It is a great and important lesson for the child to learn that he cannot always play as he lists, but that he must work and that he should work willingly and persevere though the task be hard and tedious. Man cannot play, but must work his way through life; therefore the child must be trained to work from his youth.

Children must be taught the right ethics of work. They must learn that God wants them to work (Gen. 2, 15;

2 Thess. 3, 10) and that He blesses the labor of their hands (Eph. 4, 28; Ps. 128, 2). Christ worked and did not waste His time (John 9, 4). It may be well to call the attention of children to their own parents, who toil and work for them, and to the great men in history, who achieved success by diligent application and perseverance.

Children must also learn that they are to work, not for gain or for glory, but because God wants them to work, and that every honorable work, done in the right spirit, is a service well pleasing to the Lord (Eph. 6, 5—8). We must do all we can to have children look upon their work as a privilege, which they enjoy over against those who cannot work, and not to regard it as a drudgery, which they seek to avoid. Let us inspire them with love for their work, and it will be an easy task to get them to work, and conversely, working, they will learn to enjoy their work.

Children must be trained to work by working. In assigning work to them, the teacher must be careful not to ask too much nor anything that is too hard. A task or an assignment may seem very small and easy to us, but to the child it looks quite different. Nothing is more likely to fill the child with an aversion to a special task or to work in general than when he finds he cannot do what is required and expected. On the other hand, the work should not be too easy, lest the child lose interest in it. We must also bear in mind that children must have time for rest and recreation. But work must not be treated like play. "Work while you work, play while you play."

Children should apply themselves diligently to their tasks and do their work carefully, neatly, conscientiously. They must be held to do at all times the best they can under the circumstances and never be satisfied with slipshod work. We must encourage them in their work, ackowledge their diligence and their progress, show them how to improve, etc. Thus we must lead them on to greater

How to Train a Child in Christian Virtues.

efforts and to greater achievements, directing the natural instinct to be busy into useful activity.

Work, worth-while work, is the great lesson every child must learn; for life is not all play and pleasure, but, to a large extent, labor and toil. This lesson can be learned, and the teacher must help the child to learn it. There are those who have not learned it; they are busybodies, flighty, superficial, undependable; others are very drones in the beehive of society. By training the child to work we develop not only his ability to work, but also his sense of duty and conscientiousness and diligence in the performance of duties. All these are valuable assets of character. The habit of doing work faithfully is of great consequence in school and in life. To be usefully employed will keep children and grown people out of mischief, will bring outward success and the inward satisfaction of not having wasted their time, but of having done something worth while.

Charity. — According to their Old Adam, Christian children are selfish; according to their new man, which was created in them in regeneration, they are able and willing to serve God and their neighbor in love. We must help the child not only to suppress every selfish impulse, but must especially nurse the spirit of Christian love and train him in works of charity. How is this done?

While it is true that it is the very nature of faith to "work by love," it is nevertheless necessary to instruct children on this point, even as the Bible instructs us Christians (1 John 3, 10; 4, 11; 5, 3). We must show them that God expects such works of love (1 John 3, 23), that thereby they prove themselves to be His children (1 John 4, 8. 12), that true love for the neighbor is not an idle feeling, but a strong emotion which prompts them to do good works (1 John 3, 16—18).

Train the child in these works. Even in the life of a child there are many opportunities for such works of love. Let us show our pupils how they can serve their parents at home by asking what they could do for them and by doing what they know will please them without being expressly commanded. At school they should show kindness and sympathy to one another, be ready to help, to protect, and to serve one another. Children may also be interested in doing something for the poor and needy, for the sick and the aged. Properly instructed and directed, Christian children will be glad to do such works of love. They learn to serve by serving.

In order that these works may be done in the right spirit, children must know that thereby they cannot and do not earn for themselves grace and salvation, for these are given to them freely through faith in Jesus. But because they have received these, their hearts should be filled with gratitude toward God, so that gladly they do anything that pleases Him. To serve God, it is not necessary to do great and mighty works. Small services of love which we render our neighbor the Lord Jesus will regard as having been done to Him (Matt. 25, 35—40). Let us by all means train our pupils so that Christian charity becomes an outstanding trait of their character.

"One of the greatest lessons a child can learn from his lessons in religion is that he is his brother's keeper. The instincts of childhood are naturally selfish and self-centered; the sense of reponsibility for others must be gradually trained and developed. In its neighborhood work and on many special occasions the church will have need of messenger service. Errands will have to be run, articles will have to be gathered and distributed, calls will have to be made, funds will have to be collected and a hundred other things done which children can do as well as, or better than, any one else. And it is precisely in these practical acts of homely service that the child gets his best training in the social side of religion." (*Betts.*)

Mission-Work. — Christ commanded His disciples to preach the Gospel of salvation to all nations. This is the great work of the Church on earth, and this must be the real life-work of every individual Christian. And we should neglect a very important part of the child's education if we were not to train him in mission-work and to have him participate in the missionary enterprises of the Church.

To interest children in this work, we must picture to them the needs of the heathen, who "bow down to wood and stone" or who, living in civilized countries, "have no hope and are without God in the world." Let us tell our pupils that salvation is prepared and ready for all men and that the Lord wants us Christians to bring to these people the glad tidings of pardon and peace. Let us impress upon them both their responsibility and their privilege to help in this work.

"It is not enough that the children shall be told the stories of the missionary heroes and given the picture of the needs of the people in far-away lands. Once the imagination is stirred and the emotions warmed by this instruction, an immediate and natural outlet in expression must be found if these lessons are to fulfil their end. Children should early be led into giving money for missionary purposes, and this, as far as possible, should be their own money which they have earned." (*Betts.*)

But children can also be trained to do some active mission-work. Let us get them interested in their Christian school, let us lead them to a true appreciation of the religious instruction and training they are receiving, and they will speak to other children about it. They will not only confess their faith and let their light shine before others, but they will also interest other children in their school and invite them to come. Let us train our children to become missionaries for our parochial schools, Sunday-schools, and churches.

Cleanliness, Neatness, Orderliness. — Though these pertain more to externals, they must not be neglected in the training of the child. The child should be taught to keep his body clean, to have his face and hands washed and his hair combed. His wearing-apparel should be kept neat and tidy, his clothes brushed, his shoes clean and polished. His books and papers must not be soiled, marred, or torn. He should be trained to keep his things in good condition, not to waste nor to destroy them. The desks in the schoolroom should occasionally be inspected whether they are kept in good order. Children should be held to keep the schoolroom and the school-yard clean. As a matter of training they may be asked to put their desks in order, to sweep the room, and to clean up the yard. In every way we must seek to develop in them the sense of order, neatness, and cleanliness by showing the contrast between these and their opposites and by insisting on good order, etc., at all times. It is self-evident that in these as in all other good habits in which he would train his pupils the teacher must himself set a good example.

Punctuality and Regularity. — Punctuality is the habit of keeping one's engagements, fulfilling one's promises, and performing one's duties at the appointed time. Children are inclined to do things just when they please, and even at that, they soon tire of them and become careless and negligent. Hence they must be taught to be punctual and regular in all their work. It may be a hard lesson for them to learn, but it is of some consequence for their success in life that they do learn it. A person who is irregular and unpunctual in his work is not very reliable.

Children should be at school regularly and punctually, do their work at the appointed time, and perform their duties and promises promptly. However, nothing can be accomplished by spasmodic attempts. To be punctual does not mean to be on time now and then, but regularly. Hence there must be a persistent influence in that direction until gradually the habit has been formed.

If the teacher would train his pupils to be punctual, he must himself be punctual. For why should the children be at school in time if quite often the teacher himself is fifteen minutes late? Why should they observe rules if the teacher ignores them? The example of the teacher is of utmost importance; by his own punctuality he trains the pupils to be punctual. The regular routine of daily work, which should be closely observed, has an educative influence on the children.

Manners. — The chief purpose of Christian education is to train the child in a fuller sanctification of life, so that from fear of God he will avoid what is evil and from love of God observe what is good and right. But this does not make teaching of good manners superfluous; on the contrary, Paul thus exhorts all Christians: "Whatsoever things are . . . lovely, whatsoever things are of good report, if there be any virtue and if there be any praise, think on these things" (Phil. 4, 8).

By nature the child has no manners, and he is little inclined to observe such as he may be taught. Hence it is the duty of parents and teachers to tell him what things are "lovely and of good report" among men and to train him in the observance of these things. We are not expected to drill all the formal and elaborate rules of etiquette, but there are some common-sense rules of conduct which every child should know and cultivate.

"In all education, manners should be taught as a matter of sufficient value for themselves, not merely as minor parts of health laws, good conduct, or school discipline. It is true that right manners resulting from good breeding tend toward health and good conduct and obedience, but they have also a virtue of their own, they demand for their attainment, first, control of petty irritations, capricious likes and dislikes, carelessness of speech, rudeness of action, and all forms of selfishness; and secondly, consideration for others, kindliness of will, and gentleness of words and sentiment. The daily exercise of this control and this consideration of others reacts upon the impulses or processes of the mind and tends to produce excellency of character." (*M. S. McNaught.*)

The teaching of manners is sadly neglected in many homes and in many schools. Striving for the greater aims of a Christian education, many believe themselves to be justified in ignoring these lesser details. It is true, mannerism is repulsive, but manners are very agreeable and desirable. They do not necessarily prove a Christian character; still a true Christian should also observe those things which are of good report among men. And our children should be so trained that as they grow up, they may increase in favor with God and with men (Luke 2, 52). A neat appearance and a mannerly conduct is a letter of recommendation everywhere.

As an aid in teaching good manners it may be advisable to draw up a set of the principal and most commonly accepted rules of good conduct, post them in the school, have the children copy them in their penmanship lessons, and ask them to observe them in their lives. There is ample opportunity in school for the training of children in politeness and good manners, and if the home will cooperate with the school also in this respect, much indeed can be accomplished.

XXII. Conclusion.

In the preceding chapters we have endeavored to set forth the principles of Christian education, which consists in this, that the spiritual powers and endowments bestowed upon the child in regeneration through faith in Christ Jesus be drawn out, directed, and developed so as to function in the daily life among men, in other words, that the religion of the heart may ever more become also a religion of life.

Two Extremes. — With respect to the entire educational activity there are two extremes that must be avoided: 1) doing nothing or too little for the training of the child; 2) doing too much.

The proper training of a child is a difficult, slow, and long-continued business, which requires much perseverance and patience. For this reason some parents, after a few half-hearted attempts, soon tire of it and let the child shift as he may, hoping that he will yet be sufficiently trained by his experiences in life. Others are so partial to their children that they see no need of training them in their youth. Hoping that they will outgrow the pranks of childhood, parents sometimes discover, when it is too late, that these embryonic evil tendencies have grown and developed into dangerous proportions. The Bible demands, and experience agrees to this demand, that from early infancy the child should be trained in the way he should go.

Conscientious parents and teachers, on the other hand, sometimes overdo it; they are educating and training too much. The child has absolutely no freedom of action; on every side he is hemmed in by rules and regulations. He can hardly stir without being reproved, corrected, admonished, exhorted, and told what he should do and not do. The effect of such treatment may be that for the time being the child will submit, not knowing better. But always dependent on others for guidance, he has not learned to "stand on his own feet," and as soon as the restraining discipline is removed, he will rebound and make full use of his "new liberty."

Even the Word of God may be used too much; for while it is indeed the best means for the training of children, it must for this very reason be used wisely. "A surfeit of the sweetest things the deepest loathing to the stomach brings." (*Shakespeare.*) If at every turn the child is confronted with a text from the Bible, if even in small matters of discipline he is being treated to an extensive lecture, if parents and teachers are continually preaching to him, then there is great danger that the heart of the child will become callous und that even in more serious matters the Word of God will no longer make an impression on him. Some children have "gone wrong" because they were educated too much, but not wisely.

What is to be done? How much is to be done? When is it to be done? How is it to be done? These are questions the young pedagog will ask. And these questions are extremely difficult to answer. There is no prescribed recipe, giving the exact ingredients and doses, for every case that requires treatment. A good deal also depends upon the personality of the teacher and his influence. Hardly two men will in a given case act exactly alike. Books on pedagogy can lay down only the fundamental principles. The advice of colleagues, whom he should consult in difficult cases, can give him only the general line of procedure. As to the minute details, which are often of great importance, he is thrown on his own resources and his pedagogical judgment. Let him diagnose the case as best he can, use wisely the means at his disposal, and never forget the aim he has in view in the training of that particular child.

Whoever realizes the difficulty, the importance, and the responsibility of his work as an educator of children will never have that self-sufficient feeling of being able to solve every problem that may arise. He also knows that, whatever he may do or say, he cannot make his words function in the heart of the child, he cannot make the seed grow and bring forth fruit. Therefore he will ask God for wisdom, guidance, and success.

Success Comes Slowly. — As the sapling in the forest is slowly adding ring to ring every season until, after many years, it has grown to be a sturdy oak-tree, that can weather the storm, so the growth of character is likewise a slow process, and it is only after many years of patient toil that we see the fruit of our labor. It is but gradually that impressions change into permanent attitudes and that single deeds of kindness done here and there become habits and virtues. "Education is a slow process, and it is only by a patient continuance along a well-defined path that we may hope to reach the goal." (*Kretzmann.*) The motions and promptings of the Spirit are weak at first and hardly perceptible, but by daily exercise they become stronger, until the spiritual man grows more and more to the measure of the stature of the fulness of Christ (Eph. 4, 13).

"Day after day and year after year throughout the period of training the conviction should be taking shape in the child's mind that these [Christian virtues] are the real things of life, the truest measure of successful living, the highest goals for which men can strive." (*Betts.*)

Success Is Sure. — While success in the work of education comes slowly, it is absolutely sure. Because the child is not an inanimate and senseless thing, but a rational being, which reacts to influences to which he is exposed, therefore the steady and consistent influence of education is bound to produce some reaction and to bring some result.

This result may not always measure up to our expectations, it may perhaps not even be perceptible; nevertheless the work was not in vain, something has been accomplished in the training of the child. We may not have succeeded in implanting positive Christian virtues, but we may at least have been instrumental in preventing the child from becoming worse than he now is.

The Christian educator should always feel sure of success. Employing the Word of God as the chief means of training his pupils, he should confidently believe the promise of his God: "As the rain cometh down and the snow from heaven and returneth noth thither, but watereth the earth and maketh it bring forth and bud that it may give seed to the sower and bread to the eater, so shall My Word be that goeth forth out of My mouth: it shall not return unto Me void, but it shall accomplish that which I please, and it shall prosper in the thing whereto I sent it" (Is. 55, 10. 11). The Christian teacher should never despair of success, but doing all he can for the individual child, let him firmly believe that the good Lord will bless his efforts. Though there may be no immediate response and improvement, he should know that he has sown good seed, which may yet grow and bring fruit in days to come. And even though the child will never receive the Word of God for the salvation of his soul and the sanctification of his life, still the fact that he has heard the Word of God shall be a witness unto him (Matt. 24, 14), so that he will be without excuse on the Day of Judgment.

Education a Glorious Work. — The work of teaching and training children is not very spectacular, nor is it generally regarded as highly as it deserves to be. Still it is a most important and a most glorious work, compared with which the blood-stained deeds of heroes acclaimed in history and the marvelous masterpieces of artists and architects dwindle into insignificance. Christian educators are not working in wood and stone, but are endeavoring to fashion the souls of living human beings; they are not building temples and monuments that will crumble into dust, but are laboring to build the spiritual temple in the hearts of their pupils and are molding the monument of a truly Christian character. They are not, like the civil authorities, concerned about governing the external affairs of their pupils, but are coworkers with God in shaping their temporal and eternal destiny. They truly are the builders of the nation, the generation to come will be what the educators make of the children to-day.

If all education were to be discontinued for a hundred years, the most civilized nations would sink back into illiteracy and savagery. *"Denn wo die Schrift und Kunst untergehet, was will da bleiben in deutschen Landen denn ein wuester, wilder Haufen Tataren oder Tuerken, ja vielleicht ein Saustall und eine Rotte wilder Tiere."* (*Luther.*) But Christian education is that wholesome leaven (Luke 13, 21) which quietly and steadily counteracts the corruption and the dominion of sin. If all children in the world would receive a sound and thorough Christian education, we should have less need of penal institutions than we now have. Therefore the Christian educator is the greatest benefactor of the individual child and of society in general. *„Einem fleissigen, frommen Schulmeister oder Magister, oder wer es ist, der Knaben treulich zieht und lehret, dem kann man nimmermehr genug lohnen und mit keinem Gelde bezahlen."* (*Luther.*)

Though the task be difficult, though there be many disappointments, "let us not be weary in well-doing; for in due season we shall reap if we faint not" (Gal. 6, 9). And after life's work is done, the Lord will fulfil His promise: "The teachers shall shine as the brightness of the firmament and they that turn many to righteousness as the stars forever and ever" (Dan. 12, 3).

INDEX.

Numbers refer to pages.

Abhorrence of sin, 192.
Ability to teach, 51.
Activity of the soul, rational, cognitive, 82; emotional, affective, 83; volitional, 89.
Adam, Old, makes Christian education both necessary and difficult, 195. 120.
Admonition, 164.
Affections indicate personal attitude, 84. 87; most subjective experience, 84.
Affective activity of the soul, 83.
Agencies of Christian education, 22.
Aim, Christian, of education, 113; quotations, 121.
Aim of education determines means and method of education, 93. 111.
Aims, various, of education, 111. 112.
Angell, James R., 81. 84. 88. 90. 94. 120.
Appraisal of one's calling, 49.
"Armor of God," 190.
Assurance of victory in battle against sin, 191. 209.
Attention. Ideas occupying our a. most impressive, 88. 89.
Attitudes, emotional, 84.
Avent, Joseph E., 2. 39. 78. 91. 172. 228. 229.

Babson, Roger W., 26.
Backsets, 110.
Betts, George H., 43. 45. 49. 63. 71. 77. 79. 92. 93. 98. 107. 119. 120. 122. 151. 152. 155. 158. 184. 228. 230. 243. 349.
Bodily well-being of pupils, 80; b. ailments, 100.
Body wonderfully made, 80; b. imperfect, 99.

Books, bad, 187.
Brotherhood of man, 129.
Business of the Church, 23.
Butler, Nicholas Murray, 12.

Call of teacher divine, 44.
Calling of Christian teacher, 49; important and glorious, 68. 250.
Calling of names, 125. 167. 172.
Censure, necessary, 165; must not be overdone, 166.
Character, Christian, of teacher, 69; necessary for effective influence, 70; aim of Christian training, 185; character-worth, III.
Character-building most important function of schools, IV. 26.
Charity, 241.
Cheerfulness, 53.
Child, the, 77; a creature of God, 79; depraved by nature, 98; potentially capable of all sins, 101; unregenerated, 115; regenerated, 194; has twofold moral nature, 107; save c. from sin, 211; self-willed c., 198; proud c., 201; dishonest c., 203; lying c., 204; deceiving c., 205; stealing c., 206; penitent c., 215; impenitent c., 217; backsliding c., 218; teach the c. to know the will of God, 150; and train him to do it, 156.
Childhood best for training, 15.
Child study, 79.
Christian principle of education, 113.
Christ-mindedness, 66.
Church, Christian, an educational agency, 22; business and influence of Ch., 23.

Cicero, 92.
Cleanliness, 244.
Cognition, 83.
Cognitive activity of the soul, 82.
Command wisely, 235.
Commandment, Fourth; what it means to parents and teachers, 45; to children, 183; Sixth, 207; Seventh, 206; Eighth, 221.
Comfort. Bible profitable for c., 145.
Common sense in education, 58.
Confidence of children in teacher, 59; how it is won and held, 60.
Conscience, what it is, 195; regulated by some norm, 127. 195; must be controlled by the Law of God, 196. 197; sins against c., 196; erring c., 196; witness of c. not infallible, 196; callous c., 196; treatment of c., 197. 208; c. a powerful factor in education, 197.
Consecration to calling necessary, 47; must be fostered, 48.
Constructive education, 224; fundamental prerequisite of, 224.
Consultation with parents, 39.
Convince the child, 151.
Content of knowledge determines direction of influence, 8.
Coolidge, Calvin, IV. VI. 26.
Cooperation of home and school, 37.
Correction necessary, 165; must not be overdone, 166; Bible profitable for c., 144.
Crabb, *Synonyms*, 6. 15.
Criticism of public schools, 28; of several means of training, 125.
Cultural education, 5.
Curb, the Law as a c., 132.

"Dead" knowledge, 84. 86; of the Law, 135; of the Gospel, 86.
Deceiving, sin of d., 205.
Depravity of the child, 97; a factor to be recognized, 99; d. of the heart makes the Law "weak," 133.
Diagnosis of spiritual condition, 64; and of behavior of child, 108.
Dictionary, Eclectic, 3. 90.
Difference between instruction and education, 3; in children, 10. 19; between secular and Christian education, 34; between rational man and the irrational brute, 97; in manifestation of natural depravity, 192; between printed and spoken word, 154; between knowledge and faith, 86; between Law and Gospel, 63. 132.
Diligence, 239.
Direction of influence depends on peculiar content of the idea, 8. 84. 85.
Dishonesty in children, 203.
Discipline, school, 182.
Diversity of gifts, 96.
"Divide the Word of Truth," 63. 132.
Divine truths, teach Bible truths as, 149.
Doctrine, Bible profitable for, 144.
Dominating thoughts and ideas most effective, 88. 89. 142. 150. 159.
Dominion of sin, save child from, 214.
Draft of School Regulations, quotation from, 139.

Education; see *Training*. Wider meaning of, 1; proper sense of, 2. 3; phases of, 3; intellectual, 4; social, 4; cultural, 5; moral, 6. 9; religious, 6; e. presupposes rational being,

9; not a mechanical procedure, 10; cannot be forced, 11; results of e. not uniform, 10; life an e., 12; e. a purposive endeavor, 16; e. begins in the heart, 103; e. by means of laws and rules, 74. 103; e. not exclusively Christian, 21.

Education, Christian, 21. 22; a duty, 41; means of, 125; the Word of God profitable for, 130; e. by means of the Gospel, 141; e. aims at positive results, 223; faith and sanctification of life aims of e., 114. 115. 223. 224; two extremes, 247; success slow, but sure, 249; e. important and glorious work, 68. 250.

Educative influence must be consistent and persistent, 17; teaching must be educative, 152—158.

Educator (see *Teacher*), 41; his duty, 41; natural qualifications, 51; spiritual qualifications, 61; must understand the child, 77—79.

Effect, moral, of influences of life, 13.

Efficacy of the Word of God, 130; can be hindered, 36.

Eliot, Charles W., 129.

Emotional activity of the soul, 83; attitudes, 84; e. attitudes indicate personal character, 92.

Emotions, 84; variety of, 85; are dynamic, 90.

Encouragement, 231.

Environment a powerful determinant of character, 12. 18. 19.

Equanimity, 57.

Eudemonic principle, 111.

Evolution, 79. 83. 97. 100.

Example of a Christian life necessary in every teacher, 71—74; a powerful means of training, 181.

Exhortation, 164.

Expectation of reward, 126.

Experience, Christian, of the teacher helps him to understand the Ch. e. of the child, 65.

Experiences and influences of life an educative power, 12; moral effect, 13; must not be ignored in the training of the child, 13. 18.

Expulsion from school, 177.

Expulsive power of higher affections, 189.

Extremes, two, in education, 247.

Failure, reasons for, 18. 39. 151. 155. 161. 179.

Faith, essence of, 137; a work of God, 138; wrought by means of the Gospel promise, 135. 136; functions of f., 140; f. in Christ enables the child to overcome temptation, 189; it must be nursed and strengthened, 121. 208; cannot exist in an impenitent heart, 213; dead faith, 86; f. in Christ first major objective of Christian education, 114; personal f. of the teacher, 64.

Favors, unwarranted, to children, 222.

Fear of God, 101; of punishment, 125.

Feelings indicate personal attitude, 84. 87. 90; variety of f., 85.

Flattery, 163.

Follow-up work, 161. 236.

Force, education cannot be forced, 11.

Freedom of will, 89.

Functions of faith and their relation, 140.

Gifted, poorly g. child, 52.

Gifts, natural, 96; weakened, 101.

Godliness of life second major objective of Christian education, 115; Bible proof, 116.

Index.

Goethe, W., 113.
Golden Rule, 129.
Gospel, content and effect on the heart, 135; must be taught with the view to work faith, 139; the only effectual means for Christian education, 141.
Grace, state of, must be recognized, 104.
Grillparzer, F., 206.
Group-training possible and desirable, 20.
Guide and rule, the Law, 143.

Habit, Christian life a h., 119.
Habits best formed in early youth, 120; by frequent repetition, 229.
Habituation, 110. 228.
Harding, Warren G., IV.
"Heart" center of soul life, 83. 92; cannot be reached except through the mind, 90. 93; education must begin in the heart, 103.
Herder, J. G., 154.
Home, educational agency, 24.
Honor, what it means to parents, 45; to children, 233. 234.
Humanitarian principle of education, 112.
Humility of the teacher, 67; of children, 202.
Hypocrisy, 205.
Hypocrites, 216.

Ideas; see *Thoughts* and *Knowledge*. I. possess potential power to affect the heart, 84. 91; dominating i. most effective, 88. 89. 92.
Ideational feelings, 85. 86.
Impressive teaching, 152.
Inability to make the knowledge of the mind affect the heart, 11. 153. 178.
Indifference, 75.
Individual training, 19.
Individuality of the child, 19; of the teacher, 59.
Indoctrination, 93. 150.

Inferiority complex, 191.
Influence of the world, 13; of the Church, 23; of the home, 24; mutual i., 14; we educate by the i. we exert, 181; this i. must be definite and persistent, 185.
Inhibitory influence, 84. 88; of the manner of teaching, 153.
Instruction, definition and purpose, 1; Bible profitable for i. in righteousness, 145; i. must impart clear and definite knowledge, 151; necessary, 208. 211. 227.
Insufficiency of the Law, 133.
Intellectual education, 4.
Intellectualizing religious instruction, 152.
Interest in children, 54.
Interrelation between teaching and training, 8; between cognitive, emotional, and volitional activities of the soul, 90.

Keeping the truth before our pupils, 157. 160. 161.
Kindliness, 54.
Knowledge. To impart k. aim of instruction, 1; k. of Scripture truths preliminary or medial objective of religious teaching, 114; k. must be clear and definite, 145. 150; not an end in itself, but a means to an end, 5. 87; difference between k. and faith, 7. 86; k. is power, 8; its content determines direction of influence, 8; k. of sin, 134. 212; of grace, 135. 212; of the will of God, 227; religious k. must be practical and be practised, 156; k. of Scripture doctrines, 62; and of children necessary for teacher, 77.
Kretzmann, O. P., 122. 129. 205. 249.
Kretzschmar, K., 32. 33. 34. 124.

Lack of consistency and persistency, 18; l. of cooperation between home and school cause of failure in education, 39.

Law, the, a curb, 132; a mirror, 134; a guide and rule, 143; insufficiency and weakness of the L., 133; teaching the L., we must aim to touch the heart and to work a live knowledge of sin, 134; difference between L. and Gospel, 63. 132.

Laxity, 56.

Legalism in education, 74.

Lesson in the lesson, 150.

Life an education, 12; motive of a Christian l., 117; the Christian l. a habit, 119; the Christian l. of a teacher an object-lesson for children, 71.

Liking for children, 53.

Love for children, 67; l. of sin separates from God, 194. 213; l. of Jesus necessary in teacher, 65.

Lowliness, 68.

Luther, Martin, 28. 34. 49. 78. 158. 161. 162. 168. 176. 251.

Lying, 204.

Manners, 245.

McNaught, M. S., 246.

Means of education, 125. 163. 178.

Meditation, 158.

Meekness, 67.

Memory work, 161. 162.

Method. Educative m. must be adapted to individual child, 20; the educational m., 185.

Milton, John, 121.

Mirror, the Law a m., 134; also Christian children, 135.

Mission-work, 243.

Moral neutrality, 18. 98; m. education, 6.9; twofold moral nature, 107.

Motive, proper, of a Christian life, 117.

Christian Pedagogy.

Music, 183.

Mutual influence, 14.

Naturalistic principle, 112.

Nature, a twofold moral n., 107.

Neatness, 244.

Neglect of training in childhood, 15.

"New man," the, 141. 143.

Nobility of character, III; of children, 80.

Obedience, 234; necessity of, 237; difficulty of, 237; not dependent on consent of the child, 236; of fear, 125; new o., 144.

Objectives of Christian education, 114; relation between o., 114. 117.

Object-lesson. Life of teacher an o.-l., 182.

Observe. Train child to observe the will of God, 228.

Offense, 182.

Optimism, 95.

Orderliness, 244.

Parents' power limited, 46; duty, 46. 47; responsibility, 25. 45; p. not agreeing with teacher, 221.

Patience, 55.

Pedagog, 41; see *Educator*.

Perseverance, 55.

Pessimism, 95.

Pets, 109.

Phases of education, 3; of soul activity, 82.

Philosophy of life, secular and Christian, 35; affects training of children, 36. 37.

Physical conditions affect psychological conditions, 80; ph. training, 3.

Positive results of education, 223.

Power, potential, of ideas and knowledge to affect the heart, 8. 84. 88. 148; p. to move the heart lies not in the human force of will, but peculiar content of dominating thought, 8. 132. 178. 189; the justifying p. of faith, 140; the sanctifying p. of faith, 140; the p. of sin, 214.

Praise, 163.

Prayer for the children, 178; with the children, 178; by the children, 180.

Preparation for teaching, 52; to withstand temptation, 188.

Pressure, educative, 185.

Prevention of sin and temptation, 186.

Pride, 201.

Principles, various, of education, 111.

Priority of parental authority, 37. 44.

Process, the psychological, 90.

Promise of grace unconditional, 135. 212.

Psychic nature of the child, 77; p. "machinery," 138.

Punctuality, 244.

Punishment. Fear of p. as means of training, 125; Scriptural basis for p., 168; purpose of p., 168; nature of p., 171; measure of p., 171; kinds of p., 172; the right to punish, 169; p. must be individual and corrective, 170; educational value of p., 175; corporal p., 173; rules to be observed, 175; p. of penitent children, 217.

Pupils, poorly gifted, 52.

Purity of Scripture doctrines, 88. 148.

Purposive teaching of the Law, 134; of the Gospel, 139.

Qualifications of the educator: natural q., 51; spiritual, 61.

Rational activity of the soul, 82; only r. beings can be educated, 9.

Rationalistic principle of education, 112.

Reaction, emotional, cannot be forced, 11; psychic r. different in different children, 10; r. of children to educative influences must be watched, 16; it determines the next step, 78.

Recognition of effort and improvement, 231.

Regenerated child, the, 104.

Regeneration does not make Christian training superfluous, 105; it makes it possible, 106.

Regularity, 244.

Relation of home and church with respect to Christian education, 37.

Religion, subjective, personal, 7; type of r. depends on religious doctrines, 7. 148; true r., 7; work of the Holy Ghost, 7.

Religious education, 6.

Reproof, the Scriptures profitable for, 144.

Respect, ability to gain it, 59.

Respectfulness, 232.

Responsibility of parents, 25. 45; of the educator, 11.

Results of education not uniform, 10. 19. 20.

Reward, expectation of, as a means of training, 126.

Ridicule, 172.

Right to punish children, 169.

Roosevelt, Theodore, IV.

Ruskin, John, 2.

Sanctification of life aim of Christian training, 116. 223.

Sarcasm and ridicule, 172.

Save the child from sin, 211. 214.

Schiller, F., 112.

School. Life a s., 12; every s. trains its pupils some way, 25; non-religious s., 27; public s. may not teach religion and cannot offer a Christian training, 27. 29; religious s., 29; parish-s., 31; offer systematic Christian instruction and purposive Christian train-

ing, 32; superiority of these s., 34; they are the best institution for Christian education, 44.
Schoolmaster, the Law a, 134.
School-work, 183.
Scolding, 125. 167.
Self-control, 57.
Self-will, 198.
Sense of right, 127.
Shows, bad, 187.
Sin. How to preserve a child from s., 185. 186. 198; how to save a child from s., 211; sins against conscience, 196; other sins, 207; s. that kill faith, 213; dominion of sin, 214; public sins, 216; sins whose perpetrators cannot be discovered, 219.
Singing, 183.
Social education, 4; s. and national principle of education, 112.
Soul, 81; s. depraved, 100.
State, the, has no right to teach religion, 28. 29.
Stealing, 206.
Strayer, 26.
Study, private, of the teacher, 62.
Subject-matter of instruction, 88. 146.
Success of training depends on strength and consistency of influence, 181; s. of Christian training slow, but sure, 107. 249.
Sunday-school, 29; its value, 30; its limitations, 31; teachers of S.-s., 30.

Tact, 59.
Teaching and training, 1; t. must be educative, 87. 134. 136. 139. 152—158; t. the child, 52; t. to impart knowledge, 150; to convince, 151; to impress and move, 152; to train and to do, 156.
Teacher, natural, 51, and spiritual, 61, qualifications; t. of parish-schools should take charge of Sunday-schools, 30.
Temperaments, 93; vitiated, 101.
Temptation must be kept from child, 187.
Test of one's educative ability, 230.
Things worth while to be taught, 147.
Tone, moral, of influence affects moral tone of character, 19.
Training requires some kind of teaching, 9; t. a matter of influence tending in a certain direction, 6; it must be consistent and persistent, 17; it aims to get the child to do and practise what he has learned, 156. 228; individual t., 19; childhood most opportune time for t., 15; type and success of t., 181; physical t., 5; moral t., 6; t. in Christian virtues, 223; Christian t. not superfluous for, but possible only with, regenerated children, 105. 106; the t. of children a duty of teachers, 41—50; t. a prolonged activity, 219. 249; reason and purpose of Christian t., 122. 123.
Tricks whose perpetrators cannot be found out, 219; that vex the teacher personally, 220.
"Triglot," 138.
Truthfulness, 237.
Truslit, Dr., 91.
Type of training, 181; of character depends on type of influences that fashion it, 18; of religion depends on type of religious doctrines one believes, 7. 148.

Unregenerated children, 115.
Unselfishness of the teacher, 55.
Use of the Word of God, 144.
Utilitarian principle of education, 112.

Vague and hazy knowledge of teacher cause of ineffective teaching, 62; v. ideas of little emotional and educative value, 146. 151.
Variety of feelings, 85.
Vicariousness, 78.
Victory, assurance of, in the battle against sin, 191. 209. 214.
Virtues, Christian, how to train a child in, 223. 232.
Visiting the homes of children, 39.
Vogelweide, Walter von der, 169.
Volitional activity of the soul, 89.

Warning, 166.
Washington, George, 198.
Watching children, 209.
Way of salvation, 211.
Weakness toward children, 68; w. of the Law, 133.
"Weltanschauung," secular, 35; Christian, 35; w. of the Bible most sane and rational, 113; affects the training of children, 36. 37.
Wentzlaff, Gustav G., 94. 95. 119.
Will, 89; no freedom of w., 89; a gift of God, but perverted by sin, 198.
Willingness to serve God, 225.
Wilson, Woodrow, IV.
Wisdom, pedagogical, 59.
Word, a, to the teacher, 211.
Word of God. Its use, 144; must be taught clearly, 145; in purity, 147; as divine truth, 149; convincingly, 151; impressively, 152; is profitable for education and efficacious, 130.
Worldly-mindedness, 75.
Work in school, 183; children must be trained to work, 239.